Improving Early Literacy

Strategies and Activities for Struggling Students (K–3)

Wilma H. Miller, Ed.D.

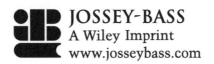

JOSSEY-BASS
A Wiley Imprint
www.josseybass.com

Published by Jossey-Bass
A Wiley Imprint
989 Market Street, San Francisco, CA 94103-1741   www.josseybass.com

Jossey-Bass books and products are available through most bookstores. To contact Jossey-Bass directly call our Customer Care Department within the U.S. at 800-956-7739, outside the U.S. at 317-572-3986, or fax 317-572-4002.

Jossey-Bass also publishes its books in a variety of electronic formats. Some content that appears in print may not be available in electronic books.

0-7879-7289-4

Printed in the United States of America
FIRST EDITION
PB Printing 10 9 8 7 6 5 4 3 2 1

Contents

Preface

Far too many young children still are failing to achieve success with beginning reading skills. These include children from all types of socioeconomic backgrounds as well as children with special needs such as learning, reading, and physical disabilities. Such children experience difficulty with initial reading skills and continue to fall further and further behind as they progress through the primary grades into the intermediate grades. What can be done to help them achieve success?

First, these children need knowledgeable, committed early childhood and primary-grade teachers, family members, and friends who will make a concerted effort to help them succeed. In addition, they need a home environment that will reinforce the reading skills that are presented in school. Therefore, both teachers and family members need to have access to a wealth of motivating, classroom-tested reading strategies and materials that can help all young children, including those with special needs, experience success in beginning reading. This book will provide numerous examples of such strategies and materials.

Improving Early Literacy: Strategies and Activities for Struggling Students (K–3) is an eminently practical resource and research-based guide for all early childhood teachers, teachers of young children with special needs, school administrators, and family members of young children. It is not a theory book about early childhood literacy, but rather a practical sourcebook containing numerous classroom-tested strategies, games, and reproducible assessment devices as well as activity sheets.

The book opens in Chapter One by providing an introduction to building early literacy. Chapter Two is devoted to assessment devices that can be used in early literacy programs. A unique feature of this chapter is that it contains two forms of an Individual Reading Inventory for accurately assessing the reading levels and reading strengths and weaknesses of children in grades 1–3. No other competing book of which I am aware contains this feature.

Chapter Three is designed to help improve the listening and oral language skills of young children. It contains several reproducible checklists as well as useful strategies and materials for doing this. This chapter is designed to be easy to implement. Chapter Four is devoted to helping young children improve competency in letter-name and sight-word knowledge. This chapter contains many classroom-tested strategies, games, and materials for helping children of varied ability levels experience optimum success with these very important elements of beginning reading.

Chapter Five deals with improving ability in phonics, an extremely important skill that normally is necessary for success in early literacy. Most competing books do not place this much emphasis on phonics. This chapter not only contains a detailed description of phonic elements and rules, but also presents a number of research-based methods for improving ability in phonics. This chapter is reader-friendly and easy to use for both early childhood educators and family members. I believe this chapter is a unique strength of my book.

Chapter Six is devoted to improving ability in word structure and context clue usage. It contains descriptions of these word identification techniques as well as numerous classroom-tested strategies, games, and reproducible activity sheets for improving beginning reading. The final chapter deals with increasing the vocabulary and comprehension skills of young children. It describes the various types of meaning vocabularies and comprehension skills and then provides practical strategies and activity sheets for improving ability in both of these areas.

Several unique features of this book include the *pre-assessment device* preceding each chapter that should effectively focus the reader's attention on the content of the chapter, and the many classroom-tested strategies and reproducible devices that will save early childhood educators and family members a significant amount of time and effort.

It is my sincere hope that this book will enable early childhood teachers and family members to provide all young children, including those with special needs, with a myriad of interesting materials that will enable them to experience early reading success. Hopefully, this success will ensure their continued progress with all reading activities as they move through school into adult life.

Wilma H. Miller

Acknowledgments

I would like to acknowledge the memory of my mother, Ruth K. Miller, who until the age of eighty, worked with me on all my writing projects. I also would like to thank the following people at Jossey-Bass who made the writing and publication of this book possible: Steve Thompson, Pam Berkman, Kate Gagnon, Jesse Wiley, Carol Jacob, and Deborah Notkin. I also want to thank Diane Turso, who was the proofreader on this book as she has been in the past for many of my publications. I am sincerely grateful to all of them for the help and encouragement they provided for me.

About the Author

A former classroom teacher, Wilma H. Miller, Ed.D., taught at the university level for thirty-three years. She is actively continuing her writing career in retirement, having authored six teacher resource books since leaving her position as professor of education at Illinois State University in Normal. She completed her doctorate in reading at the University of Arizona under the direction of the late Dr. Ruth Strang, a nationally known reading authority.

Dr. Miller has contributed over two hundred articles to professional journals and is the author of more than thirty other works in the field of reading education. Among the latter works are *Identifying and Correcting Reading Difficulties in Children* (1972), *Diagnosis and Correction of Reading Difficulties in Secondary School Students* (1973), *Reading Diagnosis Kit* (1975, 1978, 1986), *Corrective Reading Skills Activity File* (1977), *Reading Teacher's Complete Diagnosis & Correction Manual* (1988), and *Reading Comprehension Activities Kit* (1990), all published by The Center for Applied Research in Education. In addition, she has authored *Complete Reading Disabilities Handbook* (1993), *Alternative Assessment Techniques for Reading & Writing* (1995), *Ready-to-Use Activities and Materials for Improving Content Reading Skills* (1999), *The Reading Teacher's Survival Kit* (2001), *Phonics First! Ready-to-Use Phonics Worksheets for the Primary Grades* (2001), *Phonics First! Ready-to-Use Phonics Worksheets for the Intermediate Grades* (2001), *Reading Skills Problem Solver* (2002), and *Survival Reading Skills for Secondary Students* (2003), all published by Jossey-Bass.

Dr. Miller also is the author of an in-service aid for teachers entitled *Reading Activities Handbook* (1980) and several textbooks for developmental reading, including *The First R: Elementary Reading Today* (1977) and *Teaching Elementary Reading Today* (1983), all published by Holt, Rinehart and Winston. She has also published *Teaching Reading in the Secondary School* (1974) with Charles C. Thomas and *Strategies for Developing Emergent Literacy* (2000) with McGraw-Hill.

Dr. Miller's doctoral dissertation received a citation of merit from the International Reading Association in 1968. Dr. Miller also received the 1998 Outstanding Contribution to Education Award from Northern Illinois University, DeKalb.

In loving memory of my parents,
William and Ruth Miller

A Practical Introduction to Early Literacy

Have you ever met a young child who was able to read at the primary-grade level or above before entering kindergarten? Many teachers and tutors of young children have seen such a child. Do you believe that most very good readers in the intermediate grades and above were early readers? Indeed, according to research done by Durkin (1966), a number of early readers maintain their initial reading advantage into the intermediate grades. However, some children who enter kindergarten having limited emergent literacy skills learn to read very easily and well and are excellent readers in adulthood. I was an example of this type of child. When I entered school, family members were cautioned not to teach any beginning reading skills, since teachers believed that reading instruction belonged solely in school. Fortunately, today both teachers and family members understand that all students, including those with special needs, benefit from as much exposure as possible to emergent literacy skills.

This chapter opens with a pre-assessment device for early childhood teachers and tutors to ascertain their views about early literacy. Completing this informal device before reading the chapter will help you evaluate your present understanding of emergent literacy.

The chapter then briefly describes the early literacy experiences that have the most influence on school reading success. Behavioral objectives are used to summarize early literacy experiences that are appropriate for pupils with special needs, with average linguistic aptitude, and with above average linguistic aptitude. Next the chapter provides a rationale for developing literacy skills in early childhood reading programs, explains whole language instruction, and suggests elements of whole language that can be used by the same three groups. The versatile language-experience approach (LEA) and its place in early literacy programs is explained, as are the elements of the approach that can be used with children of varying abilities.

This chapter should give you a comprehensive understanding of the elements of early literacy that are crucial to subsequent success in reading and writing.

Decide whether each statement is *accurate* (true) or *not accurate* (false). Evaluate your answers after you have read the chapter. The answers are on page 319.

_____ 1. There is no single point in a child's life when literacy begins; rather it is a continuous process.

_____ 2. Learning to read always should occur before learning to write.

_____ 3. Scribbling, letter strings, and invented spelling are considered valid ways to write and spell in early literacy programs.

_____ 4. Reading to young children should begin at the age of about two.

_____ 5. Word boundaries are the "white spaces" between words.

_____ 6. A child who does "reading reenactments" is considered to be reading in a rudimentary sense.

_____ 7. A few children can read at the second-grade level or higher when they enter kindergarten.

_____ 8. Some children entering kindergarten have never had a book or story read aloud to them.

_____ 9. Most kindergarten children receive adequate rest and nutrition in their homes.

_____ 10. Kindergarten children can learn how to use a computer keyboard.

_____ 11. Each early literacy program must proceed at the child's own pace and help the child to master skills in which he or she is weak.

_____ 12. Whole language is a totally prescribed early reading program.

_____ 13. Predictable books are valuable for all types of pupils in early childhood programs.

_____ 14. "Bookmarks" is an excellent whole language strategy to use with above average young children.

_____ 15. Thematic unit teaching is the cornerstone of using whole language with young children.

_____ 16. Language-experience dictation is especially useful for young children with special needs.

_____ 17. The only early reading knowledge that a language-experience dictated story teaches is capital and lowercase letter names.

_____ 18. The language-experience approach (LEA) enhances the creativity of the young children who use it.

_____ 19. The major limitation of using the language-experience approach (LEA) is its lack of sequential skill development.

_____ 20. Most kindergarten children with special needs use scribbling and/or letter strings in place of conventional spelling when writing.

A BRIEF DESCRIPTION OF EARLY LITERACY

The *emergent* or *early literacy philosophy* states that there *is not a point in a young child's life when literacy begins; rather it is a continuous process of literacy learning that begins in infancy.* The early literacy philosophy states that children have a great deal of prior knowledge that can be built upon. This prior knowledge mainly is the result of all the experiences to which the child has been exposed. Morrow (1997) is representative of all of the researchers who have studied early literacy, and she has written the following generalizations about it:

- All literacy begins in some form from infancy on and proceeds at each child's own rate and in his or her own way.

- Most young children begin to read, write, and spell before school entrance. This includes children with special needs, although their progress may be more limited.

- Learning to read and write is a difficult task for many children.

- However, it may be quite easy for a linguistically gifted child and extremely difficult for a child with special needs.

- Learning to read, write, and spell effectively takes many years, even for a linguistically adept child.

- Ability in written language always is based on competency in oral language and may reflect it.

- Reading to children beginning in infancy is the *single most effective predictor of primary-grade reading achievement.* Reading to young children should take place daily and be pleasurable both for the reader(s) and the child. It often is called "lap reading," since the young child usually is held on the reader's lap while listening.

- Scribbling, letter strings, and invented spelling are considered acceptable ways for a young child to write in early stages of development.

- All literacy develops most effectively in lifelike situations at home and in school. Thematic unit teaching is an important element in making school learning meaningful and practical.

In the past, traditional early childhood and kindergarten programs mainly emphasized readiness for reading experiences that were not particularly educational and were often not even primarily reading related. Unstructured play and rest time also were stressed much more in past early childhood programs than they are today.

However, contemporary preschool, kindergarten, and primary-grade classrooms reflect many of the same types of experiences and materials that are found in homes that have stressed early literacy skills. Research has found that early readers, writers, and spellers have not had anyone trying to teach them literacy skills (Durkin, 1966). These children learn beginning reading skills by asking family members and friends about letters, words, and numbers. They also have parents, grandparents, siblings, and friends who model reading and writing. Often such homes have an older brother or sister who reads to younger children or plays school with them.

Early literacy programs provide lifelike and challenging literary experiences for young children. They help young children extend and refine their early literacy skills. These programs do not wait for children to "naturally" grow into reading, writing, and spelling.

The Most Useful Early Literacy Experiences

The most useful early literacy experiences are often also the cadre of experiences to which young children should be exposed in school. Many of these are discussed in greater detail in later chapters of this book. They include the following:

- Listening to books of various kinds—nursery rhymes, poetry, and other material— on a regular basis is the experience most related to subsequent school reading achievement. Unfortunately, some children, including those with special needs, enter preschool or kindergarten without ever having had any of these read aloud to them. This is true across socioeconomic groups.

- Observing family members and other adults who value reading for pleasure and information. Having good reading models is considered the second-most-important experience influencing subsequent primary-grade reading achievement.

- Taking trips and including a discussion both before and after to encourage the development of vocabulary. Although the trips obviously differ depending on circumstances, here are several examples: a zoo, a pet store, a forest preserve, a wildlife preserve, a veterinarian's office, a park, a shopping mall, a toy store, or a circus.

- Having a *print-rich environment* in the home or the classroom and answering questions about letters, words, numbers, and colors. Children exposed to a print-rich environment may learn the following concepts about print:

  - Print is different from pictures;

  - Print on a page goes from left to right and from top to bottom;

  - A capital letter differs from a lowercase letter;

  - Print is found in many places in the environment and may contain different types of information;

  - Adults read types of print in different ways—aloud to children or silently to themselves—reading has many uses and purposes;

  - A book has a title, an author, and often an illustrator;

  - The white spaces between words in print are called "word boundaries"; and

  - Anyone who is physically able can produce print with various tools—a computer word-processing system, a pen, a pencil, or crayons.

- Listening to a mass market book and then doing a *reading reenactment* (pretend reading) of the book. A young child should be encouraged to use pictures to facilitate in the reading reenactment; the child's version of the book should be welcomed, even when his or her words do not match the book.

- Playing school with an older sibling or friend is a very effective and motivating way for a young child to develop all emergent literacy skills.

- Dictating language-experiences stories and books to an adult who then transcribes them in the child's own language patterns. The adult helps the child to read the material back, stressing left-to-right progression, letter names and letter sounds, important sight words, and the concept that reading is primarily talk written down.

- Participating in all kinds of art and construction activities.

- Participating in all types of rhythm activities.

- Participating in dramatic play, such as having a make-believe veterinarian's office, or dramatizing a portion of a book that has been read aloud.

- Watching videotapes, DVDs, computer software, pictures, demonstrations, scientific experiments, dioramas, and other types of media.

EARLY LITERACY EXPERIENCES AT KINDERGARTEN ENTRANCE

By the beginning of kindergarten, children at various levels may demonstrate competency in the following early literacy skills. As soon as a child has mastered any of these skills, the skill can be checked off, and instruction and practice in the next set of skills should begin.

A. Children with Special Needs

❑ Listens to a story read aloud with a short attention span and some distractibility.
❑ Can give limited answers to lower-level (literal) comprehension questions about a story read aloud.
❑ Has been to interesting places in the immediate neighborhood such as a park, a grocery store, or a pet store.
❑ Can recognize his or her own first name in print.
❑ Can print his or her own first name somewhat correctly.
❑ Can count correctly to about 10.
❑ Can recognize and name the basic colors: *red, green, blue, black, white.*
❑ Understands that the print in books is different from the pictures.
❑ Understands that print can be found in various places such as books, television, and product labels.
❑ Understands that print is different from scribbling.
❑ Participates in art activities at a basic level and usually colors and cuts in a fairly messy manner.
❑ Displays low-level hand-eye (motor) coordination. For example, the lines on geometric figures may appear like these

❑ Can draw a person somewhat like this:

❑ Usually uses a restricted oral language code: short sentences, limited and imprecise vocabulary, nonstandard grammar, and/or a nonstandard dialect.
❑ Can use scribbling or a few letter strings in place of standard spelling.
❑ Understands some simple purposes for writing such as a letter to a friend or relative or a grocery list.
❑ Can correctly recognize and identify five or fewer lowercase letter names.
❑ Can correctly recognize and identify five or fewer capital letter names.
❑ Can identify one or two common words: *STOP, dog, cat, play, run.*

EARLY LITERACY EXPERIENCES AT KINDERGARTEN ENTRANCE *(continued)*

B. Children with Average Linguistic Aptitude

❑ Can listen to a story read aloud with attention and comprehension.

❑ Can answer lower-level (literal) comprehension questions about a story that has been read aloud.

❑ Can do a simple reading reenactment (pretend reading) of a story that has been read aloud.

❑ Can retell a very simple story (three or fewer main parts) that has been read aloud in correct sequence.

❑ Has been to interesting places in the neighborhood and understands and can use some of the specialized vocabulary of those places: a shopping mall, a toy store, a local zoo, a lake, etc.

❑ Can recognize and correctly print his or her own first name.

❑ Can count correctly approximately up to 20+.

❑ Understands that print on a page goes from left to right.

❑ Understands that a book has a title (name).

❑ Understands that a capital letter is different from a lowercase letter.

❑ Can correctly identify at least eight to ten lowercase letter names.

❑ Can correctly identify at least eight to ten capital letter names.

❑ Can correctly identify approximately five common sight words such as *STOP, dog, cat, Christmas, play, run, mother, jump, ice cream.*

❑ Can play school with an older or same-age child.

❑ Can dictate a simple language-experience story about a personal enjoyable experience.

❑ Can attempt to read his or her own language-experience story with adult support.

❑ Enjoys participating in simple art activities and cuts and colors fairly well.

❑ Can draw a fairly detailed picture of a person.

❑ Participates in spontaneous dramatic play such as playing house or playing store.

❑ Understands the purpose of a computer and can play simple computer games.

❑ Can recognize and name the basic colors and can recognize a few color words: *red, green, blue, black, white, brown, orange, pink, purple, yellow.*

❑ Displays fair hand-eye (motor) coordination; i.e., the lines on geometric figures may appear this way:

❑ Knows the name of and can draw a circle and a square.

❑ Can generally sit still about ten to fifteen minutes, usually pays attention when actively involved in an activity, and usually is fairly well behaved.

❑ Uses fairly good oral language with sentences containing six to eight words, adequate vocabulary to express him/herself, and acceptable grammar with some overgeneralizations such as *"goed"* or *"runned."*

❑ Can use random letter strings with some invented spelling such as: *J rn t sl* for *Joe ran to school.*

❑ Can provide the correct sounds for a few consonant letters.

C. Children with Above Average Linguistic Aptitude

❑ Enthusiastic about listening to a book read aloud to him or her. Very good comprehension including affective (emotional) skills and pays very good attention.

❑ Can answer both lower-level and higher-level comprehension questions about a book that has been read aloud.

❑ Can do an accurate and motivated reenactment of a mass market book that has been read aloud to him or her.

❑ Can retell a simple story or mass market book in correct sequence.

❑ Has been to interesting places and understands and uses some of the specialized vocabulary terms of the place: a zoo, a theme park, a museum, a planetarium, a wildlife preserve, an airport, a national park, etc.

❑ Can recognize and print his or her own first and last names.

❑ Can correctly count to approximately 50 to 100.

❑ Understands that print on a page goes from left to right and top to bottom.

❑ Understands that a book has a title, an author, and perhaps an illustrator.

❑ Understands that there are word boundaries ("white spaces") between the words in print.

❑ Can recognize and identify most lowercase letter names.

❑ Can recognize and identify most capital letter names.

❑ Understands that print can be found in many different places in the environment.

❑ Can identify 20+ common words by sight: *STOP, dog, cat, mother, father, play, run, ice cream, school, jump, cow, happy, funny, TV, he, she, Christmas, you, one, sun.*

❑ Can identify colors and some common color words: *red, green, blue, yellow, black, brown, white, orange, pink, purple.*

❑ Enjoys playing school with an older sibling or friend.

❑ Can dictate and successfully read back a language-experience story.

❑ Is able to learn several important sight words from each of his or her language-experience stories.

❑ Enjoys participating in challenging art activities; colors and uses scissors very well.

❑ Enjoys participating in rhythm activities.

EARLY LITERACY EXPERIENCES AT KINDERGARTEN ENTRANCE *(continued)*

❑ Can draw a detailed picture of a person.

❑ Can lead and participate in both spontaneous and planned dramatic play situations such as a veterinarian's office, television newsroom, grocery story, etc.

❑ Can use a computer for simple word processing of his or her written stories and for playing appropriate computer games.

❑ Displays good hand-eye (motor) coordination. The lines on geometric figures may look like these:

❑ Knows the name of and can draw these geometric figures: *circle, triangle, square, rectangle,* and perhaps *diamond.*

❑ Displays attention span of 15+ minutes, usually pays attention, is not easily distracted, and is usually well behaved if sufficiently challenged.

❑ Uses elaborate oral language with complex sentences, fairly precise and interesting vocabulary, and good grammar with a few overgeneralizations such as *"buyed"* or *"boughted."*

❑ Can use invented spelling to convey his or her thoughts: *i wil be getin a pupy in t fll* for *I will be getting a puppy in the fall.*

❑ Can read and understand simple predictable book such as *Is Your Mama a Llama?* (Guarino, 1989).

❑ May be able to read simple books at the first-grade level or higher.

❑ Can provide sounds for many of the consonants and vowels.

THE RATIONALE FOR DEVELOPING EARLY LITERACY SKILLS IN EARLY CHILDHOOD PROGRAMS

When young children learn early literacy skills in their home and in early childhood programs, they are more likely to be successful in kindergarten and the primary grades. Family members, family friends, and preschool teachers are very important in helping young children develop beginning reading and writing skills.

As demonstrated by the checklists in the previous section, young children's early literacy skills and exposure vary a great deal. Some young children enter kindergarten already reading at the upper primary-grade level or above, while others are not able to recognize a single alphabet letter. Some children have been read aloud to daily since infancy, while others have never heard a book or a nursery rhyme read aloud. Some have already traveled extensively before kindergarten entrance; others never have been farther away from their home than the immediate neighborhood. In addition, a number of young children do not receive adequate nutrition and rest and may spend much of their time watching television programs, including those that are not designed for young children and may be harmful for them.

Children who have had little exposure to early literacy activities and/or have special needs of various types may not be ready for beginning reading and writing instruction in school and may fall further and further behind unless a teacher, tutor, volunteer, family member, or friend makes a concerted effort to help them.

Experienced and caring kindergarten and first-grade teachers usually are able to compensate for a child's inadequate literacy experiences prior to school entrance. However, this may be especially difficult in classrooms in which there are a large number of "at-risk" children. Kindergarten teachers may need help from a teacher's aide and parent and community volunteers. First-grade teachers may also receive help from a Reading Recovery teacher who has been trained in an intervention program for "at-risk" first-grade children.

A well-trained, motivated kindergarten teacher can help a child with special needs learn the important early literacy skills by working with each child at his or her present level and proceeding at the child's own pace. The strategies and materials in this book should help a teacher, tutor, or family member do this effectively.

All young children, including those with special needs, deserve a kindergarten or first-grade reading and writing program that enhances their present strengths while compensating for their weaknesses. Such a program should provide instruction and reinforcement in beginning reading skills (including letter names and letter-sound relationships), beginning writing skills, beginning spelling skills (including invented spelling), and oral language development, as well as improving the child's sense of self-worth. Usually this becomes some variation of a whole language program, along with the language-experience approach and meaningful skills instruction emphasizing both phonic analysis and comprehension skills. Later sections of this chapter illustrate such a program.

WHOLE LANGUAGE AND ITS PLACE IN EARLY LITERACY INSTRUCTION

Whole language is a complex construct. Here is one simple definition:

> *Whole language is a philosophy that includes using relevant literature and writing and meaningful, practical, cooperative experiences in order to help students develop motivation and interest in learning.*

Whole language emphasizes child-centered learning and unifies all curriculum areas. It also emphasizes that no person becomes truly literate without being personally involved in literacy.

Crafton (1991) has identified six principles that exemplify the whole language philosophy. The following is my own adaptation of these principles, with examples.

Principle 1—Oral and Written Language Develop Whole-to-Part

The concept of whole-to-part literacy development has its beginning in what is known about how children learn to speak. From birth, young children deal with language wholes. For example, family members communicate whole meanings and encourage their young children to speak in whole words and sentences, not in letter sounds. Small pieces of language in isolation confuse young children, but they understand the relationships in whole sentences and conversations.

This whole-to-part principle contrasts with the "skills approach" to teaching reading. In a "skills" program, the names and sounds of isolated letters are stressed.

Strategy: If this principle is to be adopted from the beginning stages of early literacy, children need to read and write texts that have the characteristics of real language. They should read intact mass market books, dictated or written language-experience books, learning skills such as phonic analysis and structural analysis in the context of real books when there is a need for these skills, and use invented spelling until they learn spelling skills when they are needed in actual writing.

Principle 2—Language and Literacy Are Socially Constructed

Reading and writing are not solitary activities, but socialized learning events. Even when a person reads a book alone, he or she is having a conversation with an author. Writing, of course, is a dialogue between the writer and one or more readers. In addition, after a child has read a book alone, the child is motivated by opportunities to share his or her interpretations and reactions. Young children find it rewarding to read a book with a partner. (Book clubs are based on this premise since readers read a selected book and then share their understanding and views about it.)

Strategy: Students need opportunities to learn from their classmates as well as from their teacher or tutor. Whole language encourages collaboration and cooperation and greatly stresses the value of students learning and thinking together. Since talk is very important to learning, a whole language classroom may be a little noisy, but it always should be well managed. Whole language encourages children to think together and to expand on each other's ideas. Cooperative learning groups, interest groups, needs groups, mini-lessons, and "buddy" groups all are encouraged.

Principle 3—Literate Behavior Is Learned Through Real-Life Use

When young children use language in the home, they always have a definite purpose. For example, they ask for their favorite toy or a glass of water, or tell a parent that they love him or her. Language in the school always should have the same definite purpose and goal. Learning phonic analysis in isolation is not purposeful for young children, while reading an interesting mass market book such as *There's a Nightmare in My Closet* by Mercer Mayer is.

> *Strategy:* Children need to learn to use language for many real-life purposes. They should read and write books and stories, children's newspapers, simple poetry, environmental print, and picture books, and simple chapter books. Literacy is authentic when the child has a real personal investment in it. Teachers and tutors can help children to read and write for real purposes right now.

Principle 4—Demonstrations Are Important to Learning

Teacher or tutor demonstrations show children various elements of word identification, comprehension, writing, and spelling. Whole language emphasizes the *process* of reading and writing rather than the *product*. Teachers and tutors should share their best strategies for good reading and writing. They also should do what they request their pupils to do. For example, if children are going to write a thank-you letter, the teacher or tutor should also write a real thank-you letter.

Principle 5—All Learning Involves Risk Taking

In the past children in the primary grades were expected to read orally in a word-perfect manner. However, now beginning readers are encouraged to take risks in their reading, writing, and spelling. They are encouraged to substitute a word for an unknown word, while they are reading, if the substituted word makes sense in context. They are encouraged to guess the spelling of unknown words while writing.

Young children are encouraged in risk taking when they are learning to speak. Approximations of correct words are celebrated and encouraged. Similar approximations of correct words while reading and while spelling likewise should be celebrated by teachers, tutors, and family members.

Principle 6—Learners Must Take Responsibility for Their Own Learning

According to the whole language philosophy, children must take responsibility for their own learning. This concept assumes that all children are natural learners and want to learn. Very young children take responsibility for learning to speak. Children can take responsibility for their own early literacy by choosing mass market books to read for pleasure or information and choosing writing topics. Teachers and tutors should allow students to direct their learning as much as possible. This means allowing students to take appropriate risks and proceed at their own pace. They should be helped to understand that it is *their own* learning.

Since whole language is a philosophy and not a teaching approach, a variety of elements typically may be found in a whole language classroom. Some of these are

- Whole-to-part reading and writing;
- Collaboration among children;
- Risk taking;
- Authentic or "real" learning experiences;
- Teaching and learning that emphasize *process* not *product*;
- Student-involved discussions, demonstrations, multi-media, and experiments;
- Student, not teacher, ownership of learning;
- Learning experiences that stress reflection and evaluation;
- The teacher or tutor acting as a *facilitator*, rather than a director, of learning;
- A child-centered and child-regulated classroom, where as much as possible the children select the topics of the curriculum and the means by which they are learned;
- All students are active participants in their learning;
- Skills are taught in the contexts of books, stories, paragraphs, and sentences, not in isolation; for example, phonic worksheets and workbooks normally would not be used;
- All elements of literacy (listening, speaking, reading, and writing) are emphasized, because a literate person is one who can use them all;
- Thematic unit teaching is typical and usually the theme is taken from the content areas of social studies or science, and all listening, speaking, reading, writing, and spelling activities are based on it. Some common themes are our neighborhood, community helpers, school helpers, animals, zoo animals, the reasons for recycling, our city (town), the rain forest, and cultural differences in our classroom;
- Literacy instruction takes place throughout the day with large blocks of time being set aside specifically for literacy;
- Commercial materials such as basal readers or phonic materials do not dictate the curriculum so materials are used as a means to an end, not an end in themselves;
- Different classroom organizational patterns are used, such as whole-class instruction, small-group skills instruction, needs groups, interest groups, mini-lessons, "buddy" groups, cross-age groups, and cross-grade groups. The groups generally are short-term and very flexible, meaning that young children can easily move from group to group; and
- All of these cueing systems are stressed in whole language programs:
  - Semantic (meaning) cues
  - Syntactic (grammar or word order) cues
  - Graphophonic (visual/phonic) cues
  - Combination (a combined system such as using both meaning and phonic cues)

WHOLE LANGUAGE AND CHILDREN WHO HAVE SPECIAL NEEDS

Several elements of whole language seem to be especially useful with young children who have special needs. Here is a brief description of them.

Print-Rich Environment

All preschool, kindergarten, or primary-grade whole language classrooms should have many examples of functional print available for children to look at. This print should be placed so that each child can associate the words with what they represent. As an example, a *desk, chair, table, window, door, book, floor,* and/or *rug* can be labeled so that the children can associate the abstract symbol with the concrete object, thus giving meaning to it. Although a print-rich environment is most associated with the whole language approach, it also is useful in any early literacy program.

Big (Oversized) Books

Big or *oversized books* are very much identified with early childhood early literacy programs. Big books are often used in the *shared book experience* described later in this section. Big books measure from about 14 by 20 inches to about 24 by 30 inches. Some of the simpler big books are best for children as young as two or three, while others can be used through the third-grade level. Although they can be used in a whole-class setting, they often are most effective in a small-group setting. The teacher or tutor usually places the big book on an easel so that all children can see it easily.

NOTE: Whether reading from a big book or a normal-sized book, the adult should genuinely enjoy all books that he or she reads aloud to young children.

Big books are very effective because their size makes it easy for children to see the print and pictures clearly. As the teacher or tutor runs his or her hand underneath the print, children can easily notice the word boundaries ("white spaces"), target letters and words, the differences between print and pictures, and left-to-right progression. Many big books also are *predictable,* making it easy for children to try to read along and to perhaps learn some letter names and sight words.

NOTE: Not all big books are predictable, and those that are not probably will be difficult for young children with special needs.

A teacher or tutor can make a cassette tape recording while he or she is reading a big book aloud so that pupils can listen at a later time while looking at it. Big books as well as all mass market books should be reread a number of times to young children if they are to be used most effectively. When children seem to be enjoying a big book (or any book), it should be used with them for several days. The adult can leave big books on a chart easel or some other appropriate place so that children can "play school" with them or look at them again.

A number of companies are currently publishing big (oversized) books. A list of some of them can be found in Appendix I.

Shared Book Experience

The *shared book experience* helps students learn concepts about print, such as that reading goes from left to right and top to bottom and that sentences are made up of words and words are made up of letters. The shared book experience is very similar to the *lap reading* or bedtime story reading during which a family member reads to a child. A shared book experience can use a big (oversized) book or, perhaps less effectively, a normal-sized picture book.

Before a teacher, tutor, or family member reads to a group of children or to one child, he or she should introduce the title, author, and illustrator of the book and have children make predictions about the book contents from its title and cover. The adult also can activate the children's prior knowledge and help them set purposes for reading, such as learning about the theme of the book, getting to know the characters, or simply listening for pleasure. As the reader shares the book, he or she should move a hand under the print to emphasize left-to-right progression and teach that printed words represent concepts. A shared book reading should be *interactive*, encouraging the children to make numerous predictions, share comments, and ask questions.

As a book is read aloud for a second or third time, have children try to read familiar phrases or predictable parts along with you. This is the main reason that the shared reading usually should feature big or normal-sized books that are predictable.

Here is one set of guidelines for following up on a shared reading experience:

- Read the book aloud and have children try to read the predictable parts with you.

- Read one line of the book aloud and have the children together repeat the line of print.

- Read most of each sentence in the book, leaving out one important word in that sentence and have children try to supply the missing word.

- Have children try to read the entire book along with you. For this, it is more important to select a *predictable book* for the shared reading experience than a big book.

- For follow-up activities the children can do any of the following:
  - Dramatize the book.
  - Illustrate the book.
  - Construct a puppet based on the book.
  - Look at a videotape of the book.
  - Listen to a musical version of the book.

Predictable Books

Predictable books are very useful with students who have special needs. Predictable books have repetitive language patterns, thus allowing children to guess (predict) the next portion of the book.

Predictable books can make use of rhyme, repetition of words, phrases, sentences, and refrains, as well as such patterns as cumulative structure and turn-around plots. Predictable books encourage children to make predictions or guesses about words, phrases, sentences, events, and characters that may be found next.

Here is a brief description of various kinds of predictable books:

- *Chain or circular story*—The plot is structured so that the ending leads back to the beginning.

- *Cumulative book*—Each time a new event occurs, all the previous events in the story are repeated.

- *Familiar sequence*—This book is organized by a recognizable theme such as numbers, colors, or days of the week.
- *Pattern stories*—The basic scene is repeated with some variation.
- *Question and answer*—The same or similar questions are repeated.
- *Repetition of phrases*—Word order in a phrase or sentence is repeated.
- *Rhyme*—Rhyming words, refrains, or patterns are used.
- *Songbooks*—A familiar song with predictable elements such as repetitive phrases are the basis for the book.

All books become somewhat predictable when they are read repeatedly to young children, as should be the case. Since fairy tales may be familiar to many children, they may be considered predictable, as may mass market books if they have very good plots and familiar topics. Books that contain pictures that exactly parallel the print often are predictable, especially if the children can see the pictures as the book is being read.

Here are several suggestions for using predictable books with children who have special needs:

- Select books that you very much enjoy.
- Begin with books that have clearly defined patterned language such as *Bright Star, Bright Star, What Do You See?* and gradually move toward books that have less clearly defined patterns.
- Read the title and show the picture on the cover to the children. Ask: "What do you think this book might be about?" Help them use the title and cover picture to make predictions about the book's content. Many children with special needs as young as the age of four should be able to look at the title and cover of a predictable book and make predictions about its content. This should occur before listening to the book and later before doing a pretend reading (reading reenactment) of the book.
- Read the book aloud. When you come to a predictable line, encourage the children to read the line with you. Show them where the line is located in the print.
- However, be sure to allow the story lines and rhymes to carry the meaning of the book. Do not stop at points in a predictable book that interrupt the flow of patterned language since that will damage the book's value.

A list of recommended predictable books of various types can be found in Appendix II.

WHOLE LANGUAGE AND CHILDREN WHO HAVE AVERAGE LINGUISTIC SKILLS

In addition to the strategies that work for children with special needs, several whole language strategies may be especially useful with children who have average linguistic skills. Some of these are explained here.

Thematic Unit Teaching and Collaborative Learning

Thematic unit teaching and *collaborative learning* are the heart of every whole language classroom. Most teaching and learning in whole language classrooms occurs in child-selected and child-organized thematic units. Thematic unit teaching presents skills from all the content areas using a single unit topic.

Thematic unit teaching relies on collaboration among children and between teacher or tutor and children. Children work cooperatively with each other and with an adult(s) in researching their own selected objectives. Children participate in various kinds of collaborative learning, including cooperative learning groups, "buddy" or partner groups, needs groups, interest groups, and with cross-grade or cross-age reading partners. Keep reading for more detail on these forms of collaborative learning.

Cooperative learning group—This kind of group usually consists of two to five or six children with different reading abilities. Each child participates in those tasks in which he or she is able and then shares what was learned with others in the group or class. As much as possible, this group is child-directed. As an example, if a cooperative learning group in third grade studies the topic "The Importance of Recycling," several children might read simple trade books on this topic; others might research it on the World Wide Web; while others might draw some simple recycling illustrations or diagrams. In addition, children could watch videotapes or DVDs on recycling.

"Buddy" (partner) reading—*"Buddy" reading* takes place when two children decide to be reading buddies for a period of time. Each child then reads a copy of the selected book either silently or orally. When one buddy needs help, either in word attack or comprehension, he or she can ask the buddy. The buddies can have different or similar reading abilities.

Needs groups—These usually are short-term groups formed so that a teacher or tutor can present or review mini-lessons on important reading, writing, or spelling skills that one or more children need to learn at that time.

Interest groups—These groups are formulated by the children depending on their unique needs. The teacher or tutor rarely has input into the formulation of an interest group. These short-term groups are disbanded when the interest(s) that the group was formulated to research are finished.

Cross-age and cross-grade reading partners—In this type of grouping, an older and a younger child work together on selected reading skills. The partners may be an older child who has reading problems and a younger child who either is reading on grade level or has reading problems, or two children with similar reading levels who are in different grades. Since an older student, even if reading disabled, is often a better reader than a younger reader, an older student can experience success and enhance self-esteem by working with a younger child.

The *themes* should develop from young children's actual life experiences and should interest them. In true whole language instruction, young children themselves select all the topics that they study. However, the teacher or tutor usually has to provide some direction, especially with very young children. Sample topics include *zoo animals, animal babies, animals that can be children's pets, community helpers, different kinds of rocks, cowboys and cowgirls, spending the summer at a lake, our immediate neighborhood, the farm, protecting the environment, dinosaurs,* and *the veterinarian's office.*

Thematic unit teaching in early childhood usually is based on the content areas of social studies or science or (less commonly) on one of the following: one book, the books written by one author, or one genre of literature.

Unit teaching helps students make connections between listening, speaking, reading, and writing, as well as among the content areas. An early literacy unit always should be developed around a genuine theme or core idea.

Message Boards

Message boards emphasize the social and authentic aspects of whole language. A classroom bulletin board can be designated as the class message board. When children enter a classroom at the beginning of a school year, they should find a note that the teacher, teacher's aide, or tutor has left for them on the message board. Tell children that all messages must be signed and that they must not hurt any child's feelings. Personal messages from a teacher, tutor, or classmates help children to understand that they are valued members of the class.

Mailboxes

An early childhood teacher or tutor can construct *mailboxes* and provide each child with a designated space for his or her mailbox. Mailboxes can be constructed from cardboard dividers. At the beginning of the school year the teacher, teacher's aide, or tutor places a short letter in each mail slot. The teacher, tutor, and children then discuss how the mailboxes will function in the classroom. Children should be encouraged to write letters at any free time during the school day. Stress that all letters must be signed and be written with an awareness of other children's feelings. Assign children the job of being sure that the mailboxes have an adequate supply of notebook paper, personalized stationery that the children have made, and envelopes.

Mini-Lessons

Mini-lessons are brief discussions or demonstrations of some aspect of reading or writing, designed to highlight the kind of thought or procedure in which a good reader/writer might participate. Mini-lessons are developed from a teacher's or tutor's observations of the reading or writing skills in which children are weak. Very briefly, here is the basic procedure for using mini-lessons in early childhood literacy programs.

1. When teachers or tutors observe specific missing skills that are causing children difficulty, a mini-lesson may be appropriate. In reading, these may be sight word vocabulary, phonic analysis, word structure, use of context clues, literal or higher-level comprehension, or oral or silent reading fluency. In writing, they could be spelling, use of correct grammar, or writing content.

2. Teachers or tutors should design a brief lesson(s) to present and/or review one aspect of the learning activity. Mini-lessons should be concise and emphasize only one reading or writing strategy. On the average, mini-lessons last about five to ten minutes.

3. A mini-lesson begins with the teacher or tutor helping students notice the observations that lead to instruction. For example, a mini-lesson on phonics can focus on the use of the schwa (ə) sound.

4. After the mini-lesson, children can be asked where they see an opportunity to use the information from the lesson in their current reading or writing. For example, third-grade children could be asked to write down all the words containing the schwa (ə) sound from a short reading selection.

5. After the reading or writing time, the teacher or tutor asks: Did it help you? Will you use this strategy again? When do you think this strategy will be the most useful for you?

6. When mini-lessons are a regular part of the curriculum, children should participate in planning the lessons.

7. Mini-lessons should be repeated throughout the school year as teachers observe a need for them.

Me Boxes

Me Boxes are collections of items that reflect the interests, prior knowledge, personal experiences, and family background of their owners. When children are encouraged to share aspects of their own lives, they can more successfully read and write material that reflects their interests.

To begin using this strategy, the teacher or tutor brings a small box filled with his or her personal items to share early in the school year. The items should reflect the teacher's or tutor's unique interests, experiences, family, hobbies, or mementos that have special significance. For example, I might put the following in my Me Box: a small stuffed dog, a book that I have recently read, an artifact from my trip to Kenya, a pine cone from northern Wisconsin, and/or a picture of me walking with my dog. Then the teacher or tutor takes each item out of the Me Box and talks about why each is significant.

Subsequently the teacher or tutor asks the children to bring their own Me Boxes to school. Shoe boxes are easy to obtain and work well. Each child shares his or her Me Box with the class. After all the Me Boxes have been shared, have each child dictate or write a story or a description about the items contained in the Me Box. Although not all the items contained in a Me Box have to be included in the story or description, the more complete the list is, the more predictable the material. After the children have shared their stories with the rest of the class, display the Me Boxes with the writing placed under each box.

Here is a story that accompanied a Me Box constructed by a third-grade boy. It contained two small stuffed dogs, photographs of his dogs playing ball, a baseball, and a rock from his collection:

> This story is about me.
> My name is Ben, and I am in third grade at Heartland School.
> I have two dogs that are named LeRoy and Ellie.
> LeRoy is a yellow lab and Ellie is a black lab.
> I really like to play ball with them at Birch Lake in the summer.
> I like to play baseball in the summer too.
> I have a big rock collection.

WHOLE LANGUAGE AND CHILDREN WHO HAVE ABOVE AVERAGE LINGUISTIC SKILLS

Along with the strategies described so far, several whole language strategies seem very useful with children who have above average linguistic skills. The descriptions in this section have been adapted from Crafton's book *Whole Language: Getting Started . . . Moving Forward* (1991).

Literacy Celebrations

Literacy celebrations reinforce the positive experiences that go with reading. They have two purposes:

1.   Praising the meaning-making process by calling attention to higher-level thinking.

2.   Presenting children's interpretations or discoveries.

Process celebrations can be classroom displays that emphasize in-process thought such as several drafts in writing. *Culminating celebrations* take place when classmates join a child to praise his or her reading or writing progress.

Bookmarks

Bookmarks encourage children to write their responses on small pieces of paper while they are reading. Children using bookmarks can write down difficulties and continue reading, knowing that they will later be able to talk about these difficulties with their teacher, tutor, or classmates.

The teacher cuts notebook paper, construction paper, or tag board into strips about two inches wide. Then he or she models this strategy by showing the children sample responses to reading, written on a bookmark. Each child is given several bookmarks to use while reading self-selected materials. If two children are reading "buddies," they can write comments on a bookmark(s) together.

If they wish, children can share the comments they wrote on the bookmarks with the teacher, tutor, a group, or the entire class. If the teacher or tutor would like, children can hand in the bookmarks to help the teacher understand which strategies the children may need to learn or review. The teacher or tutor also can answer questions or comments directly on the bookmarks.

Here is a bookmark that was written by a second-grade child with above average linguistic skills after she read *The Tortilla Factory* (Paulsen & Paulsen, 1998).

The Tortilla Factory

How did the yellow corn seeds know when to start to grow?

I didn't understand how the workers know when to pick the corn.

Is eating corn tortillas good for a person?

I never ate tortillas. What do they taste like?

I would like to make tortillas here at school sometime.

Do the farm workers from Mexico get paid very much for picking food like corn?

Exit Slips

Exit slips are an easy way to help children think about what they have learned and to determine areas that need additional study. Exit slips may be used after any learning experiences or at the end of a school day. Reading teachers and tutors can use the following strategy with above average readers in the primary grades:

- Talk about the importance of decision making, such as what to include in a letter to a friend or relative, what to wear to school on a particular day, or how to ask a friend or relative for help in solving a simple problem.
- Give one 3-inch by 5-inch index card to each child.
- Ask each child to write down one thing that he or she has learned (in the day or during the learning experience) on one side of the index card. Have the child write down one question that he or she still has. Encourage children to ask any question that seems meaningful and relevant to them.
- Collect the cards and examine them.
- Choose several questions to use the next morning. Questions can be answered either orally or by writing on each child's card, or other children can be encouraged to answer them. Selected questions can be used for future study or to help a teacher or tutor choose topics for future mini-lessons.

Book Talks

Book talks can be used to emphasize books that other children might like to read for fun. Children can give book talks anytime when they have read books that they want to recommend.

A book talk in an early childhood program may include any of these elements:

- A favorite part of the book;
- A favorite character in the book;
- The most interesting incident in the book;
- A retelling of the most important events, being sure not to give away the ending;
- How this book is like or different from other books that the child has recently read; and/or
- Why the child would or would not want to read another book by the same author.

Before using book talks, the teacher or tutor should explain why book talks are helpful. Children can give book talks to a small group, large group, or the entire class. If a child wants to, he or she can make brief planning notes for the talk. A child also can construct advertising posters or develop a simple costume to wear while giving the talk.

Observation Journals

Observation journals are a useful strategy for above average readers/writers. To keep an observation journal, children follow this basic procedure:

1. Children and teacher or tutor choose an area of social studies or science they would like to directly observe. Classroom pets are useful for this purpose, as are classroom plants.

2. Teachers or tutors tell children that they will be involved in original research as they make observations, conduct simple experiments, ask questions, and then use their observation journals to record their discoveries.

3. The class brainstorms questions they might want to investigate. Children and teachers divide themselves into small groups based on common prior knowledge and interests.

4. The small groups are given ten to fifteen minutes to begin their investigations. They observe, discuss, and record observations.

5. After the observations, group members meet to formulate new questions or refine previous ones in preparation for the next observations. At this time, groups may want to suggest experiments to help answer their questions. They use their journals to plan the experiments and to record explorations.

6. Children are encouraged to analyze their observations and to draw conclusions.

Here is an example from a second-grade student, using invented spelling.

Our tertl lives in a glas bol.
There is a rock in the bol for him.
He likes to et flys.
Wen I hold a ded fly in my fngrs for him, he stiks his nek up and gets it from my hand.
He has lived in our room at skol for a lon tim.

The Language-Experience Approach (LEA) in Early Literacy Programs

The *language-experience approach* (LEA) is an excellent way for young children to learn and review letter names, letter sounds, sight words, word structure, and comprehension skills and to understand the concept that "reading is primarily talk written down." LEA dictation can begin as early as the age of three for a child who has good linguistic aptitude, and somewhat later for students who have less competency in oral language development. LEA was primarily researched and written about by the late Roach Van Allen, professor emeritus at the University of Arizona, under whom I studied in the 1960s. At that time, Allen was speaking and writing about the language-experience approach in much the same way as it is used today. According to Allen (1976), LEA is mainly based on the following philosophy:

What I think about is important.
What I can think about, I can say.
What I can say, I can write or someone else can write it for me.
I can read what I have written or what someone else has written for me.

The language-experience approach is a very effective way of teaching and practicing letter names, letter sounds, sight words, word structure, context, and comprehension. Students usually can read their own LEA dictated charts and stories much better than they can read any other print materials.

Here is a brief description of how to use LEA dictation to improve early literacy skills:

1. Provide the child or children with a highly motivating experience so that they will have something interesting about which to dictate. This opportunity can be provided in the home, in an early childhood program, or in kindergarten or early first grade. The dictated stories are very motivating since they reflect the children's own unique experiences. Here are some motivating experiences:

   - A trip to a pet store, a zoo, a wildlife preserve, a humane society animal shelter, a library, an airport, a grocery store, a toy store, a shopping mall, a park, a post office, a doctor's office, a hospital, a dairy farm, a grain farm, a peanut factory, a dairy, a candy factory, or a fire station, among countless others. The unique attractions of each community can be the basis for a dictated language-experience story.

   - An art or construction activity such as constructing a simple puppet, making construction paper flowers, finger painting, making a kite, furnishing a simple playhouse, making paper umbrellas, constructing a Valentine, making a May basket, making a paper turkey, making a construction paper snowman, or formulating a simple collage, among many others.

   - A cooking or baking activity, including deviled eggs, making butter, bread, edible alphabet letters, cookies of various kinds, frosting cupcakes, vegetable soup, jam or jelly, muffins, fudge, peanut brittle, or lasagna.

   - A visual or aural activity, such as watching a videotape, viewing a DVD, observing experiments, watching demonstrations, listening to a book being read, or listening to an audiotape.

2. Have an interesting preliminary discussion with the children during which the motivation for the LEA dictation is discussed. As an example, the teacher and children can discuss a zoo trip in detail using correct vocabulary and stressing the order in which the different animals were seen.

3. Have the child or children dictate the language-experience chart (on large chart paper) or the LEA book (on regular or oversized paper) trying to motivate the children to dictate in complete sentences. If you want, an LEA story can be transcribed in a blank book. (Blank regular-sized and oversized books can be purchased inexpensively from Bare Books, Treetop Publishing Company, 220 Virginia St., Racine, WI 53405, and from most teachers' supply stores.) Do not structure the dictation or else the LEA chart or book will reflect the language of the adult instead of the child or children. Most reading specialists believe that the exact language patterns of the child or children should be used, including a nonstandard dialect, but any offensive language should be changed. If a child's

language patterns are changed, he or she may feel rejection, since that is the only language that he or she has.

4. Once the story or stories are dictated, here are some guidelines for using them:

- Read the experience chart or story aloud several times, placing a hand under each word as you read it, being sure to stress one-to-one oral language and written word relationships. The reading teacher or tutor also can stress left-to-right progression by moving a hand in a sweeping movement under each sentence as he or she reads it aloud.

- Present and/or review several beginning reading skills from each chart or story. In addition to letter-name identification, letter-sound relationships, and sight word identification, other skills that can be stressed are concept of words and word boundaries, beginning word structure, and use of context (meaning) clues.

- All of a child's stories can be bound into a "book," reread several times, and then sent home with the child to read to family members or friends. The LEA charts can be duplicated for other children in the class to read. The charts can be kept on a chart holder and reread a number of times as a class or a group.

- Each child can illustrate his or her dictated stories, using such varied art media as watercolor paints, finger paints, tempera paints, chalk, markers, crayons, colored pencils, or construction paper cutouts. The dictated and illustrated stories can be bound into a teacher-made, child-made, or pre-made book and laminated. The books can be fastened with spiral binding (available at printing stores and office supply stores), three large rings, yarn, staples, or other means. The books should be as attractive as possible so that other children and the child's family and friends will want to look at them. Making them attractive also indicates that the teacher or tutor, as well as family members and friends, values the child's thoughts.

- Each published LEA book can be put in the literacy center or library corner of the classroom for children to look at and read. Often young children, including those with special needs, find child-dictated or child-written books among the most interesting materials they want to examine and read, if possible.

- Each child in the latter part of kindergarten or first grade can make a *word bank*. A word bank is a collection of all the words that the child has found interesting and useful from individual and group LEA charts and stories. The child, if he or she can, or the teacher, tutor, or family member, prints each word on a piece of tag board about 1 inch by 3 inches with a dark-colored marking pen or crayon. The child then files the words in a large brown envelope, a shoe box, or some other appropriate container. The child should review his or her word bank words on a regular basis, use them in an oral or written sentence, and then return them to the word bank. The word bank can be used along with a classroom word wall as an easy-to-find source for the spelling of commonly used and meaningful words.

Here are some words from an LEA story about a deer that observed a young child and his dog one summer day: *dog, deer, watched, backed, walked, again, afraid,* and *bark.*

The preceding steps in LEA dictation of both experience charts should be modified depending on each child's abilities and interests and each teacher, tutor, or family member's preferences. Here are two LEA stories dictated by first-grade children:

My Dog and a Deer

My dog and I live in the big woods.
We went for a walk by our house one day.
We saw a beautiful deer in a yard by our house.
The deer looked and looked at my dog and me.
We walked by him, and he just watched us.
As we were by him, he backed up a little.
He looked some more at us.
We walked closer again, and he just watched us.
Then he backed up a little again.
We walked closer again, and he just watched us.
After a while, he slowly walked away from us.
The deer didn't seem afraid of us at all.
My dog didn't bark at the deer one time.

The Black Bear

My dad and I were driving on a road in the woods one day.
All of a sudden, we saw a big animal coming out of the woods.
Then we saw what it was.
We were surprised that it was a big black bear.
He ran right across the road in front of our car.
We're lucky we didn't hit him.
The bear was running very fast.
I'm glad that we were in our car.
I wouldn't have wanted to meet that bear if we were walking.

Some LEA resources can be found in Appendix III.

THE LANGUAGE-EXPERIENCE APPROACH FOR CHILDREN WHO HAVE SPECIAL NEEDS

Some elements of the language-experience approach are especially well-suited to children who have special needs.

1. To motivate children with special needs to dictate a language-experience chart or story, a teacher, tutor, or family member can use the following experiences successfully:

   - A trip to an interesting, challenging place with many opportunities to discuss what is expected beforehand and what was seen on the trip. Some places of interest are a pet shop, a zoo, a toy store, a farm, a railroad train ride, and a fire station.

- A simple art or construction activity in which *process* instead of *product* is stressed. Some examples include finger painting, making a simple puppet such as a stick puppet using tongue depressors and construction paper, making a construction paper snowman, building a snowman outside in winter, "dressing up" to play house, and making a drawing in instant pudding.

- A simple cooking or baking activity with a two-step or three-step recipe perhaps using rebuses (pictures). Here are examples: frosting pre-made cupcakes; baking prepared refrigerated cookies; spreading peanut butter, jam, or jelly on bread; dishing up ice cream; and mixing up precut vegetables or fruits to make a salad.

- A simple visual or aural activity like watching a videotape, listening to a picture book or simple chapter book being read aloud, or looking at some motivating pictures.

2. Children with special needs can participate in a simple preliminary discussion before dictating a brief, language-experience chart or story if the discussion is somewhat structured by a teacher, tutor, or family member. Some special-needs children may have to be motivated to participate in such a preliminary discussion, since their oral language skills may be somewhat limited.

3. Children with special needs can participate to some extent in language-experience chart or story dictation. However, they often may not participate in whole-class dictation. In a small-group dictation, each special-needs child may be asked to contribute one sentence for the chart. With some help, each child can usually do this. It often is more difficult for a special needs child to dictate an entire language-experience story or book since he or she often may have quite limited oral language skills. If this is the case, the following may help:

   - A highly motivating initiating experience;

   - A language-experience book with only one dictated sentence per page;

   - Trying to record the child's exact oral language as much as possible; or

   - Using a pre-made teacher-constructed book or commercial blank book for the transcribed story. Many special-needs children cannot construct their own experience books.

4. These are the skills that a special-needs child usually can learn from a dictated experience chart or experience book:

   - Left-to-right progression, by watching the teacher, tutor, or family member's hand move left-to-right under each sentence;

   - Letter-name recognition and identification, especially of initial consonant sounds;

   - Several simple motivating sight words from the chart or story;

- Beginning concept of word boundaries; and

- Fluency practice through rereading each transcribed experience chart or story a number of times.

5. A dictated language-experience story or chart can be illustrated using crayons, markers, or finger paints. These seem to be the simplest for such children.

6. The teacher, tutor, or family member can print one or two easy, meaningful words for inclusion in each child's *word bank*.

THE LANGUAGE-EXPERIENCE APPROACH FOR CHILDREN WITH AVERAGE LINGUISTIC SKILLS

Some of the elements of the language-experience approach seem especially useful with children who have average linguistic skills. These experiences should be an extension of the elements summarized in the previous section.

To motivate children to dictate or write (using letter strings or invented spelling) a language-experience chart or story, a teacher, tutor, or family member can use the following experiences successfully:

- A wider range of places may be appropriate for trips: a wildlife preserve, a zoo, an airport, a railroad train station, a police station, a fire station, a dairy farm, a grain farm, the post office, and a local sporting event.

- A simple art or construction activity that stresses *process* more than *product*s may work. A few examples are watercolor or tempera painting; making a fairly complex puppet such as a sock puppet using an old sock, red felt for a mouth, and a sewing machine; constructing a kite; constructing a playhouse out of cardboard boxes; making a May basket; making a simple collage; and making crayon etchings with fall leaves.

- A cooking or baking activity with a simple recipe, perhaps using rebuses (pictures). Here are some possibilities: making butter, deviled eggs, vegetable soup, edible alphabet letters, and baking cookies, muffins, or scones.

- A visual or aural activity, including the examples given above for children with special needs.

Children with average linguistic aptitude usually can participate quite effectively in a brief preliminary discussion before dictating (most likely) or writing (using letter strings or invented spelling) a language-experience chart or story with only minimal structure by a teacher, tutor, or family member. Many children with average linguistic skills use standard English with mostly correct grammar with the exception of some overgeneralizations such as "*runned*" or "*goed.*"

Children with average linguistic skills usually can use a language-experience chart or story dictation effectively. They often are able to participate in whole-class, small-group, and individual dictation. They usually enjoy small-group and individual dictation the most. The story or book always should be transcribed exactly as it was dictated, including nonstandard language patterns.

It is usually most efficient to use a pre-made teacher-constructed or commercial blank book. However, a child with average linguistic skills can construct and illustrate an experience book with help from an adult or classmate(s) if he or she wants.

Here are some additional skills beyond those for children with special needs that a child with average linguistic aptitude often can learn from a dictated experience chart or story:

- Letter-name recognition and identification of consonants and vowels;

- Recognition and identification of some sight words that are found in the language-experience charts and stories;

- Concept of word boundaries (the "white spaces") between words;

- Beginning understanding of simple suffixes such as "*s*," "*ed*," and "*ing*"; and

- Motivation to read his or her own language-experience books or those of his or her classmates.

A dictated or child-written language-experience chart or story can be illustrated in more ways by children with average linguistic skills. Some additional options are markers, colored chalk, watercolor paints, tempera paints, and construction paper cutouts.

An adult or the child can print several important words for inclusion in the child's *word bank.*

THE LANGUAGE-EXPERIENCE APPROACH FOR CHILDREN WITH ABOVE AVERAGE LINGUISTIC SKILLS

Here are elements of the language-experience approach that prove to be especially useful with young children who have above average linguistic skills. These experiences are an extension of the elements discussed in the two previous sections. These elements are the highest level of the language-experience approach and should be the goals for all children, if possible.

The following experiences can successfully motivate children who have above average linguistic skills to dictate (less often) or write a language-experience chart or story using invented spelling:

- A trip to an even wider range of locations, including a planetarium, a museum, a children's discovery museum, a television station, a theme park, a hospital, a candy factory, an airport, a trout farm, a fishery, and a weather station.

- An art or construction activity that emphasizes both *process* and *product.* For these children, *product* can be important, but should never receive excessive emphasis. A few additional examples for this group include making a quite complex puppet such as a papier-mâché puppet head out of Styrofoam, a cardboard neck tube, instant papier-mâché, poster paints, and white glue; constructing a make-believe veterinarian's office; making snowflakes out of white construction paper; constructing a make-believe grocery store; making a collage; and origami.

- A cooking or baking activity using somewhat more complex recipes. Here are several examples: baking bread, baking a birthday cake, cooking a Thanksgiving dinner, cooking lasagna, making pizza, making fudge, and making peanut brittle.

- A visual or aural activity such as these: watching an educational videotape or DVD, listening to a mass market book being read aloud, viewing demonstrations, and observing scientific experiments.

Children with above average linguistic skills can participate very effectively in a preliminary discussion before dictating (less often) or writing a language-experience chart or story using invented spelling with very limited or no help. Most children with above average linguistic skills use standard English with mainly correct grammar.

Children with above average linguistic skills can participate very effectively in language-experience dictation. However, they may more enjoy writing an entire language-experience story or book independently using invented or traditional spelling. Although they may want to use a pre-made teacher-constructed book or a commercially available blank book for a written experience book, most such children prefer to construct their own experience book, entirely independently or with minimal help.

The following are additional skills that a child with above average linguistic skills usually can learn from a dictated, or more commonly, written language-experience chart or story:

- Letter-name identification of all the upper- and lowercase alphabet letters;
- Letter-sound relationships (phonics) of the consonants and, to a lesser extent, the vowels;
- Identification of a number of the words that are found in his or her dictated and written experience stories and books and those of his or her classmates;
- Understanding of the use of sentence context in which a word that makes sense is substituted for an omitted word in an experience chart or story;
- Ability to fluently read his or her own language-experience stories and books and those of classmates; and
- Strong motivation to read his or her own language-experience books or those of classmates.

A dictated or child-written language-experience story or book can be illustrated in several different ways by children with above average linguistic skills. Additional media appropriate for these children include watercolor paints and cloth, among others.

The child with above average linguistic skills can print several important words from his or her charts and stories in his or her *word bank*. Later the child can use the words from the word bank in the following ways: alphabetizing, classifying, and reviewing them for later immediate identification.

Assessment Devices in Early Literacy Programs

Do you think that most children in first grade are adept at taking standardized tests? If you answered "No," you are correct. Young children can have more difficulty with the mechanics of taking a test than with the actual skills the test is evaluating. For example, they can have trouble responding on computer-scored answer keys even if they know the correct answers. Most young children respond much more easily and accurately to informal devices of various types. Informal assessment devices usually quite accurately reflect the actual reading, writing, and spelling strengths and weaknesses of young children. This chapter primarily contains *reproducible informal assessment devices* that teachers, tutors, and family members can duplicate and immediately use.

Completing the chapter's informal pre-assessment device to determine your knowledge and attitudes about assessment in early childhood programs will help you evaluate your present understanding of standardized and informal early childhood assessment devices. Then the chapter presents a very brief description of standardized tests and the major advantages and limitations of using them in early literacy programs. Following that is a very brief discussion of informal assessment devices in early literacy programs, with a summary of the major advantages and limitations of using them in early childhood programs.

The major portion of the chapter consists of numerous reproducible informal assessment devices. After reading this chapter, early childhood teachers and tutors as well as family members will understand assessment much better and will be able to assess effectively the literacy strengths and weaknesses of the children with whom they interact.

Decide if each statement is *accurate* (true) or *not accurate* (false). Evaluate your answers after you have read the chapter. The answers are on page 319.

_____ 1. The influence of testing reading in early childhood programs is greater now than at any other time in the history of the United States.

_____ 2. Most standardized reading tests are criterion-referenced.

_____ 3. A major advantage of using standardized tests is the ease of scoring and reporting for teachers and tutors.

_____ 4. "Teaching for a test" may take valuable time away from other classroom activities such as creative writing, art, and rhythm activities.

_____ 5. A few young children who score well on a standardized test may still not enjoy reading for pleasure or information.

_____ 6. Informal assessment devices help teachers and tutors make minute-to-minute decisions about teaching reading and writing.

_____ 7. Learning how to administer and evaluate some informal assessment devices may take considerable time.

_____ 8. A Concepts About Books Checklist can evaluate a child's understanding of where to begin reading on a printed page.

_____ 9. A Concepts About Print Checklist may evaluate a child's understanding of word boundaries.

_____ 10. A novice reading teacher can learn to administer and evaluate a running record quite easily.

_____ 11. A running record evaluates a child's substitutions, self-corrections, and requests for teacher or tutor help, among other elements.

_____ 12. A limitation of an Individual Reading Inventory (IRI) is the time involved to administer and evaluate it accurately.

_____ 13. A self-correction is counted as an error on an Individual Reading Inventory (IRI).

_____ 14. A child's interests may influence his or her performance on an Individual Reading Inventory (IRI).

_____ 15. A child's performance on an Individual Reading Inventory (IRI) always should be considered a tentative indicator of his or her actual independent, instructional, and frustration reading levels.

_____ 16. The retelling or tell-back strategy was first used around 1920 as the major way of testing reading comprehension.

_____ 17. Multiple forms on an Individual Reading Inventory (IRI) often are not completely parallel.

_____ 18. The questions on an Individual Reading Inventory (IRI) always should be passage dependent.

STANDARDIZED TESTS AND THEIR MAJOR ADVANTAGES AND LIMITATIONS

Standardized tests are formal tests with standard directions, precise time limits, and rigid scoring. A reading teacher or tutor cannot vary from the procedures that are contained in the test if the results are going to be considered accurate.

Most standardized tests are norm-referenced. This type of test helps a teacher compare his or her pupils' scores with a standardized sample similar in age, grade level, sex, geographic location, and socioeconomic status. Usually the norms on such a test are reported as follows:

- *Raw Score*—The total number of correct answers on the test. This score is meaningless until it is changed into a percentile rank, stanine, grade equivalent, or standard score.

- *Percentile Rank*—The point on a scale of *1* to *99* indicating what percentage of pupils scored equally or lower. As an example, a percentile rank of *56* means that *56 percent* of the pupils who took the test scored the same or less.

- *Grade Equivalent Score*—This score characterizes a child's performance as equivalent to that of other students in a target grade. As an example, a grade equivalent score of *2.2* indicates that the child answered the same number of items correctly as the average second-grade student in the second month of school. The grade equivalent score does not indicate on what level the child is performing (i.e., a score of *2.2* does not indicate that a child can actually read at the beginning of the second-grade level, just that he or she can read as well as other second-grade students).

- *Stanine*—The point on a nine-point scale with *5* being the average stanine. The word *stanine* is a combination of the words "standard" and "nine." The stanines *4, 5,* and *6* are average points, with *1, 2,* and *3* being below average, and *7, 8,* and *9* above average. Stanines are valuable when comparing subtests of norm-referenced tests.

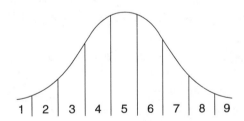

- *Scaled Scores*—A continuous ranking from *000* to *999* of a series of norm-referenced tests from the lowest to the highest. These scores may be useful for comparing scores from several different tests as they are the only scores that can be *averaged.*

In the primary grades children often are given a *standardized achievement test* to determine their reading progress. The reading portions are vocabulary (word meaning), sentence and simple paragraph comprehension, and occasionally, word study. These tests attempt to find children who need additional reading testing or to determine the amount of reading progress a child has made during the school year. Standardized tests are simple to administer and score. They are evaluated by computer, and the school district is given a computer printout of the complete results. They usually are mandated by school districts, and often are an example of *high-stakes testing*.

IMPORTANT NOTE: Results from such a test always should be interpreted very cautiously, especially when the test is given to any child outside the average, including children who are culturally or linguistically diverse. *This is especially true in first, second, and third grades.*

The most common contemporary standardized achievement tests all are available in a variety of forms and on various grade levels from beginning reading onward. They include:

- *Iowa Test of Basic Skills*—AGS Publishing
- *Metropolitan Achievement Test*—Harcourt Educational Measurement
- *Stanford Achievement Test*—Harcourt Educational Measurement

Criterion-referenced tests or *mastery tests* are a much less common type of standardized test. Instead of using norms, the results are reported in terms of a *standard* or *criterion*. These are formal measures designed to focus on a child's mastery of a specific reading skill or skills. A child has to receive a prescribed score (usually the *80 percent* accuracy level) to demonstrate mastery in the tested skill. These tests sometimes are criticized because the criterion level is arbitrary. The difference between passing and not passing may be very small. In addition, some children can learn isolated reading skills very well but still are not able to read whole stories or books effectively.

Two types of standards that are often identified with criterion-referenced assessment are *benchmarks* and *rubrics*. A *benchmark* is a written description of a key task that children are expected to perform successfully. For example, a benchmark for short vowel phonemes (sounds) might be: *Is able to provide a word that contains a short /a/, short /e/, short /i/, short /o/, or short /u/.* A *rubric* is a written description of what is expected in order to meet a certain level of performance and is accompanied by samples of typical performance. The main advantage of a rubric is that it provides criteria or standards for task assessment.

Here are the major advantages to using standardized tests for early literacy:

- Teachers and tutors, including those who are inexperienced, find them easy both to give and to evaluate.
- They take a limited amount of time to administer.
- Most are norm-referenced, so the teacher or tutor can easily compare the results achieved by a class or an individual student with those of a standardization sample that is similar in various ways.
- They are *reliable* and *valid*. *Test reliability* means that a child who takes equivalent forms of a test usually achieves about the same results. *Test validity* means that the test evaluates what it is supposed to evaluate.

Here are the major limitations of standardized tests:

- They may *overestimate* a child's instructional reading level due to guessing multiple-choice answers correctly. Some students may guess at all of the items on a test, finish it, and therefore receive a fairly high score, while a child who actually reads the items on a test may not finish it.

- *Taking the test* may be more difficult than the material that is included on the test, especially for young children who have learning disabilities or cultural or linguistic differences from the norm sample. For example, a child who knows the answer may not be able to fill in the answer bubble.

- Many standardized tests can evaluate a child's prior knowledge and experience, assuming middle-class experiences and culture. The score that a child from a class or ethnic background outside the norm earns on a standardized test is likely to be significantly lower than his or her actual reading level.

- The items on a standardized test may not be *passage dependent*. If they can be answered only on the basis of the reader's prior knowledge and experiences without reading the material, they are not testing the child's actual reading level.

- Although the grade equivalent score is very commonly used, it is subject to considerable misinterpretation, as explained at the beginning of this section. The grade equivalent score typically represents a child's frustration reading level rather than the instructional reading level.

- Since most standardized tests are strictly timed, they often penalize the slow, but careful, reader who cannot finish the test during the prescribed time limit.

- Children must be given the proper level of the test. If a child with special needs is given a test that is too difficult, the score is likely to be incorrect.

- Some children have a high degree of test anxiety and are poor test takers. Standardized tests usually underestimate these children's actual instructional reading level.

The results from standardized tests should never be used as a sole deciding factor to group young children in a classroom or place them in a special program. In addition, they should not be used to evaluate teachers or tutors. Standardized test scores can be greatly influenced by factors such as the examiner-examinee relationship, the child's health on the day of the test, the test format, the physical conditions in the classroom, and the time of the day or year.

INFORMAL ASSESSMENT IN EARLY LITERACY PROGRAMS

Informal (or *process-oriented*) *assessment* is an important part of instruction and should take place continuously. Informal assessment often is more useful in determining a child's literacy strengths and weaknesses than are standardized tests, especially if the informal assessment is done by experienced teachers.

Informal assessment devices are especially important to determine the early literacy levels of young children. I recommend that informal assessment be used more often than standardized tests.

Informal assessment can take many forms, including checklists, miscue analysis, Individual Reading Inventories (IRIs), conferences and interviews of various types, retellings, response journals, observation journals, creative book reports, holistic scoring of writing, and portfolio assessment. Reproducible examples of informal assessment devices are included in this chapter.

Here are the major advantages of using informal assessment devices in early childhood literacy programs:

- They are more authentic than most standardized devices.

- They emphasize the *process aspects* of reading, writing, and spelling rather than the *product aspects*.

- They usually are more relevant to what is being taught.

- They evaluate the whole language approach effectively. Traditional tests view reading as a group of discrete subskills.

- They are usually more accurate reflections of the accomplishments and attitudes of children with special needs than standardized tests.

- They usually reflect the different styles of teaching and learning more effectively than standardized tests.

- They do not have rigid directions and time limits, which often penalize a slow, but accurate, reader.

Here are the major limitations of informal assessment devices:

- They can be time-consuming to construct and/or evaluate, especially without access to reproducible informal assessment devices like the ones in this book.

- A reading teacher or tutor may need a significant investment in time and effort to become adept at giving and evaluating them.

- They usually are neither statistically reliable nor valid. Although they may be extremely valuable, they do not meet the statistical requirements for reliability and validity.

- They may make it difficult to evaluate children by predetermined criteria such as traditional report cards and grades.

- Their results often do not meet the requirements of administrators, school boards, state boards of education, the federal government, or family members.

- Although they may not be easy to locate, this book is one resource for reproducible informal assessment devices.

Reproducible Informal Assessment Devices

The remainder of this chapter consists of reproducible informal assessment devices. Each one includes a brief description of the device, easy-to-understand directions for administering and evaluating it, and a reproducible copy of the device. These devices include:

Concepts About Books Checklist
Concepts About Print Checklist
Running Records
Individual Reading Inventories
Checklist of Primary-Grade Writing Behaviors

Concepts About Books Checklist

This checklist assesses young children's understanding of the various elements found in trade books and how to use them effectively. This checklist can be given to children as young as three years old (if they have excellent linguistic skills) or as old as seven years (if they have special needs). It should primarily be used with children in kindergarten and perhaps beginning first grade.

Young children must master all of the concepts included on this checklist if they are to make good subsequent progress in reading.

CONCEPTS ABOUT BOOKS CHECKLIST: EMERGENT LITERACY LEVEL

	Often	Sometimes	Not Yet
1. Knows that a book is for reading.	_____	_____	_____

For a Children's Trade Book

	Often	Sometimes	Not Yet
2. Can point out the front, middle, and back.	_____	_____	_____
3. Can point out the top, middle, and bottom.	_____	_____	_____
4. Knows that a reader reads the print, not the pictures.	_____	_____	_____
5. Can point out where to begin reading on a page.	_____	_____	_____
6. Can point out the title and knows its purpose.	_____	_____	_____
7. Can point to the author's name and understands what the author has done.	_____	_____	_____
8. Can point to the illustrator's name and understands what the illustrator has done.	_____	_____	_____
9. Can make accurate predictions about the content from the title.	_____	_____	_____
10. Can make accurate predictions about the content while it is being read.	_____	_____	_____
11. Is able to turn the pages correctly.	_____	_____	_____

Concepts About Print Checklist

This checklist is appropriate for kindergarten children who have above average linguistic skills, for first graders who have average linguistic skills, and for children in second and possibly third grade who have below average linguistic skills. Young children need to master all of the concepts as quickly as possible, certainly before entering fourth grade. If any child, including those with special needs, does not have competency in one or more of the reading subskills evaluated by this checklist, he or she should have instruction and/or reinforcement in them until mastery is attained. In general, the items on this checklist are presented in an easy-to-difficult sequence.

CONCEPTS ABOUT PRINT CHECKLIST

	Often	Sometimes	Not Yet
1. Can identify environment print such as *STOP, McDonald's, Christmas, Exit,* and *Sale,* among many others.	_____	_____	_____

On a Printed Page of a Children's Trade Book

	Often	Sometimes	Not Yet
2. Can point to a *letter.*	_____	_____	_____
3. Can point to a *word.*	_____	_____	_____
4. Can point to a *word boundary* (*white spaces*).	_____	_____	_____
5. Understands that the print goes from left to right.	_____	_____	_____
6. Understands the use of a period.	_____	_____	_____
7. Understands the use of a comma.	_____	_____	_____
8. Understands the use of a question mark.	_____	_____	_____
9. Can recognize all of the lowercase letter names in isolation.	_____	_____	_____
10. Can recognize all of the lowercase letter names in context.	_____	_____	_____
11. Can recognize all the uppercase letter names in isolation.	_____	_____	_____
12. Can recognize all the uppercase letter names in context.	_____	_____	_____
13. Is able to use picture clues as a word-identification technique.	_____	_____	_____
14. Can identify sight words such as *to, of, was, they, is, down, do, one, for,* and *have* in isolation.	_____	_____	_____
15. Can identify sight words such as *said, her, there, as, out, you, the, my,* and *what* in context.	_____	_____	_____

Name: _____ Grade: _____

CONCEPTS ABOUT PRINT CHECKLIST *(continued)*

	Often	Sometimes	Not Yet
16. Can suggest a rhyming word (can include some nonsense words) for a word that is provided: *cat, fat, hat, mat, pat, sat, vat.*	_____	_____	_____
17. Can provide a word that begins with *b, c (k and s sounds), d, f, g (g and j sounds), h, j, k, l, m, n, p, q(u), r, s, t, v, w, x, y, z.*	_____	_____	_____
18. Can provide a word that begins with a consonant blend: *bl, cl, fl, gl, pl, sl.*	_____	_____	_____
19. Can provide a word containing each of these long and short vowel sounds: */a/—ape, apple; /e/—eel, egg; /i/—ice, it; /o/—oat, octopus; /u/—use, up.*	_____	_____	_____
20. Can attach consonants to a rime: *b-ill, d-ill, f-ill, g-ill, h-ill, k-ill, m-ill, p-ill, s-ill, t-ill, w-ill.*	_____	_____	_____
21. Can attach a consonant blend to a rime: *br-ing, cl-ing, fl-ing, spr-ing, str-ing, sw-ing.*	_____	_____	_____
22. Can blend phonemes (sounds) into words.	_____	_____	_____
23. Can divide (segment) phonemes (sounds) into words.	_____	_____	_____
24. Uses word placement or grammar clues to identify unknown words.	_____	_____	_____
25. Can correctly predict unknown words by using context clues along with phonics (letter-sound relationships).	_____	_____	_____

Running Records

Running records are an effective way of assessing a young child's reading progress. A running record is an individual assessment device that requires only the child's own copy of the material that he or she is going to read aloud and paper and a pencil or pen for the reading teacher or tutor. (An inexperienced adult may find a pencil easier.) Since running records evaluate oral reading in a number of ways, not including comprehension, I recommend that the child also briefly retell the material that he or she has read.

A running record has two main purposes: (1) to determine whether a child's reading materials are on the instructional reading level and (2) to ascertain information about the child's word identification processes. Although running records are especially useful in first grade, they also may be used for children in second and third grades who have special needs.

As used in the first-grade early intervention program *Reading Recovery* and explained in Clay (2002), even though running records are considered informal assessment devices, they must be given according to a standardized format. Running records may be recorded (as long as the fair-use provision of the copyright law is adhered to or permission is obtained from the publisher) on a photocopy of the reading material that the child is reading or (more common and preferred) on a blank piece of paper (Learning Media, 1991).

To determine whether a child's reading materials are at the correct difficulty level and to ascertain whether a child is making correct use of cueing strategies, including meaning (use of semantic or context clues), visual (sight word or phonic clues), or syntactic (grammar or word order clues), take a running record on a book, reader, or simple textbook that the child has already read.

To assess a child's ability to read more difficult materials and to apply cueing strategies independently, take a running record on material that the child has not yet read. If the book is fairly short, take a running record from the entire book. If the book is long, take a running record from a sample of one hundred to two hundred words.

Competency in taking a running record requires considerable practice and concentration. Tape recording the child's oral reading is good practice and I recommend it; however, true proponents of the running record caution against this. After taking a running record, record the number of words in the entire selection, the number of errors that the child made, the number of self-corrections made (very important), and the accuracy rate. Table 2.1 shows the symbols and instructions for keeping a running record.

Although Clay (2002) recommends 90 percent as an adequate accuracy rate in oral reading, 95 percent undoubtedly is preferable. A child's reading errors must be analyzed to determine what reading strategies he or she is using. Incorrect reading strategies should be corrected as quickly as possible. Think about the following questions:

- Does the child use picture clues as an aid to meaning?

- Do the child's errors make sense? Are they *semantically* (contextually) acceptable? Does the child read for meaning?

- Does the child use visual or *sound-symbol* (phonic) cues? Are the child's errors similar in appearance and sound to the target word?

- Does the child use *syntactic* (word order or grammar) cues?

Table 2.1.   Running Record Symbols

Symbols	Text	Example
Each work read correctly is marked with a check mark.	Black bears eat very little meat.	✓ ✓ ✓ ✓ ✓ ✓
Substitutions are written above the line.	Black bears often live in the woods, swamps, and parklands away from people.	✓ ✓ ✓ ✓ ✓ ✓ ✓ swims/swamps ✓ parks ✓ ✓ ✓ /parklands
Self-corrections are marked SC.	They will not hurt a person if he or she stays away from them.	✓ ✓ ✓ harm/sc ✓ ✓ /hurt; ✓ ✓ ✓ ✓ ✓ ✓ ✓ ✓
A dash is used to indicate no response.	Today black bears often are seen close to towns.	✓ ✓ ✓ – ✓ ✓ ✓ ✓ /often
A dash is used to indicate an insertion of a word.	Today black bears often are seen close to towns.	✓ ✓ ✓ ✓ ✓ ✓ ✓ by ✓ /–
A T is used to indicate that a child has been told a word.	Today black bears often are seen close to towns.	✓ ✓ ✓ T ✓ ✓ ✓ ✓ /often
The letter A indicates that the child has asked for help.	Today black bears often are seen close to towns.	✓ ✓ ✓ A ✓ ✓ ✓ ✓ /often
At times the child becomes so confused by a misreading that it is suggested that he or she "try that again" (coded TTA). Brackets are put around the section that has been misread, the entire misreading is counted as one error, and the child reads it again for a new score.	They usually live on grasses and other plants in the spring, fruits and berries in the summer, and nuts and acorns in the fall.	TTA [fry ✓ beans ✓ ✓ ✓ / fruits berries]
A repetition is indicated with an R. Although not counted as errors, repetitions are often part of an attempt to puzzle out a difficult term. The point to which the child returns in the repetition is indicated by an arrow.	When a person meets a black bear, the bear usually will run away from him or her.	✓ ✓ ✓ ✓ ✓ ✓ ✓ ✓ ✓ / T ✓ ✓ ✓ ✓ ✓ ✓ / usually↓ R

- Does the child integrate clues? Balance the use of meaning clues with sound-symbol clues? Avoid relying too heavily on just one type of word identification cue?

- Does the child self-correct errors, especially those that interfere with comprehension? Is the child aware when reading errors do not make sense in the material?

- What reading strategies does the child need to master?

You also can observe whether or not a child reads from left to right and from top to bottom and whether there is one-to-one correspondence (voice-print match). For more comprehensive information about how to analyze and interpret running records, consult Clay (2002) for more detail.

How to Evaluate a Running Record

Exhibit 2.1 shows a passage on the first-grade level given to a second-grade child named Emmie. A detailed analysis of Emmie's performance on this running record and some recommendations for her classroom reading teacher or tutor are given later in this chapter.

Exhibit 2.1.   Black Bears

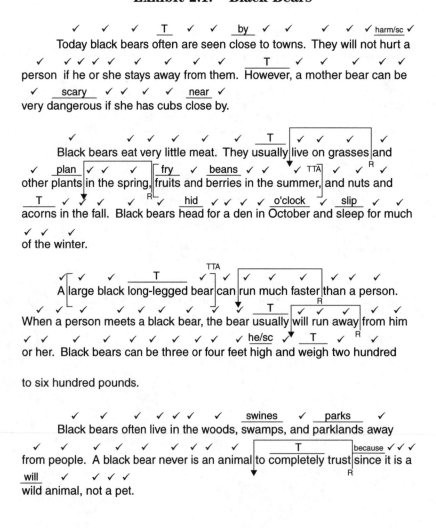

Emmie's Performance on the Running Record

The passage Emmie read aloud contained *160* words. She made *23* miscues. Dividing *23* by *160* obtains a reading error percentage of about *13* or *14 percent*. Therefore, Emmie read the passage at about the *86–87 percent* level of accuracy. This passage is at her frustration (hard) reading level. Although Clay (2002) feels that a *90 percent* accurate rate is acceptable, I believe that a child should have an accuracy level of *95 percent* or better to read with fluency and ease.

Let's examine Emmie's errors line by line on a copy of the passage, shown in Exhibit 2.2.

Exhibit 2.2.   Black Bears

✓   ✓   ✓   T   ✓   ✓   by ✓   ✓   ✓   ✓ ✓ harm/sc ✓
Today black bears often are seen close to towns. They will not hurt a

One error—one substitution. The self-correction is not counted as an error.

✓   ✓ ✓ ✓ ✓   ✓   ✓   ✓   ✓   T   ✓   ✓   ✓   ✓ ✓
person if he or she stays away from them. However, a mother bear can be

One error—one "teacher told the word"

✓   scary   ✓ ✓   ✓   ✓   near ✓
very dangerous if she has cubs close by.

Two errors—two substitutions

✓   ✓   ✓   ✓   ✓   ✓   T   ✓ ✓   ✓   ✓
Black bears eat very little meat. They usually live on grasses and
R

One error—one "teacher told the word." The repetition is not counted as an error.

✓   plan ✓ ✓   ✓   fry ✓   beans ✓ ✓   ✓ TTA ✓   ✓   ✓
other plants in the spring, fruits and berries in the summer, and nuts and
R

Four errors—three substitutions and one "try that again." The repetition is not counted as an error.

T   ✓ ✓   ✓   ✓   ✓   hid ✓ ✓ ✓ ✓ o'clock ✓   slip ✓   ✓
acorns in the fall. Black bears head for a den in October and sleep for much

Four errors—three substitutions and one "teacher told the word"

✓ ✓   ✓
of the winter.

No errors

TTA
✓ ✓   ✓   T   ✓ ✓ ✓   ✓   ✓   ✓ ✓   ✓
A large black long-legged bear can run much faster than a person.
R

Two errors—one "teacher told the word" and one "try that again." The repetition is not counted as an error.

✓ ✓ ✓   ✓   ✓   ✓   ✓   ✓ ✓   T   ✓ ✓ ✓
When a person meets a black bear, the bear usually will run away
R

One error—one "teacher told the word." The repetition is not counted as an error.

✓   ✓ ✓ ✓   ✓   ✓   ✓ ✓   ✓   ✓   ✓ ✓ he/sc ✓   T   ✓   ✓
from him or her. Black bears can be three or four feet high and weigh

One error—one "teacher told the word." The self-correction is not counted as an error.

Exhibit 2.2 (continued).   Black Bears

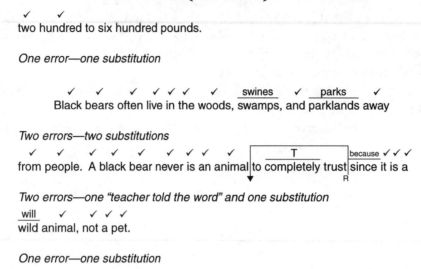

two hundred to six hundred pounds.

One error—one substitution

Black bears often live in the woods, swamps, and parklands away

Two errors—two substitutions

from people. A black bear never is an animal to completely trust since it is a

Two errors—one "teacher told the word" and one substitution

wild animal, not a pet.

One error—one substitution

Emmie demonstrated several reading strengths. She had a fairly good sight vocabulary. Some of her substitutions made sense in context, while others did not.

She had a positive attitude and did not become easily frustrated. However, Emmie showed the following weaknesses in her oral reading of the passage:

- She may not always be reading for understanding. A number of her substitutions did not make sense in context.

- Since Emmie made only two self-corrections, she was not monitoring her comprehension effectively. This major problem also was illustrated when she substituted words that did not make sense. Self-monitoring must be stressed significantly in her reading improvement program.

- Emmie needs to learn to take more risks. Her teacher had to supply seven words for her (almost 5 percent of the words in the passage). That indicates not only that the material was much too difficult for her, but also that she did not attempt to identify the words either by semantic cues, visual cues, syntactic cues, or a combination.

- Because she made six repetitions while reading this passage, she needs much easier reading material. Repetitions often are a child's way of "stalling for time" while he or she examines the next few words.

- Emmie needs to look more carefully at the words. Sometimes she looked at only the initial consonant or consonant blend and did not look at the rest of the word.

- She needs instruction and/or practice in using visual (sight word and phonic) cues and especially in *cross-checking cues* (semantic, visual, and syntactic). She needs to use visual cues along with semantic (meaning) and syntactic (grammar) cues.

- Perhaps most importantly, Emmie needs to read much easier, highly motivating material on her *independent* (easy) and *high instructional* (with teacher support) reading levels. Easier material will go a long way in helping her overcome her reading miscues.

To summarize, Emmie's teachers should provide her with easy, interesting reading materials that are on her independent (easy) or high instructional (with some teacher support) reading levels to improve her confidence and fluency. This will also greatly improve her reading comprehension and self-monitoring skills. She must always be sure that her reading makes sense. She also should be given some practice in phonic skills and considerable practice in cross-checking cues (semantic, visual, and syntactic).

Individual Reading Inventory

The *Individual Reading Inventory* (IRI), also called an *informal reading inventory*, is an informal assessment device designed to determine a child's *independent* (easy), *instructional* (with teacher support), and *frustration* (difficult) reading levels and specific reading strengths and weaknesses. An IRI is usually only given to disabled readers or children with learning disabilities, although it can be helpful in evaluating any child.

The main purposes of an IRI are the following:

- To ascertain a child's prior knowledge and interests;
- To determine a child's ability to predict the content of a passage;
- To determine a child's *approximate* independent, instructional, and frustration reading levels;
- To estimate a child's listening comprehension ability;
- To learn about a child's progress in word identification, using the three main cueing systems (semantic, visual, and syntactic), oral reading fluency, and literal and interpretive comprehension skills;
- To enable the teacher, tutor, or family member to closely observe a child engaging in a variety of reading tasks; and
- To determine a child's skills in self-monitoring or metacognition.

The Individual Reading Inventory varies in format depending on who is giving it. The version contained in this book can be given by any adult. A Title I reading teacher or a tutor can give an IRI to most of the children with whom he or she is working near the beginning of the school year. However, at that time, he or she may want to give a running record instead, because a running record may yield more accurate results for some first-grade children and be less intimidating. A classroom teacher may want to give an IRI to a few disabled readers in his or her classroom early in the school year. A teacher of learning disabled pupils can give an IRI to most students, remembering that it may be too difficult for young readers. A reading volunteer will probably want to give an IRI to most pupils early in the sessions unless the children are reading at the early first-grade level or lower. A family member can give an Individual Reading Inventory anytime he or she wants to informally assess a child's reading progress.

NOTE: Giving too many informal assessment devices near the beginning of the school year may overwhelm the children and perhaps hinder subsequent progress.

Here are the main steps of an IRI:

1. *Establish rapport with the child.* This is important if you do not know the child well. If you already are well acquainted, immediately proceed to the next step. If not, ask the child some informal questions about his or her interests, hobbies, reading, and pets, among other things. You also can ask about his or her perception of reading skills.

Ask questions about his or her family life only if this is pertinent to the assessment and can be done tactfully and with sensitivity.

2. *Give the graded word lists.* The graded word lists of the IRI included in this book begin at about the pre-primer reading level and continue through the fifth-grade reading level. Each graded word list contains *twenty-five* words. The child reads each word aloud and continues until he or she misses about *five* words (*20 percent*) or reaches an obvious frustration reading level. The examiner also can stop when the child misses three words in a row. This often is called the *ceiling level.* The main purposes of the lists are to determine how well a student identifies words in isolation in comparison to (sentence) context, to observe what types of visual cues (sight, phonic, or word structure) the child uses to identify words, and to determine at about what level the child should begin reading the graded oral reading passages.

3. *Give the graded oral (silent) reading passages.* These are a series of narrative and content passages that begin at the pre-primer level and continue through the fifth grade. Some may be used for assessment of silent reading or listening comprehension. A child usually begins with a passage at least *one grade level* below his or her estimated instructional reading level. This judgment may be made from the child's performance on the word lists and the examiner's observation of previous reading performance.

Advantages and Limitations of Using an IRI

Major advantages of using an IRI for informal assessment of reading in early childhood programs include:

- Different forms of an IRI can be used as a pre-test and post-test of a child's reading progress. The pre-test is given before the teaching begins, and the post-test when the teaching is completed.

- The reading levels determined from an IRI usually are more accurate than those from a group-administered standardized test, because standardized tests allow children to randomly guess answers.

- An IRI allows the examiner to observe a child while he or she is reading orally. The examiner can notice if a child uses meaning cues, visual cues, and syntactic cues and also cross-checks the three different cueing systems. In addition, the examiner can notice other aspects of the child's reading performance, such as one-to-one correspondence, answers to comprehension questions, distractibility, oral reading fluency, word-by-word reading, and evidence of frustration.

- An IRI enables the examiner to observe a child's *pattern of errors*, to notice whether a child has made numerous omissions, substitutions, insertions, repetitions, reversals, pauses, or words supplied by the examiner. The IRI in this book also enables the examiner to recognize whether the child's miscues (errors) are usually *major* or *minor.*

- The IRI in this book uses activation of prior knowledge and interests that obviously cannot be assessed in a group-administered standardized test. This is a very important element of reading comprehension.

- The IRI in this book contains comprehension questions at both the explicit (literal) and implicit (interpretive, critical, and applied) levels. The child is given credit for sensible answers to the implicit questions, even if other answers are provided in the inventory.

Here are the main limitations of using an IRI:

- Since an IRI is given individually, it is somewhat time-consuming to give and evaluate. Running records usually take less time.

- A child's performance on an IRI may be greatly affected by his or her prior knowledge or interest in a specific subject. For example, a fifth-grade student in northern Wisconsin predicted that a passage about a *steel plow* would be about a snow plow. In actuality, the passage was about a steel plow used in farming. However, the child from northern Wisconsin had never seen a plowed field. An examiner must review all the passages on an IRI to determine how free from culture and gender bias they are and how interesting they would be to the specific children involved.

- Learning how to evaluate an IRI can be challenging, since each one differs on how to count and score miscues and has a different scoring system. An examiner should study the IRI in this book carefully before attempting to give, score, and evaluate a child's performance. In this IRI, for example, miscues that interfere with comprehension (major miscues) are weighted more heavily than those that do not (minor miscues), and dialect differences and self-corrections are not counted as miscues.

- Although the criteria for determining the independent, instructional, and frustration reading levels on an IRI are based on both research and many years of practical experience, they are nonetheless arbitrary and should be recognized as such.

To summarize, an IRI is a useful informal assessment device for determining a child's *approximate* reading levels and reading strengths and weaknesses in early childhood reading programs. It can be used as a supplement to a running record or in place of one. The main advantages of running records are that the actual material that the child recently has read or will soon read is used and that the running record is faster to give and score. However, both should be used at various times in early childhood reading programs.

IRI findings should be interpreted cautiously. Don't think of them as completely accurate, but as *tentative indicators* of a child's reading levels and skills, which should be modified when necessary.

Administering the Graded Word Lists and Reading Passages of an IRI

When administering IRI graded word lists, have the child begin with a word list *at least one reading level below* his or her estimated instructional reading level. Then the child continues pronouncing the words on the lists until he or she misses *three words* in a row or is able to pronounce fewer than *80 to 90 percent* of the words on the list.

Before the child begins reading the first appropriate reading passage, ask the questions that determine prior knowledge and interest in the material. Then have the child begin reading the graded oral reading passage that corresponds to the level at which *80 to 90 percent* of the words on a list were recognized.

A child should begin reading at a low enough level to avoid frustration at the outset. If either an initial graded word list or an initial passage is too hard, the child may not want to continue and try to do his or her best.

As the child reads each of the passages aloud, mark any oral reading miscues on your copy of the passage. Here is my recommended system for marking oral reading miscues:

- *Omission*—Circle the entire word or letter sound.

- *Insertion*—Insert with a caret.

gray
∧

- *Substitution/mispronunciation*—Draw a line through a substitution or mispronunciation and write it in.

spaniel
~~spend~~

- *Reversal*—Use the transposition symbol.

- *Repetition*—Use a wavy line to indicate a repetition of two or more words.

in the truck

- *Words Aided*—If a child gives no answer after about five seconds, provide the word for him or her and cross it out.

~~timber~~

Learning to mark oral reading miscues can be quite difficult. Focusing on the marking system may make an examiner fall behind in marking miscues and observing the important characteristics of the reading, such as excessive substitutions, repetitions, words aided, or word-by-word reading. Thus, an examiner normally tape records a child's reading so that he or she can mark the miscues later. Even an experienced IRI administrator may want to tape record a child's oral reading of the passages. A child may be self-conscious about reading aloud if he or she notices the examiner marking the miscues. This is particularly common in children who have reading or learning disabilities.

When a child has finished reading a passage aloud, ask the comprehension questions for that passage. The answers can be scored at that time or when the tape recording is played back. After a child has answered the comprehension questions, ask him or her to assess how well he or she has performed. An experienced examiner can ask the child to retell the major points of the passage instead of asking the comprehension questions.

Have the child stop reading when he or she has reached the frustration (difficult) reading level. This level is the point at which a child makes numerous miscues, has poor comprehension, appears tense and nervous, and wants to stop.

Evaluating the Graded Word Lists and Reading Passages of an IRI

The graded word lists and reading passages of an IRI help determine the child's approximate reading level, evaluate his or her pattern of oral reading miscues, observe self-corrections, and determine the child's strengths and weaknesses in reading.

As a child pronounces each word on a graded word list, mark his or her response by placing a + for a correct answer and a – or *0* for an incorrect answer. If a child pronounces a word phonetically, in addition to the – or *0* write the phonetic spelling of the word. If you have printed the words on a list on individual cards, place them in two different piles—correctly pronounced words and incorrectly pronounced words. Word lists can be scored when replaying the tape recording.

Then determine the child's *approximate reading level* on each of the word lists. This demonstrates the child's ability to *pronounce words in isolation*. Use the following *approximate percentages* to make this determination:

- 99 percent or more of the words on a list correctly identified—*independent reading level*

- 90 to 98 percent of the words on a list correctly identified—*instructional reading level*

- Fewer than about 89 percent of the words on a list correctly identified—*frustration reading level*

After a passage is read, the examiner asks him- or herself these questions:

- Did the child have excellent, good, or inadequate prior knowledge for reading this passage?

- Was the child able to access (activate) his or her prior knowledge for reading this passage?

- Did the child have sufficient interest in reading this passage so that a lack of interest did not significantly hinder his or her comprehension?

Use these guidelines to evaluate the IRI in this chapter.

1. Count any error that interferes significantly with comprehension as a *major oral reading miscue* and deduct one point.

2. Count any deviation from the printed material that does not seem to interfere significantly with comprehension as a *minor oral reading miscue* and deduct one-half point.

3. Count an addition that does not interfere significantly with the meaning of the material as half a miscue. Most additions do not.

4. Do not count a self-correction that occurs within a short period of time as an error. Usually a self-correction indicates that a child is attempting to read for meaning.

5. Count a repetition that occurs on *two or more words* as half a miscue.

6. Do not count more than one miscue on the same word.

7. Do not count a miscue on any proper noun.

8. Deduct one point for any word that a child cannot pronounce after about five seconds *if that word interferes with comprehension*. Deduct one-half point *if that word does not interfere significantly with comprehension*.

9. Do not count miscues that exemplify a child's cultural or regional dialect. To consider this point, the examiner must, of course, be fairly familiar with the child's basic speech patterns.

Next, evaluate the child's answers to the comprehension questions. On the first line by each question under the word *Score*, write the number *1* for a correct answer and the number *0* for an incorrect answer. On the second line by each answer under the word *Appropriateness*, write a + for a detailed and thoughtful answer or a ✓ for a completely illogical answer. Leave the space blank for answers in the middle ground. If more than one-third of the child's answers have been marked with a ✓, the child may not have a real understanding of the purpose of the passage and not comprehend it very well.

Then determine the child's *comprehension score* on each of the graded passages.

- *Independent reading level*—six questions correct
- *Instructional reading level*—four or five questions correct
- *Frustration reading level*—three or fewer questions correct

If an examiner uses retelling instead of the comprehension questions to determine a child's reading levels, he or she may have to make a judgment call. This may be too difficult for a novice teacher.

After evaluating a child's oral reading miscues and comprehension levels, the examiner can determine the child's *approximate* independent, instructional, and frustration (difficult) reading levels. Various IRIs use different classification schemes for determining these levels. The percentages included in this book are based on the fairly limited research in this area, along with logical analysis and the results of thousands of children who have used the graded reading passages found in my previous publications.

The characteristics of the three basic reading levels used in the IRI contained in this book are the following:

- *Independent (easy) reading level*—The child is about *99 percent* accurate in word identification and has about *95 percent* or better comprehension.

- *Instructional (with teacher support) reading level*—The child is about *90 percent* accurate in word identification and has *75 percent* or better comprehension.

- *Frustration (difficult) reading level*—The child is less than about *90 percent* accurate in word identification and has less than about *50 percent* comprehension.

Adding three sublevels to these three basic levels helps accurate selection of reading materials for children.

- *Low independent reading level*
- *High instructional reading level*
- *Low instructional reading level*

NOTE: I recommend weighting the child's performance on comprehension more highly than weighting his or her performance in word identification. Comprehension is always the ultimate goal of the reading process.

An examiner also can informally assess a child's self-monitoring of his or her comprehension by observing the answers to the questions following the comprehension questions. As an example:

How well do you think you answered these questions?

very well _____
all right _____
not so well _____

Make an informal comparison between each child's answer on these questions and his or her actual score on the comprehension questions.

Individual Reading Inventory: Grades 1–5

Here are two forms of an IRI primarily designed for grades 1 through 3. However, word lists and passages are included through the fifth-grade level, since some children in the upper primary grades may be able to read to that level. The word lists and passages up to the fifth-grade level may be needed to establish these children's instructional or frustration reading levels.

Duplicate two sets of the word lists: one for the child to pronounce and another on which to record the scores. Duplicate one set of the appropriate graded reading passages without the various instructor notes and questions or the formula for scoring. This is the set from which the child reads aloud. Also duplicate a complete set containing the questions and the formula for scoring. This is the set that you use to evaluate. The child's materials can be laminated for durability.

The following code has been placed on each of the graded word lists and reading passages so that the child is not able to determine the levels of the word lists and passages that he or she is going to read. This is especially important for children with reading or learning disabilities.

Pre-Primer Level	**PP**
Primer Level	**P**
First-Grade Reading Level	**1**
Second-Grade Reading Level	**2**
Third-Grade Reading Level	**3**
Fourth-Grade Reading Level	**4**
Fifth-Grade Reading Level	**5**

The following books contain additional sets of graded words lists and graded reading passages that you can use for pre-testing and post-testing or for different kinds of administration, such as oral-silent-oral, silent-oral, oral-silent, or silent-oral-silent.

Miller, W. (1995). *Alternative assessment techniques for reading and writing* (pp. 158–215). San Francisco: Jossey-Bass.

Miller, W. (1993). *Complete reading disabilities handbook* (pp. 64–95). San Francisco: Jossey-Bass.

Miller, W. (2003). *Survival reading skills for secondary students* (pp. 11–48). San Francisco: Jossey-Bass.

IRI 1: WORD LISTS

PP	P	1
1. will	1. that	1. once
2. and	2. good	2. why
3. black	3. laugh	3. again
4. big	4. tree	4. give
5. see	5. cake	5. every
6. red	6. one	6. many
7. to	7. they	7. paint
8. help	8. out	8. walk
9. an	9. was	9. would
10. me	10. away	10. street
11. back	11. white	11. found
12. up	12. your	12. can't
13. funny	13. thank	13. snow
14. little	14. have	14. open
15. can	15. now	15. much
16. said	16. please	16. father
17. I	17. very	17. buy
18. see	18. yellow	18. love
19. you	19. hold	19. give
20. ride	20. two	20. say
21. jump	21. tree	21. brown
22. blue	22. about	22. birthday
23. not	23. fly	23. kind
24. are	24. could	24. street
25. play	25. all	25. children

2

1. friend
2. breakfast
3. squirrel
4. beautiful
5. surprise
6. everyone
7. myself
8. their
9. been
10. should
11. which
12. hurt
13. carry
14. does
15. finish
16. save
17. grandfather
18. lazy
19. write
20. upon
21. brave
22. cupcake
23. always
24. light
25. grow

3

1. thought
2. eight
3. remember
4. planet
5. special
6. mystery
7. mountain
8. country
9. ocean
10. enough
11. earth
12. strange
13. built
14. unusual
15. diamond
16. escape
17. wander
18. travel
19. decide
20. storm
21. magic
22. impossible
23. close
24. enough
25. museum

IRI I: WORD LISTS *(continued)*

4	**5**
1. predict	1. manager
2. pavement	2. ambulance
3. island	3. region
4. theater	4. territory
5. experience	5. gentle
6. weight	6. photograph
7. enormous	7. argument
8. original	8. plateau
9. dignity	9. scientist
10. protection	10. surgery
11. vicious	11. intense
12. pollution	12. horizon
13. canoe	13. salmon
14. parachute	14. vinegar
15. modern	15. prevent
16. ancient	16. parallel
17. decorate	17. telegram
18. interrupt	18. orchard
19. coward	19. muscle
20. exercise	20. considerable
21. machine	21. qualify
22. scientific	22. burden
23. pronounce	23. navigate
24. legend	24. organize
25. windshield	25. grief

BEN'S BLACK DOG*

Ben has a black dog.

The dog's name is Jan.

Jan is a little dog.

Ben and Jan like to play ball.

Jan has a red ball.

Jan likes to run after the ball.

Ben and Jan like to go for a walk.

Ben plays with Jan.

Ben and Jan have fun.

Ben likes Jan a lot.

Jan likes Ben too.

Do you want a dog?

I do.

*The readability level of this passage was computed by the Spache Readability Formula.

BEN'S BLACK DOG

Before Reading

Assessing Prior Knowledge and Interest

1. What are some things a child and a dog can do to have fun together?

2. Do you think that you will like to read this story about a boy and his dog? Why? Why not?

After Reading

Number of words in this selection _____68_____
Number of word identification miscues _____

Word Identification Miscues

Independent reading level _____0–1_____
Low independent reading level approx. _____2_____
High instructional reading level approx. _____3–4_____
Instructional reading level approx. _____5–6_____
Low instructional reading level approx. _____7–8_____
Frustration reading level _____9+_____

Assessing Comprehension

Score *1* for a correct response and *0* for an incorrect response in the appropriate column. Score ✓ for any answers that are clearly illogical or + for any answers that are very good.

	Score	**Appropriateness**
Reading the Lines (Literal Comprehension)		
1. What color is Ben's dog? (*Black*)	_____	_____
2. What color is Jan's ball? (*Red*)	_____	_____
Reading Between the Lines (Interpretive Comprehension)		
3. Why do you think that Ben and Jan like to play ball together? (*It's fun; Jan likes to run after the ball; they can do it together*)	_____	_____
4. Why do you think that Ben likes Jan? (*They are friends; they can go for a walk together; they can play ball together*)	_____	_____

	Score	Appropriateness

Reading Beyond the Lines (Applied Comprehension)

5. Do you like big dogs or little dogs better? Why? (*Any logical answer—some examples: big dogs—you can play rougher with them; they run and swim better; you don't have to be so careful that you will hurt them. Little dogs—don't eat so much; you can hold them in your lap*)   _____   _____

6. What are some things you would need to do to take care of a dog? (*Any logical answer—some examples: give it food; give it water; take it outside to go to the bathroom; take it for a walk; play with it; brush and comb it*)   _____   _____

Number of comprehension questions correct _____

Comprehension Score

Independent reading level _____6____
Instructional reading level ____4–5____
Frustration reading level __3 or fewer__

Self-Monitoring of Comprehension

How well do you think you answered these questions?

very well _____
all right _____
not so well _____

P

THE BROWN DEER[*]

I walked out of my house one day.

I saw a brown deer in my yard looking at me.

When I walked to him, the deer backed up a little and stopped.

He looked and looked at me when I walked to him again.

Then the deer backed up a little and stopped to look at me.

I went back into my house.

When I came out a little later, the deer was back in my yard.

He looked and looked at me again as I walked to him.

The deer did not let me walk up to him, but I was by him.

I think he liked me.

I liked that brown deer a lot. I want to see him again one day.

---

[*]The readability level of this passage was computed by the Spache Readability Formula.

THE BROWN DEER

Before Reading

Assessing Prior Knowledge and Interest

1. What do you think a deer in someone's yard could be doing?

2. Do you think that you will like to read this story about the brown deer? Why? Why not?

After Reading

Number of words in this selection _____124_____
Number of word identification miscues _____

Word Identification Miscues

Independent reading level _____0–2_____
Low independent reading level approx. _____3–4_____
High instructional reading level approx. _____5–7_____
Instructional reading level approx. _____8–11_____
Low instructional reading level approx. _____12–13_____
Frustration reading level _____14+_____

Assessing Comprehension

Score *1* for a correct response and *0* for an incorrect response in the appropriate column.
Score ✓ for any answers that are clearly illogical or + for any answers that are very good.

	Score	Appropriateness
Reading the Lines (Literal Comprehension)		
1. Where was the deer? (*In a person's yard*)	_____	_____
2. How did the person feel about the deer? (*He or she liked the deer*)	_____	_____
Reading Between the Lines (Interpretive Comprehension)		
3. Why do you think the deer kept on backing up and stopping? (*He was a little afraid of the person; he had never seen a person before*)	_____	_____
4. Why do you think that the person liked seeing the deer? (*A deer is a beautiful animal; the deer was not very afraid*)	_____	_____

Score   **Appropriateness**

Reading Beyond the Lines (Applied Comprehension)

5. Would you like to see a deer close up in a
   yard someday? Why or why not? (*Any logical
   answer—some examples: YES a deer is a
   beautiful animal; I love animals; NO I am
   afraid of a deer; I don't like animals*)   _____   _____

6. Where would a person live if he or she can
   see a deer in their yard? (*Any logical
   answer—some examples: in the woods; in
   a small town near the woods; in an area
   away from a city*)   _____   _____

Number of comprehension questions correct _____

Comprehension Score

Independent reading level _____6_____
Instructional reading level _____4–5_____
Frustration reading level ___3 or fewer___

Self-Monitoring of Comprehension

How well do you think you answered these questions?

       very well _____
       all right _____
       not so well _____

THE BEAR THAT RAN FAST*

In the summer Beth lives in the woods in a house by a lake. She goes for a walk on the road by her house every morning. When she is walking, she may see deer, but she had never seen a bear.

One morning this summer, Beth was taking her walk. Two cars stopped, and the man in each car told her to watch out for a bear. They had seen a bear when they were driving.

Beth watched for the bear for a time, but she stopped thinking about it after a little while. When she walked to the top of a little hill, Beth looked up and saw a black bear about 20 feet away! It was not a very big bear. Beth was very, very surprised.

When the bear saw Beth, it ran. It ran very fast across the road. The bear wanted to get away from Beth as soon as it could. The bear was afraid of Beth. That is why it ran so fast.

Beth was happy to see the bear, but she doesn't want to see a bear that close again!

*This true story happened in northern Wisconsin during summer, 2003. The readability level of this passage was computed by the Spache Readability Formula.

THE BEAR THAT RAN FAST

Before Reading

Assessing Prior Knowledge and Interest

1. Do you know how fast a black bear can run?

2. Do you think that you will like to read this story about the bear that ran fast? Why? Why not?

After Reading

Number of words in this selection _____*187*_____
Number of word identification miscues _____

Word Identification Miscues

Independent reading level _____*0–3*_____
Low independent reading level approx. _____*4–6*_____
High instructional reading level approx. _____*7–11*_____
Instructional reading level approx. _____*12–18*_____
Low instructional reading level approx. _____*19–20*_____
Frustration reading level _____*21+*_____

Assessing Comprehension

Score *1* for a correct response and *0* for an incorrect response in the appropriate column. Score ✓ for any answers that are clearly illogical or + for any answers that are very good.

	Score	**Appropriateness**

Reading the Lines (Literal Comprehension)

1. What does Beth do every morning in the summer? (*Go for a walk*)   _____   _____

2. Why did the bear run so fast? (*It was afraid of Beth*)   _____   _____

Reading Between the Lines (Interpretive Comprehension)

3. Why do you think that Beth goes for a walk every morning? (*She likes to walk; she likes the fresh air; she likes to look at the woods and animals*)   _____   _____

4. Why was Beth surprised to see a bear that was close to her? (*She had forgotten about what the men in the cars told her; she had never met a bear while she was walking before*)   _____   _____

Score   **Appropriateness**

Reading Beyond the Lines (Applied Comprehension)

5. Would you like to see a bear while you were
   walking on a road in the woods? (*Any logical
   answer—some examples: YES it would be
   exciting; I like bears; NO I would be really
   scared; I don't like bears*)   _____   _____

6. How might a person act if he or she saw a
   bear close by while he or she was walking?
   (*Any logical answer—some examples: run
   away from the bear; stop and watch the
   bear; yell at the bear; stand very still*)   _____   _____

Number of comprehension questions correct _____

Comprehension Score

Independent reading level _____6_____
Instructional reading level _____4–5_____
Frustration reading level __3 or fewer__

Self-Monitoring of Comprehension

How well do you think you answered these questions?

   very well _____
   all right _____
   not so well _____

TWO GRAY WOLVES[*]

Joan is a lady who walks with her two small dogs every day. One afternoon while she was walking with them, the two dogs started barking and barking. Joan was surprised to see two gray timber wolves looking at her from about sixty feet away.

While Joan's dogs kept on barking, the one wolf started walking slowly to her and her dogs. Joan picked up some very small stones from along the road and threw them near the wolf. She didn't want to hit the wolf but just scare him. The wolf then stopped and looked at Joan and her dogs for a while. After a little while, the wolf walked back to the other wolf, and the two wolves walked away together. When the wolves were out of sight, Joan's dogs stopped barking.

Joan and her dogs were very lucky. Timber wolves are wild animals that don't like dogs very much. The wolves could have hurt either Joan or her dogs. However, all wild animals usually try to stay away from trouble if they can. People who live in the woods usually do not see wolves, as they often stay out of sight deep in the woods.

---

[*]This true story happened in northern Wisconsin during summer, 2003. The readability level of this passage was computed by the Spache Readability Formula.

TWO GRAY WOLVES

Before Reading

Assessing Prior Knowledge and Interest

1. What do you know about gray timber wolves?

2. Do you think that you will like to read this story about two gray wolves? Why? Why not?

After Reading

Number of words in this selection _____*198*_____
Number of word identification miscues _____

Word Identification Miscues

Independent reading level _____*0–3*_____
Low independent reading level approx. _____*4–6*_____
High instructional reading level approx. _____*7–11*_____
Instructional reading level approx. _____*12–18*_____
Low instructional reading level approx. _____*19–20*_____
Frustration reading level _____*21+*_____

Assessing Comprehension

Score *1* for a correct response and *0* for an incorrect response in the appropriate column.
Score ✓ for any answers that are clearly illogical or + for any answers that are very good.

	Score	**Appropriateness**

Reading the Lines (Literal Comprehension)

1. How many timber wolves were there? (*Two*)   _____   _____

2. What did Joan throw at the timber wolves?
   (*Some small stones*)   _____   _____

Reading Between the Lines (Interpretive Comprehension)

3. Why do you think that Joan's dogs kept on barking loudly? (*They had never seen wolves before; they were trying to warn Joan; they were afraid of the wolves*)   _____   _____

4. Why do you think that wild animals try to avoid trouble? (*They may be afraid they could get hurt; they prefer to stay with their own kind of animals; they are not used to other kinds of animals or people*)   _____   _____

Score   Appropriateness

Reading Beyond the Lines (Applied Comprehension)

5. Would you like to meet two timber wolves
    when you were walking with a dog? (*Any logical
    answer—some examples: YES it would be
    exciting; I always have wanted to see a wolf;
    NO it would be scary; they might hurt me
    or my dogs*)   _____   _____

6. What could the timber wolves have done to
    Joan and her dogs? (*Bitten them very badly;
    chased them; tried to injure or kill them*)   _____   _____

Number of comprehension questions correct _____

Comprehension Score

Independent reading level _____6_____
Instructional reading level _____4–5_____
Frustration reading level _3 or fewer__

Self-Monitoring of Comprehension

How well do you think you answered these questions?

very well _____
all right _____
not so well _____

GOLDEN HAMSTERS[*]

Golden hamsters have been kept as pets for about fifty years. Hamsters are members of a group of animals called *rodents.* The word "*rodent*" comes from a Latin word meaning "*to gnaw.*" All rodents have sharp front teeth called *incisors* (ĭn-ʹsī-zərz) that they use to gnaw almost anything.

All hamsters only eat plant food. In the wild they live on grain and seeds, roots, and fruit. When a hamster is kept as a pet, it eats "hamster mix" purchased at a pet store or a home-made mix made of broken up crackers, rolled oats, and crumbled bread. A hamster likes to store food in its cheek pouches to eat later. In the wild a hamster is a night animal that sleeps during the day and actively looks for food at night.

A pet hamster must have a cage made of hard wood or metal so it cannot gnaw through its cage. The cage must have saw-dust or dried peat and sand on the floor for *litter.* It also must have an exercise wheel so the hamster can keep on running. Hamsters also like to play with tubes from toilet paper or kitchen towels. They also enjoy gnawing on wooden spools and small blocks of wood.

A hamster must be given clean water every day, and its water bowl also should be washed. The cage should be completely cleaned once a week.

A hamster usually lives to be about two years old. It can be a good pet for a child if it is taken care of properly.

Copyright © 2005 by John Wiley & Sons, Inc.

---

[*]The readability level of this passage was computed by the Spache Readability Formula.

GOLDEN HAMSTERS

Before Reading

Assessing Prior Knowledge and Interest

1. What do you know about golden hamsters?

2. Do you think that you will like to read this story about golden hamsters? Why? Why not?

After Reading

Number of words in this selection _____256_____

Number of word identification miscues _____

Word Identification Miscues

Independent reading level _____0–4_____
Low independent reading level approx. _____5–9_____
High instructional reading level approx. _____10–14_____
Instructional reading level approx. _____15–22_____
Low instructional reading level approx. _____23–26_____
Frustration reading level _____27+_____

Assessing Comprehension

Score *1* for a correct response and *0* for an incorrect response in the appropriate column. Score ✓ for any answers that are clearly illogical or + for any answers that are very good.

	Score	Appropriateness
Reading the Lines (Literal Comprehension)		
1. Hamsters are members of what group of animals? (*Rodents*)	_____	_____
2. How often should a hamster's cage be completely cleaned? (*Once a week*)	_____	_____
Reading Between the Lines (Interpretive Comprehension)		
3. Why do you think that it is convenient to feed a hamster prepared "hamster food"? (*It saves the owner time and trouble; it may be better for the hamster*)	_____	_____
4. Why do you think that the hamster's cage should be completely cleaned once a week? (*The hamster might get sick otherwise; it might not smell or look very good otherwise; the hamster might not enjoy its cage otherwise*)	_____	_____

Score   **Appropriateness**

Reading Beyond the Lines (Applied Comprehension)

5. Would you like to own a hamster for a pet?
   Why? Why not? (*Any logical answer—some
   examples: YES I like hamsters; I like small
   animals; it would be easy to take care of; NO
   I don't like hamsters; hamsters look like rats;
   it would be too much trouble*)   _____   _____

6. What would be the hardest part of taking
   care of a hamster for you? (*Any logical
   answer—some examples: cleaning the
   cage; not letting it escape from the cage;
   getting its food ready to eat*)   _____   _____

Number of comprehension questions correct _____

Comprehension Score

Independent reading level _____6____
Instructional reading level ____4–5____
Frustration reading level _3 or fewer_

Self-Monitoring of Comprehension

How well do you think you answered these questions?

   very well _____
   all right _____
   not so well _____

HOW TREES GROW[*]

Although oak trees live up to 1,000 years, they, like all trees, start from a tiny seed. All seeds need sunlight, water, and soil to grow. Nature finds a way to scatter the seeds from plants so they can grow away from the shadow of their parent.

Maple trees produce seeds with "wings" to be blown by the wind. When a squirrel buries nuts for the winter when food is scarce for him, he may have planted a tree. When birds eat berries, cherries, and other fruit, they may spit the seed out, or it will pass through them undigested and be scattered in their droppings. Other seeds may be carried on water.

If you watch an acorn grow, you will see that it produces two shoots. Whichever way you plant the acorn, one shoot grows down to form a root while the other shoot grows up to become a tree trunk. Most trees produce thousands of seeds each year, but only one seed needs to survive and grow for the tree to replace itself.

Conifer trees have male and female *cones* instead of flowers. You may have seen large quantities of fine yellow powder at the foot of a pine tree. This is *pollen* from the male pine cones, and it is carried to the female cones by the wind. Female cones are larger than male cones. Once female cones are pollinated, they begin to harden and close up. They can remain closed for several years while the seeds ripen inside. On a warm day when the cone is ready, it will open to allow its single-winged seeds to be carried away by the wind.

Some cones, like those of the *lodgepole pine,* only release their seeds after a fire. This is nature's way of recreating a forest after it has been burned.

Copyright © 2005 by John Wiley & Sons, Inc.

---

[*]The readability level of this passage was computed by the Dale-Chall Readability Formula.

HOW TREES GROW

Before Reading

Assessing Prior Knowledge and Interest

1. What do you think that all seeds need to have to grow?

2. Do you think that you will like to read this story about how trees grow? Why? Why not?

After Reading

Number of words in this selection _____306_____
Number of word identification miscues _____

Word Identification Miscues

Independent reading level _____0–5_____
Low independent reading level approx. _____6–11_____
High instructional reading level approx. _____12–18_____
Instructional reading level approx. _____19–30_____
Low instructional reading level approx. _____31–37_____
Frustration reading level _____38+_____

Assessing Comprehension

Score *1* for a correct response and *0* for an incorrect response in the appropriate column. Score ✓ for any answers that are clearly illogical or + for any answers that are very good.

	Score	Appropriateness
Reading the Lines (Literal Comprehension)		
1. How long can oak trees live? (*Up to 1,000 years*)	_____	_____
2. How many shoots does an acorn produce? (*Two*)	_____	_____
Reading Between the Lines (Interpretive Comprehension)		
3. What do you think happens when there are too many trees in a forest? (*The new seedling trees cannot get sunlight, water, and food from the soil*)	_____	_____
4. Why do you think that a fire can be helpful to a forest? (*The forest may currently be too thick to be able to allow all the trees to live; some trees only release their seeds after a fire; some of the trees may be too old to live and should burn up*)	_____	_____

Score   **Appropriateness**

Reading Beyond the Lines (Applied Comprehension)

5. Examine a seed produced by a maple tree. How
    far away do you think that the seed could travel?
    (*Any logical answer—some examples: a block;
    several blocks; a mile or farther depending on
    how strong the wind is*)   _____   _____

6. How could you use pine cones to identify
    trees? (*Any logical answer—some examples:
    compare the pine cones to those illustrated
    in a book about trees; compare the pine
    cones to those illustrated in an article
    about pine trees found on the World
    Wide Web*)   _____   _____

Number of comprehension questions correct _____

Comprehension Score

Independent reading level _____6_____
Instructional reading level _____4–5_____
Frustration reading level _3 or fewer_

Self-Monitoring of Comprehension

How well do you think you answered these questions?

      very well _____
      all right _____
      not so well _____

SNOWBOARDING[*]

Snowboarding is as close to flying as a person can get. Snowboarding is a popular sport that includes many of the features of surfing and skateboarding and is also somewhat like skiing.

The snowboard is a fiberglass, metal-edged board that is several feet long and looks something like a very wide ski. Plastic or metal bindings hold the person's boot to the board.

After stepping into the bindings, you are standing sideways to your direction of travel like a surfer. You face forward and bend your knees. Once you're gliding down a hill, you use your toes and heels to pressure the board's edges to change direction and stop.

A skilled snowboarder enjoys the thrills and excitement of sweeping down a mountainside or twisting and flipping his or her way over the jumps, rails, and banks of a snowboard park.

Snowboarding is a fairly new sport. However, some people say it is on its way to becoming the nation's number one mountain sport. During the 1980s the modern snowboard came into existence. High-back bindings also were introduced. These made it possible to control a board even on hard-packed snow. Soft boots were another invention.

In 1982 national snowboarding championships were held for the first time, and the next year the world snowboarding championships were held. By the 1990s most ski areas welcomed snowboarders, and snowboarding had become the "king of the mountain." By 2000 there were about four million snowboarders in this country.

At most mountain resorts you can rent snowboards, boots, and other equipment. There also are "snowboarding" schools where beginners can learn the basic snowboarding skills after a few lessons and several days of practice. Maybe you will be able to learn snowboarding someday.

Copyright © 2005 by John Wiley & Sons, Inc.

[*]The readability level of this passage was computed by the Dale-Chall Readability Formula.

SNOWBOARDING

Before Reading

Assessing Prior Knowledge and Interest

1. What do you know about the sport of snowboarding?

2. Do you think that you will like to read this story about snowboarding? Why? Why not?

After Reading

Number of words in this selection _____289_____
Number of word identification miscues _____

Word Identification Miscues

Independent reading level _____0–5_____
Low independent reading level approx. _____6–10_____
High instructional reading level approx. _____11–16_____
Instructional reading level approx. _____17–25_____
Low instructional reading level approx. _____26–31_____
Frustration reading level _____32+_____

Assessing Comprehension

Score *1* for a correct response and *0* for an incorrect response in the appropriate column. Score ✓ for any answers that are clearly illogical or + for any answers that are very good.

	Score	**Appropriateness**
Reading the Lines (Literal Comprehension)		
1. How long is the typical snowboard? (*Several feet*)	_____	_____
2. What kind of boots do snowboarders use? (*Soft*)	_____	_____
Reading Between the Lines (Interpretive Comprehension)		
3. Why do you think that the typical snowboarder likes this sport so much? (*It is exciting; it is challenging; it is out in the fresh air; it is fun*)	_____	_____
4. Why do you think snowboarding will become even more popular in the next few years? (*More people will hear about it; more people will see it on television*)	_____	_____

Score   **Appropriateness**

Reading Beyond the Lines (Applied Comprehension)

5. Would you like to go snowboarding sometime?
   (*Any logical answer—some examples: YES it
   would be exciting; I like winter and snow; it
   would be fun; I like being outdoors in the winter;
   NO I would be afraid; I don't like snow; I don't
   like the cold; I wouldn't want to get hurt*) _____ _____

6. How could you learn to be a safe
   snowboarder? (*Any logical answer—some
   examples: read a book about snowboarding;
   go to a "snowboarding" school; snowboard
   with a friend who is good at the sport;
   take lessons on safe snowboarding*) _____ _____

Number of comprehension questions correct _____

Comprehension Score

Independent reading level _____6_____
Instructional reading level _____4–5____
Frustration reading level __3 or fewer__

Self-Monitoring of Comprehension

How well do you think you answered these questions?

> very well _____
> all right _____
> not so well _____

IRI 2—WORD LISTS

PP	P	1
1. green	1. around	1. birthday
2. not	2. know	2. street
3. look	3. very	3. brown
4. play	4. what	4. snowman
5. three	5. cake	5. flower
6. make	6. where	6. could
7. black	7. please	7. around
8. jump	8. have	8. many
9. blue	9. mother	9. again
10. help	10. laugh	10. every
11. in	11. that	11. once
12. big	12. they	12. never
13. get	13. your	13. paint
14. saw	14. two	14. can't
15. to	15. find	15. why
16. an	16. away	16. much
17. me	17. all	17. give
18. ride	18. out	18. father
19. I	19. thank	19. from
20. up	20. white	20. ask
21. it	21. what	21. walk
22. in	22. good	22. open
23. see	23. children	23. again
24. will	24. same	24. call
25. red	25. hold	25. wish

2

1. together
2. grandfather
3. beautiful
4. squirrel
5. brave
6. finish
7. their
8. carry
9. light
10. been
11. better
12. write
13. friend
14. save
15. does
16. which
17. today
18. hurt
19. until
20. should
21. cupcake
22. strong
23. everyone
24. eyes
25. sorry

3

1. mountain
2. strange
3. enough
4. escape
5. special
6. remember
7. ocean
8. earth
9. idea
10. mystery
11. unusual
12. several
13. thankful
14. country
15. decide
16. planet
17. though
18. built
19. close
20. wiggle
21. discover
22. hour
23. precious
24. enemy
25. either

Name: _____   **Grade:** _____

4 **5**

4	5
1. experience	1. scientist
2. island	2. typical
3. coward	3. intestines
4. original	4. argument
5. knowledge	5. grease
6. protection	6. plateau
7. theater	7. dissolve
8. decorate	8. territory
9. dignity	9. apparent
10. design	10. photograph
11. imitate	11. intense
12. parachute	12. international
13. pollute	13. region
14. contradict	14. ceremony
15. vicious	15. merchant
16. enormous	16. gentle
17. force	17. manage
18. legend	18. qualify
19. critical	19. physical
20. bound	20. ceremony
21. windshield	21. operation
22. dozen	22. responsible
23. official	23. burden
24. canoe	24. amount
25. motion	25. navigate

MY NEW PUPPY*

I have a new puppy.

She is black and white.

She is very little.

She likes to play ball.

She likes to play with me too.

My puppy is funny.

She likes to run after me.

I like her a lot.

She likes me too.

She is my friend.

My puppy's name is Jill.

Do you want a puppy?

I did.

Copyright © 2005 by John Wiley & Sons, Inc.

---

*The readability level of this passage was computed by the Spache Readability Formula.

MY NEW PUPPY

Before Reading

Assessing Prior Knowledge and Reading

1. What are some of the things a child and a dog can do together?

2. Do you think that you will like to read this story about a child and a dog? Why? Why not?

After Reading

Number of words in this selection _____*61*_____
Number of word identification miscues _____

Word Identification Miscues

Independent reading level _____*0–1*_____
Low independent reading level approx. _____*2*_____
High instructional reading level approx. _____*3–4*_____
Instructional reading level approx. _____*5–6*_____
Low instructional reading level approx. _____*7–8*_____
Frustration reading level _____*9+*_____

Assessing Comprehension

Score *1* for a correct response and *0* for an incorrect response in the appropriate column. Score ✓ for any answers that are clearly illogical or + for any answers that are very good.

	Score	Appropriateness
Reading the Lines (Literal Comprehension)		
1. What color is the puppy? (*Black and white*)	_____	_____
2. What is the puppy's name (*Jill*)	_____	_____
Reading Between the Lines (Interpretive Comprehension)		
3. Why do you think the child likes the dog? (*It's cute; it's pretty; it's fun to play with; it feels soft*)	_____	_____
4. Why do you think the puppy is little? (*It's young; it's not very old; it is a small kind of dog*)	_____	_____

Score   Appropriateness

Reading Beyond the Lines (Applied Comprehension)

5. Would you like to have a puppy? Why? Why
    not? (*Any logical answer—some examples:
    YES it would be fun; I like dogs; NO a puppy
    is too much trouble; a puppy goes to the
    bathroom in the house; a puppy takes too
    much time to train*)   _____   _____

6. What are some of the things you would need
    to do to take care of a puppy? (*Any logical
    answer—some examples: feed it; give it fresh
    water; teach it to go outside to go to the
    bathroom; take it for a walk; play with it;
    brush and comb it*)   _____   _____

Number of comprehension questions correct _____

Comprehension Score

Independent reading level _____6_____
Instructional reading level _____4–5_____
Frustration reading level _____3 or fewer_____

Self-Monitoring of Comprehension

How well do you think you answered these questions?

    very well _____
    all right _____
    not so well _____

THE PUPPY SCHOOL*

Jim's new black puppy Ben is going to school.

A school for puppies is not like a school for children.

Puppies can't learn to read or write like boys and girls do.

At school puppies learn to walk with a leash.

They learn to come when they are called and to sit down.

They also learn to play with and get along with other puppies.

Jim will learn how to work with his puppy at the school.

Jim wants his puppy Ben to do well at the school.

He wants Ben to be the very best puppy in the school.

I hope that Ben does very well at the puppy school, don't you?

*The readability level of this passage was computed by the Spache Readability Formula.

THE PUPPY SCHOOL

Before Reading

Assessing Prior Knowledge and Reading

1. What do you think that puppies learn to do at a puppy school?

2. Do you think that you will like to read this story about a boy who takes his puppy to school? Why? Why not?

After Reading

Number of words in this selection _____ *113* _____
Number of word identification miscues _____

Word Identification Miscues

Independent reading level _____ *0–2* _____
Low independent reading level approx. _____ *3–4* _____
High instructional reading level approx. _____ *5–7* _____
Instructional reading level approx. _____ *8–11* _____
Low instructional reading level approx. _____ *12–13* _____
Frustration reading level _____ *14+* _____

Assessing Comprehension

Score *1* for a correct response and *0* for an incorrect response in the appropriate column. Score ✓ for any answers that are clearly illogical or + for any answers that are very good.

	Score	**Appropriateness**

Reading the Lines (Literal Comprehension)

1. What color is Ben? (*Black*) _____ _____

2. At the puppy school what is one thing Ben will learn how to do? (*Walk with a leash; come when he is called; sit down*) _____ _____

Reading Between the Lines (Interpretive Comprehension)

3. Why do you think it is important for a puppy to learn to come when he or she is called? (*It may keep him or her from being hit by a car; it may keep him or her out of trouble; its owner may need to have him or her come right then*) _____ _____

4. Why do you think Jim wants Ben to do very well at the puppy school? (*He wants a well-behaved dog; he wants to be proud of Ben; he wants Ben to be easy to live with*) _____ _____

Score   **Appropriateness**

Reading Beyond the Lines (Applied Comprehension)

5. Would you like to train puppies at a puppy school someday? Why? Why not? (*Any logical answer—some examples: YES I love puppies; I would like to train puppies to be well behaved; NO I don't like puppies; puppies are too silly; puppies are too hard to train; a puppy school would be very confusing*) _____   _____

6. Would you like to take your own puppy to a puppy school? (*Any logical answer—some examples: YES it would be fun to be around so many puppies; I would like to learn how to teach my puppy new things; NO it would be too noisy; it would be too confusing*) _____   _____

Number of comprehension questions correct _____

Comprehension Score

Independent reading level _____6_____
Instructional reading level _____4–5_____
Frustration reading level _____3 or fewer_____

Self-Monitoring of Comprehension

How well do you think you answered these questions?

       very well _____
       all right _____
       not so well _____

FINDING A BABY DEER*

One day Jenny and Joe were walking in the big woods.

Suddenly they saw a baby deer lying in the woods by itself.

It was brown with white spots all over its body.

A baby deer is called a fawn, and it is very helpless when it is little.

When Jenny and Joe came near to the deer, it just stayed still and looked at them.

Jenny wanted to pick up the fawn, but Joe told her that she shouldn't do that.

Jenny thought that the mother deer might have left her baby and gone away.

However, Joe knew that mother deer often leave their babies in the woods for a while.

They always return for them later.

That is why a person must never pick up a baby deer and take it anywhere else.

Then its mother could never find it, and it would have no one to help it.

*The readability level of this passage was computed by the Spache Readability Formula.

FINDING A BABY DEER

Before Reading

Assessing Prior Knowledge and Reading

1. What do you think a person should do if he or she finds a baby deer alone in the woods?

2. Do you think that you will like to read this story about two children who found a baby deer in the woods? Why? Why not?

After Reading

Number of words in this selection _____*150*_____
Number of word identification miscues _____

Word Identification Miscues

Independent reading level _____*0–2*_____
Low independent reading level approx. _____*3–5*_____
High instructional reading level approx. _____*6–8*_____
Instructional reading level approx. _____*9–12*_____
Low instructional reading level approx. _____*13–14*_____
Frustration reading level _____*15+*_____

Assessing Comprehension

Score *1* for a correct response and *0* for an incorrect response in the appropriate column. Score ✓ for any answers that are clearly illogical or + for any answers that are very good.

	Score	Appropriateness
Reading the Lines (Literal Comprehension)		
1. What did Jenny and Joe find in the woods? (*A baby deer; a fawn*)	_____	_____
2. What color was the baby deer (fawn)? (*Brown with white spots all over it*)	_____	_____
Reading Between the Lines (Interpretive Comprehension)		
3. Why do you think Jenny wanted to pick up the baby deer (fawn) when she saw it? (*She thought that its mother had abandoned it; she thought that its mother was dead; she was afraid it would starve; she was afraid it was hurt*)	_____	_____

	Score	Appropriateness

4. Why do you think a mother deer might leave her baby alone in the woods for a while? (*She might be looking for food somewhere else; she might have heard a strange noise; she might be looking for another place to hide her baby*)   _____   _____

Reading Beyond the Lines (Applied Comprehension)

5. If you found a baby deer alone in the woods, would you pet it? Why? Why not? (*Any logical answer—some examples: YES I would like to touch a baby deer; it would be fun to touch a baby deer; NO it might frighten the baby deer; it might accidentally hurt the baby deer*)   _____   _____

6. What are some of the things you could do if you found a baby deer lying near the side of a road? (*Any logical answer—some examples: find a grown-up to help; leave it alone; don't touch it*)   _____   _____

Number of comprehension questions correct _____

Comprehension Score

Independent reading level _____6_____
Instructional reading level _____4–5_____
Frustration reading level _____3 or fewer_____

Self-Monitoring of Comprehension

How well do you think you answered these questions?

very well _____
all right _____
not so well _____

THE "LOANED" GOLDEN RETRIEVER[*]

Last summer my old golden retriever dog became sick and died. I missed her very much, and I was very sad.

One of my neighbors has a big golden retriever that is seven years old. He had seen my dog and me walking for many years. He knew that I missed my dog and was unhappy.

One afternoon he brought his dog Willie to my house for a visit. Willie stayed near me and let me pet him whenever I wanted. I also took him for a walk on his leash. When it was time for Willie to go home, he didn't want to go. He is so big that he couldn't sit on the front seat of my car. His front legs had to be on the floor of my car.

Willie's owner brought him over to my house two more times. I played with him and took him for walks. When it was time for him to go home, Willie always wanted to stay with me. I couldn't get him up to go home. Since he is so big, I had to pull and pull at him with his leash. I was happy that Willie didn't want to go home. I guess he liked me a lot.

Now I have a new black puppy named Honey so I am not sad anymore. My neighbor will not have to loan Willie to me again, but Willie always will be my friend.

---

[*]The readability level of this passage was computed by the Spache Readability Formula. This is a true story that happened in northern Wisconsin during summer, 2003.

THE "LOANED" GOLDEN RETRIEVER

Before Reading

Assessing Prior Knowledge and Reading

1. Why do you think that someone would "loan" a person a golden retriever?

2. Do you think that you will enjoy reading this story about a "loaned" golden retriever? Why? Why not?

After Reading

Number of words in this selection _____*242*_____
Number of word identification miscues _____

Word Identification Miscues

Independent reading level _____*0–4*_____
Low independent reading level approx. _____*5–8*_____
High instructional reading level approx. _____*9–13*_____
Instructional reading level approx. _____*14–21*_____
Low instructional reading level approx. _____*22–25*_____
Frustration reading level _____*26+*_____

Assessing Comprehension

Score *1* for a correct response and *0* for an incorrect response in the appropriate column. Score ✓ for any answers that are clearly illogical or + for any answers that are very good.

	Score	Appropriateness

Reading the Lines (Literal Comprehension)

1. What kind of dog is mentioned in this story? (*A golden retriever*) _____ _____

2. What is the name of the golden retriever in this story? (*Willie*) _____ _____

Reading Between the Lines (Interpretive Comprehension)

3. Why do you think the person in this story was sad because his or her dog died? (*The person loved the dog; the person and the dog had been together for a long time; the person was lonely; the person didn't like to live alone*) _____ _____

Score　　**Appropriateness**

4. Why do you think that the neighbor loaned his
    golden retriever to the person in this story?
    *(He felt sorry for him or her; he was a kind
    person; he also loved dogs and knew how the
    person in the story felt; he wanted to help
    the person)*　　　　　　　　　　_____　　_____

Reading Beyond the Lines (Applied Comprehension)

5. Would you ever "loan" your dog to someone?
    *(Any logical answer—some examples: YES
    I would like to help someone whose dog had
    died; I understand how the person in the
    story felt when his or her dog died; NO I
    would be afraid to let anyone else take care
    of my dog; I would not trust anyone else
    with my dog)*　　　　　　　　　　_____　　_____

6. What are some of the things that might
    happen to a dog who was "loaned" to
    someone? *(Any logical answer—some
    examples: it might get lost; it might try to
    go back home; it might miss its owner; it
    might not want to go home; it might run
    away; it might be very lonesome for
    its owner)*　　　　　　　　　　_____　　_____

Number of comprehension questions correct _____

Comprehension Score

Independent reading level _____*6*_____
Instructional reading level _____*4–5*_____
Frustration reading level _____*3 or fewer*_____

Self-Monitoring of Comprehension

How well do you think you answered these questions?

　　　　very well _____
　　　　all right _____
　　　　not so well _____

GUINEA PIGS*

Guinea (gin e) pigs are furry, funny animals that have been kept as children's pets for many years. Another name for guinea pigs is cavy.

The best place to buy a guinea pig is in a pet store when it is six to eight weeks old. Baby guinea pigs have a full set of teeth and can walk around and eat solid food when they are only several days old. If a child buys only one guinea pig, he or she must give it a great deal of attention so that it does not become lonely.

Guinea pigs come in several different coat types and many different colors and markings. The coat can be smooth and short-haired, rough-haired, or long-haired. The ones with a smooth or rough coat are the easiest to keep clean and well-groomed.

Pet guinea pigs live in sturdy hutches or cages. A hutch usually is the best choice because it has two rooms—a living room and a bedroom for the guinea pigs. The living area of the hutch has a wire mesh front, and the food bowl is kept in the living room. The water bottle is attached to the wire mesh. The hutch should be large enough, and it should be kept in a place that is warm enough.

Pet guinea pigs eat grass, hay, cereal, and fresh vegetables. They should be fed twice a day at breakfast and an evening meal. Cereal is an important part of a guinea pig's food. Guinea pigs should have vitamin C in the form of fruits and vegetables. Since guinea pigs do not use their front feet as hands, their food should be cut into small chunks.

When you get a new guinea pig, stroke it, talk to it, and play with it every day. Guinea pigs also must file their teeth down all the time by chewing on hard objects like a piece of wood.

Copyright © 2005 by John Wiley & Sons, Inc.

*The readability level of this passage was computed by the Spache Readability Formula.

GUINEA PIGS

Before Reading

Assessing Prior Knowledge and Reading

1. What do you know about guinea pigs?

2. Do you think that you will like to read this story about guinea pigs? Why? Why not?

After Reading

Number of words in this selection _____ *320* _____
Number of word identification miscues _____

Word Identification Miscues

Independent reading level _____ *0–5* _____
Low independent reading level approx. _____ *6–10* _____
High instructional reading level approx. _____ *11–16* _____
Instructional reading level approx. _____ *17–25* _____
Low instructional reading level approx. _____ *26–31* _____
Frustration reading level _____ *32+* _____

Assessing Comprehension

Score *1* for a correct response and *0* for an incorrect response in the appropriate column. Score ✓ for any answers that are clearly illogical or + for any answers that are very good.

	Score	**Appropriateness**
Reading the Lines (Literal Comprehension)		
1. What is another name for a guinea pig? *(Cavy)*	_____	_____
2. Where can a pet guinea pig live? *(A hutch or cage)*	_____	_____
Reading Between the Lines (Interpretive Comprehension)		
3. Why do you think it is best to buy a young guinea pig between six and eight weeks of age? *(They are easier to train; they become your pet more easily; they may be cheaper to buy)*	_____	_____
4. Why do you think that the hutch should be cleaned regularly? *(To prevent illness; to make it nicer for the guinea pig)*	_____	_____

Score   **Appropriateness**

Reading Beyond the Lines (Applied Comprehension)

5. Would you want a guinea pig for a pet? Why? Why not? *(Any logical answer—some examples: YES I like animals; it would be lots of fun; it would be interesting; NO I wouldn't like that small a pet; I don't like animals)*   _____   _____

6. What would you do if your guinea pig's teeth were too long? *(Any logical answer—some examples: have an adult take it to the vet; ask an adult what to do; give it a piece of wood to chew on)*   _____   _____

Number of comprehension questions correct _____

Comprehension Score

Independent reading level _____ 6 _____
Instructional reading level _____ 4–5 _____
Frustration reading level _____ 3 or fewer _____

Self-Monitoring of Comprehension

How well do you think you answered these questions?

      very well _____
      all right _____
      not so well _____

LOONS*

Have you ever heard anyone say, "You're crazy as a loon"? The expression probably got started because of the loon's strange call that sounds somewhat like crazy laughter. However, loons are not crazy but are remarkable in many ways.

Loon chicks go for their first swim when they are only a few hours old, and in no time at all they can swim as well as their parents. If a baby loon gets tired while it is swimming, it can ride on its mother's back until it is rested.

The common loon got its name because it is the loon we most often see. In the spring and summer it has bright red eyes, a black-and-white checkerboard coat, and a "necklace" of white markings around its neck. At the end of the summer it sheds this coat and grows a drab gray winter outfit and almost loses its necklace. Both the male and female loon have the same markings.

In the summer a loon lives in northern and wilderness lakes. However, when its home lake freezes over in the late fall, the loon flies south since it cannot find fish from a frozen lake.

A loon's body is perfectly suited to live in the water. Its body is shaped like a torpedo so it can cut through the water easily and smoothly. To propel itself the loon has big webbed feet set back toward its tail, which gives the loon extra paddle power in the water.

A loon is a superb diver and underwater swimmer. It dips, dives, and soars underwater as though it were flying. To dive the loon plunges forward with its neck arched and pushes down with its strong feet. The loon, who is so graceful on water, is very awkward on land. Because a loon's legs are near

*The readability level of this passage was computed by the Spache Readability Formula.

the back of its body and its feet are large and webbed, it has trouble walking on land.

Loons usually live in pairs on lakes. In early June the loon pair chooses a place for the female to lay her eggs. The mother and father take turns sitting on the eggs to keep them safe and warm for thirty days.

LOONS

Before Reading

Assessing Prior Knowledge and Reading

1. What do you know about loons?

2. Do you think that you will like to read this story about loons? Why? Why not?

After Reading

Number of words in this selection _____*362*_____
Number of word identification miscues _____

Word Identification Miscues

Independent reading level _____*0–5*_____
Low independent reading level approx. _____*6–10*_____
High instructional reading level approx. _____*11–16*_____
Instructional reading level approx. _____*17–25*_____
Low instructional reading level approx. _____*26–31*_____
Frustration reading level _____*32+*_____

Assessing Comprehension

Score *1* for a correct response and *0* for an incorrect response in the appropriate column.
Score ✓ for any answers that are clearly illogical or + for any answers that are very good.

	Score	**Appropriateness**

Reading the Lines (Literal Comprehension)

1. What color are a loon's eyes in summer? *(Red)* _____   _____

2. Where do loons live in the summer?
   (Northern lakes; lakes) _____   _____

Reading Between the Lines (Interpretive Comprehension)

3. Why do you think a baby loon may tire easily
   when it is swimming? *(It is very young; it is
   not strong; it is not used to swimming)* _____   _____

4. Why do you think that a loon does not like
   to spend much time on land? *(It is not safe
   on land; it feels clumsy on land; it has enemies
   on land; it is hard for a loon to walk on land)* _____   _____

Score **Appropriateness**

Reading Beyond the Lines (Applied Comprehension)

5. Would you like to see a loon? Why? Why not?
    *(Any logical answer—some examples: YES it
    sounds interesting to see; I would like to hear
    its cry; I like all animals and birds; NO I don't
    like the out of doors; I would not want to hear
    its cry)*   _____   _____

6. Where could you find out more about loons?
    *(Any logical answer—some examples: the
    World Wide Web; a print or online
    encyclopedia; trade books; from an adult
    who has studied loons)*   _____   _____

Number of comprehension questions correct _____

Comprehension Score

Independent reading level _____6_____
Instructional reading level _____4–5_____
Frustration reading level _____3 or fewer_____

Self-Monitoring of Comprehension

How well do you think you answered these questions?

very well _____
all right _____
not so well _____

WATER-SKIING*

Water-skiing is a tremendously exciting sport both for children and adults. However, much equipment is needed for water-skiing.

A ski boat with at least a 25-horsepower motor is needed, and the front passenger seat of the ski boat should face the back of the boat or swivel enough to face the back since the person sitting there is called the observer and must watch the skier for the driver. A ski boat also must have a towing hitch or a towbar. A pylon is used with inboard motorboats, while a towbar is used with outboards. To keep the skier away from the boat's motor, the tow rope should be 75 feet long. It should be made of a material that floats and have a breaking strength of 1,500 pounds.

Children's water-skis, called junior skis, are made of wood, and their tips curve upward so they can go over the water more easily. Each ski has a foot binder on top in the middle, and a small fin on the underside at the back. The foot binder holds the skier's foot in the ski, while fins help to steer the skis better in the water.

An extremely important piece of equipment is the flotation device, preferably a ski vest. A water-skier also should be a good swimmer since water-skiing is done in deep water.

There are some safety rules that every water-skier should observe. A water-skier should be very familiar with the area where he or she is going to ski. Skiing always should be done in water more than five feet deep. Never ski without an observer in the boat who watches the skier and tells the driver if the skier falls or signals. A final safety rule is that a skier never should be brought closer than 150 feet to the shore, dock, or other boaters.

*The readability level of this passage was computed by the Spache Readability Formula.

WATER-SKIING

Before Reading

Assessing Prior Knowledge and Reading

1. What do you know about the sport of water-skiing?

2. Do you think that you will like to read this passage about water-skiing? Why? Why not?

After Reading

Number of words in this selection _____307_____
Number of word identification miscues _____

Word Identification Miscues

Independent reading level _____0–5_____
Low independent reading level approx. _____6–10_____
High instructional reading level approx. _____11–16_____
Instructional reading level approx. _____17–25_____
Low instructional reading level approx. _____26–31_____
Frustration reading level _____32+_____

Assessing Comprehension

Score *1* for a correct response and *0* for an incorrect response in the appropriate column.
Score ✓ for any answers that are clearly illogical or + for any answers that are very good.

	Score	Appropriateness
Reading the Lines (Literal Comprehension)		
1. What is the minimum horsepower needed on a ski boat? *(25)*	_____	_____
2. What are children's water-skis called? *(Junior skis)*	_____	_____
Reading Between the Lines (Interpretive Comprehension)		
3. Why do you think the tow rope should be very strong? *(So it will not break, causing the skier to fall; there is a lot of pressure on the tow rope when the boat is traveling fast)*	_____	_____
4. Why is a flotation device so important in water-skiing? *(If the skier falls, he or she will not drown; it will keep the skier afloat if he or she falls)*	_____	_____

Score   Appropriateness

Reading Beyond the Lines (Applied Comprehension)

5. Would you like to learn to water-ski? Why?
   Why not? *(Any logical answer—some examples:*
   YES it would be fun; it would be exciting; it
   would be great; NO it would be scary; I don't
   know how to swim; I don't like the water; I'm
   afraid of the water)   _____   _____

6. How much practice do you think it takes to
   be an expert water-skier? *(Any logical*
   answer—some examples: many years; a
   long time; many hours of practice)   _____   _____

Number of comprehension questions correct _____

Comprehension Score

Independent reading level _____6_____
Instructional reading level _____4–5_____
Frustration reading level _____3 or fewer_____

Self-Monitoring of Comprehension

How well do you think you answered these questions?

        very well _____
        all right _____
        not so well _____

CHECKLIST OF PRIMARY-GRADE WRITING BEHAVIORS

Checklists are an excellent way for early childhood teachers to evaluate the writing skills of young children, particularly because they do not require any special materials or teaching strategies. They can be a part of the regular primary-grade curriculum. Here is a reproducible checklist of primary-grade writing behaviors that can be used in second and third grades, or with older students who have special needs. Feel free to duplicate this checklist and use it in its present form or modify it in any way.

Copyright © 2005 by John Wiley & Sons, Inc.

Name: _____ **Grade:** _____

CHECKLIST OF PRIMARY-GRADE WRITING BEHAVIORS

		Usually	Sometimes	Not Yet
1.	Is able to print his or her own first name correctly.	_____	_____	_____
2.	Holds the pencil or marker correctly.	_____	_____	_____
3.	Enjoys using writing materials such as unlined and lined paper, pencils, markers, and materials for making his or her own books.	_____	_____	_____
4.	Seems to enjoy most writing activities.	_____	_____	_____
5.	Can dictate words, phrases, sentences, and stories that he or she wants someone to record.	_____	_____	_____
6.	Uses invented spelling when required instead of asking the teacher or classmates for help.	_____	_____	_____
7.	Uses traditional spelling when writing most words in personal writing.	_____	_____	_____
8.	Is able to use correct spacing between words, sentences, lines, and the end of the page while writing.	_____	_____	_____
9.	Is able to write with interest and enthusiasm for about 15 to 20 minutes.	_____	_____	_____
10.	Can write at a rudimentary level in varied genres such as creative expression, narration, exposition, persuasion, and description.	_____	_____	_____
11.	Can brainstorm with some help to select a topic for writing.	_____	_____	_____
12.	Can write an acceptable rough (first) draft of his or her selected topic.	_____	_____	_____
13.	Can successfully edit his or her rough (first) draft, making additions, deletions, and organizational changes.	_____	_____	_____

CHECKLIST OF PRIMARY-GRADE WRITING BEHAVIORS *(continued)*

	Usually	Sometimes	Not Yet
14. Understands and uses correct mechanics such as complete sentences, capital letters, periods, commas, question marks, and exclamation points.	_____	_____	_____
15. Has a beginning, middle, and ending in his or her writing if appropriate.	_____	_____	_____
16. Is willing and able to give advice to his or her classmates about writing at writing conferences.	_____	_____	_____
17. Is able to "publish" his or her writing in an acceptable form such as a language-experience booklet.	_____	_____	_____
18. Is able to reread his or her own writing.	_____	_____	_____
19. Is able to share his or her own writing with classmates.	_____	_____	_____
20. Listens with interest to the writing of his or her classmates.	_____	_____	_____
21. Is able to use the word-processing program of a computer if one is available.	_____	_____	_____

3

Listening and Oral Language Skills

Do you believe that there is a significant difference between the oral language skills of children with average or above average linguistic aptitude and those with special needs of various kinds? Do you think that such a difference may impact the primary-grade reading achievement of such children? If you answered "yes" to both questions, you are correct. Young children with average or above average linguistic skills often use longer and more complex sentence structure and more precise vocabulary than do children with special needs. In addition, a child with delayed oral language development also may have delayed reading achievement in the primary grades.

This chapter opens with a pre-assessment device. Completing this informal device will evaluate the reader's present knowledge about the importance of both listening and oral language skills. The chapter then includes a very brief description of listening and a reproducible checklist of listening skills, followed by practical strategies and materials (including games) for improving competency in listening skills. Finally, I provide a very brief description of oral language and a reproducible checklist of oral language skills, with a brief summary of strategies and materials for improving oral language skills in early childhood programs as well as several games to promote oral language development.

After reading this chapter, the reader should better understand the importance of listening skills and oral language skills on primary-grade reading achievement as well as how to promote these skills effectively.

Decide whether each statement is *accurate* (true) or *not* (false). Evaluate your answers after you have read the chapter. The answers are on page 320.

_____ 1. The listening skills of both children and adults can be improved significantly with practice.

_____ 2. Auditory memory is the ability to hear sounds at various levels of frequency.

_____ 3. In critical listening, a child understands, evaluates, makes decisions, and formulates opinions.

_____ 4. A listening center is sometimes called a listening post.

_____ 5. Communication by speech enables humans to connect with others for professional and personal reasons.

_____ 6. Oral language skills develop at about the same time as do written language skills.

_____ 7. The behaviorist theory presents an accurate picture of how young children develop oral language skills.

_____ 8. Some linguists state that language develops entirely innately.

_____ 9. One type of oral language development may be called a restricted oral language style.

_____ 10. The constructivist theory of language acquisition states that children create language using an innate set of rules.

_____ 11. Most children progress through the same stages of oral language development, although at different rates.

_____ 12. Children use telegraphic speech at about the age of four.

_____ 13. Most children have developed all speech sounds by the age of eight years.

_____ 14. Conversing with a child can help to improve his or her confidence while speaking.

_____ 15. Young children's dramatic play is enhanced by using props and learning centers in classrooms.

_____ 16. Show-and-tell is always a motivating, worthwhile activity for improving oral language skills.

_____ 17. Costumes can be useful in improving the oral language skills of young children.

_____ 18. Games are the most effective way of improving oral language skills.

LISTENING

Listening consists of *hearing, attending, discriminating,* and *remembering.* The listening skills of both children and adults can be improved with motivated practice. As an example, the typical person listens to about *50 percent* of what he or she hears and understands about *25 percent* of that. According to Pinnell and Jaggar (1992), active involvement following listening activities probably is more effective than are passive activities. In contrast to listening, *hearing* is a process involving nerves and muscles and usually is fully developed by the age of four or five.

Here are a number of terms that directly relate to improving listening skills:

- *Auditory acuity*—The ability to hear sounds at different levels of frequency. Hearing impairment of the high tones makes it harder to hear consonant sounds, while impairment of the low tones makes it harder to hear vowel sounds.

- *Auditory perception*—The processing of sounds in the brain and the ability to sustain attention span while listening. It also includes the skills of following directions and identifying the intensity, pitch, and tempo of sounds.

- *Auditory memory*—The ability to hear and remember a sequence of sounds. Auditory memory ability is most often evaluated by having someone repeat a series of numerals either in the same order in which they were given or in reverse order. The typical adult can repeat about seven numerals in the original order, although a few can repeat ten or more. A young child can repeat significantly fewer than seven numerals; auditory memory is a skill that improves with maturation and experience.

- *Auditory discrimination*—The ability to discriminate or differentiate between various types of sounds. While reading, auditory discrimination usually means the ability to differentiate between the various consonant or vowel sounds. Many young children, especially those with special needs, have difficulty differentiating between the short vowel sounds, especially *short /e/* and *short /i/.*

The various types of listening are

- *Appreciative listening*—Finding pleasure and entertainment in hearing music, poems, nursery rhymes, jingles, and finger plays. Listening programs are well served by beginning with appreciative activities.

- *Purposeful listening*—Listening to follow directions and then providing the appropriate responses.

- *Discriminative listening*—Becoming aware of changes in pitch and loudness and how sounds are differentiated in the environment. Also discriminating among speech sounds.

- *Creative listening*—Imagination and emotions are motivated by listening experiences. The listener expresses thoughts spontaneously and easily through words or actions or both.

- *Critical listening*—Understanding, evaluating, making decisions, and constructing opinions on material the person has heard. To motivate critical listening, ask questions such as these: "*What happens when all of us in the class talk at the same time? Why should a child interrupt or not interrupt a classmate when he or she is speaking?*" The child should think through the possible answers, decide the best solution to the problem, and present a point of view.

PP

ABILITY IN LISTENING SKILLS

		Usually	Sometimes	Not Yet
1.	Can hear the high tones and consonant sounds.	_____	_____	_____
2.	Can hear the low tones and vowel sounds.	_____	_____	_____
3.	Can discriminate between the *short /e/* and *short /i/* sounds.	_____	_____	_____
4.	Can hear, remember, and repeat at least three numerals in correct order.	_____	_____	_____
5.	Can identify the pitch of sounds.	_____	_____	_____
6.	Can discriminate between the consonant sounds.	_____	_____	_____
7.	Can discriminate between the vowel sounds.	_____	_____	_____
8.	Enjoys listening to and participating in chants.	_____	_____	_____
9.	Enjoys listening to and participating in finger plays.	_____	_____	_____
10.	Seems to listen critically and make critical judgments within the limits of his or her prior knowledge.	_____	_____	_____
11.	Enjoys listening to trade books, CDs, or cassette recordings at a listening post (station) in the classroom.	_____	_____	_____
12.	Enjoys listening to books with a listening theme. (These are books that stress listening carefully, critically, and with appreciation.)	_____	_____	_____
13.	Is able to play a listening game successfully.	_____	_____	_____
14.	Seems to remember what he or she has heard.	_____	_____	_____
15.	Is able to successfully participate in a Directed Listening-Thinking Activity (DL-TA).	_____	_____	_____
16.	Is an attentive listener to trade books that are read aloud.	_____	_____	_____

ABILITY IN LISTENING SKILLS *(continued)*

	Usually	Sometimes	Not Yet
17. Is an attentive listener to conversations with classmates or teacher (tutor).	————	————	————
18. Is an attentive listener to a classroom activity such as sharing time (show-and-tell).	————	————	————
19. Enjoys listening to music of various kinds.	————	————	————
20. Is able to identify the voices of the various school personnel.	————	————	————

Notes:

_____

_____

_____

_____

_____

_____

_____

_____

Improving the Listening Skills of Young Children

Here are some strategies and materials that can be used to improve the listening skills of young children. They can be used in their present form or modified in light of the abilities, needs, and interests of particular children.

The Directed Listening-Thinking Activity (DL-TA)

The *Directed Listening-Thinking Activity* (DL-TA) was developed by the late Russell G. Stauffer of the University of Delaware (Stauffer, 1980). It is a variation of the popular *Directed Reading-Thinking Activity* (DR-TA), also developed by Stauffer. The DL-TA helps young children gain meaning from books and develop story structure. It consists of the following steps:

1. Have the child predict the book content after hearing the title.

2. Have the child ask questions that can be answered by hearing the book read aloud.

3. Have the child actively listen to the book being read aloud, verifying or altering his or her predictions. The child should engage in interactive story reading such as commenting on pictures, pointing to various words and letters, and interacting with the content.

The DL-TA stimulates active, involved listening and encourages oral language development. In addition, it increases the story comprehension of young readers.

Listening Posts (Listening Centers)

Listening posts or *listening centers* are often used in preschools, kindergartens, and first grades. A listening post is a part of a classroom in which a child can listen to various books, CDs, or cassette recordings with headphones or where he or she can simply be alone.

Headsets plugged into a jack or terminal can help to block out room noise, while partitions can cut down on distractions. Listening posts can contain the following:

- Large packing boxes lined with soft fabrics and pillows;
- Old, soft armchairs; or
- A bunk or loft.

A child can listen to commercial or teacher-prepared read-along tapes (*read-alongs*) of appropriate books. Usually teacher-prepared read-along tapes are better since professional readers often read too rapidly for young children to follow. Cassette recordings of the following songs are very popular with young children:

"Old MacDonald Had a Farm"
"Five Little Frogs"
"One, Two, Buckle My Shoe"
"Itsy-Bitsy Spider"
"Hokey-Pokey"

"Five Little Pumpkins"
"Baa, Baa, Black Sheep"
"Down by the Bay"
"The Wheels on the Bus Go Round and Round"
"Farmer in the Dell"

Chants, Finger Plays, and Action Verses

A teacher or tutor can use *chants*, *finger plays*, and *action verses* to improve a child's listening skills, as well as the oral language skills of young children. These usually have regular and predictable sound and word patterns. Useful examples can be found in Appendix V, along with lists of books that contain further examples.

Games for Improving Listening Skills

Here are brief descriptions of several games that can improve the listening skills of young children. They can be adapted to the interests, needs, and abilities of specific pupils.

Guess What Makes This Sound

Objective

To identify the source of common sounds.

Materials Needed

Assemble various items such as a drum, an alarm clock, sandpaper, a baby doll that cries, a New Year's Eve noisemaker, a washboard, a tambourine, paper to crumple, dishes to rattle, a baby rattle, and so forth. Stand where the children cannot see any of the objects that will be used to make noises. This activity can be placed on a cassette tape to be placed at a listening post (station).

Playing the Game

For each sound, have the children guess what is making the sound that they hear. As a variation, clap rhythms behind the screen and have the children try to imitate the rhythms. Use patterns of loud and soft claps and slow and fast claps.

I'm Going on a Trip

Objective

To motivate young children to listen extremely carefully.

Materials Needed

None.

Playing the Game

Have one child in the class or group say, "*I'm going on a trip, and I'm taking a coat with me.*" He or she selects another child to continue the game. That child says, "*I'm going on a trip, and I'm taking a coat and mittens with me.*" The game continues with children trying to remember all of the previous items that are going to be taken on the trip in correct order in addition to their own item. The winner is the child who is able to remember the most items in the correct order without forgetting any of them.

Does This Sound Crunchy?

Objective

To provide practice in auditory discrimination and auditory memory skills.

Materials Needed

Celery sticks, carrot sticks, a raw potato, a piece of flannel cloth, marshmallows, a cotton ball for each child, a turnip, an ear of corn, and so forth.

Playing the Game

Place all the materials in a bag that you hold behind your back. Then reach in and pull out a celery stick as you begin to sing, "Celery sticks are green and thin, green and thin, green and thin" (to the tune of "Mary Had a Little Lamb"). Then pass a cotton ball to each child and sing the song again crunching the cotton ball when you reach the end of the song. You can follow up with "What other things do you think are crunchy?"

You can then introduce the other objects to the children along with appropriate songs in each case.

ORAL LANGUAGE

Oral language is a crucial element of reading instruction. Humans are wired to need to communicate with others. Oral language enables us to interact with others, understand our world, and reveal ourselves. Human beings have an innate understanding of the rules that govern language. If they did not, language learning would not occur in young children. Most children possess an intuitive set of rules for how different parts of speech are used. Oral language, therefore, always is *constructive*, *interactive*, and *functional*. Oral language also is *stable*, *versatile*, and *predictable*.

Reading teachers and tutors should be aware of several important relationships between oral language and reading. They are as follows:

- In all children oral language skills develop to a fairly high degree of proficiency before reading or writing develops.
- Oral and written language share the same grammar (syntactical structure) and vocabulary.
- Children use their knowledge of oral language in learning to read and write.
- All children pass through the same stages of oral language, but at different times.
- Most children with special needs develop oral language skills later than do children with average or above average linguistic aptitude.
- Oral language and reading are keys to subsequently developing more complex cognitive capabilities.

THEORIES OF ORAL LANGUAGE DEVELOPMENT

No single theory can provide a comprehensive explanation for the oral language development of young children. However, it appears that a combination of the leading theories provides the best explanation. Here are brief descriptions of the most common theories.

The Behaviorist Theory

The *behaviorist theory* is accurate, but incomplete. The psychologist B. F. Skinner (1957) defined language as the observed and produced speech that occurs between a speaker and a listener. He stated that thinking is the internal process of language and that thought begins through interactions of speaker and listener. Skinner also wrote that thought is initiated between a parent and child. According to the behaviorists, a child's acquisition of language is both encouraged and developed by imitating the language of adults and other children and by the positive reinforcement that the child receives.

Obviously, babies and young children learn many spoken words by listening to adults or older children and imitating their speech before the imitation has concrete meaning. However, the behaviorist theory can only be partial, since children learn some oral language by constructing it instead of merely imitating it. However, this theory accounts for a young child's use of a word such as *"runned"* for *"ran."*

The Nativist Theory

The *nativist theory* also has some element of truth, and it too can be a partial explanation. Chomsky (1965), McNeil (1970), and Lennenberg (1967) are proponents of the nativist theory. These well-known linguists state that oral language develops entirely innately. For example, young children discover how language works for themselves by internalizing grammar rules. They can do this without the modeling, practice, and reinforcement provided by the adults and older children in their environment. Therefore, the nativists state that oral language development is innate to humans and depends on maturation. The nativists believe that children learn new oral language patterns and generate new rules for the new elements of language.

This theory has some merit, since a horse obviously cannot use oral language. Therefore, oral language as we know it is innate only to humans. However, the nativist theory cannot account for imitation in oral language learning, nor for the part social interaction and construction of oral language play in speech.

The Interaction Theory

The *interaction theory* states that oral language is mediated through interactions designed to elaborate and extend meanings (Neuman & Roskos, 1993). As an example, when babies make cooing or other verbal sounds, family members and friends are excited and provide positive reinforcement. The baby then responds to this positive reinforcement by repeating the same cooing sounds. As babies mature, they begin to construct both consonant and vowel sounds. The typical six-month-old baby usually makes sounds like *ma-ma*, *da-da*, and *ba-ba*.

If the child says *da-da*, family members and friends usually encourage him or her to continue saying *da-da*. Thus the child receives more positive reinforcement that encourages similar oral language play. The pre-linguistic *"chats"* form the foundations of listening, speaking, and writing, according to the interaction theory. As the child continues to develop oral language skills, he or she experiments with additional words. As an example, when the young child is playing with a stuffed toy cat, he or she may say *"kitty, kitty, kitty."* An adult or older child may say: *"Yes, that's a nice little kitty."*

Through the expansion and positive reinforcement of words, the child develops oral language skills. The adult often extends the young child's words by asking questions such as: *"What can you tell me about your pretty black kitty? What do you like to do with it?"* Such language extension encourages a young child to think and understand. This type of oral language development may be called the *elaborated language code (style)*. In this type of oral language development, an interested adult or older child tries to elaborate on, extend, and clarify the speech of a young child. This type of oral language development often leads to a high degree of emergent literacy skills and success in beginning reading activities both at home and at school (Miller, 1967).

However, in some families a baby's cooing and babbling may be considered a nuisance and a waste of time. Without interaction and positive reinforcement, a young child may use a predominantly restricted oral language code (style), which may lead to slower emergent literacy skills and less success in beginning reading (Miller, 1967).

The Piagetian and Vygotskian Theories

Piaget's theory of cognitive development is based on the concept that children learn through their activities. He stated that children's understanding of the world is related to their sensory experiences or actions. According to Piaget, a child's first words are egocentric, centered on his or her own actions. Young children mainly talk about themselves and what they do. Therefore, their beginning oral language is related to the events, objects, and events that they have directly experienced through seeing, hearing, touching, tasting, and smelling (Piaget & Inhelder (1969).

In addition, *Vygotsky's theory of basic learning* is related to oral language development. According to Vygotsky, children learn higher cognitive functions by internalizing social relationships. As an example, adults first provide children with the name of objects and help them to make suggestions. As children become more adept at this, adults and older children gradually withdraw scaffolding and support. Vygotsky also described the *zone of proximal development*, a range of social interaction between an adult and a child. Supposedly, the child can perform within that range, but only with support (Vygotsky, 1978). According to this theory, adults and older children should interact with young children by encouraging, motivating, and supporting them.

The Constructivist Theory

The *constructivist theory* is a contemporary and useful theory emerging from the work of Piaget and Vygotsky, extended by such linguists as Brown, Cazden, and Bellugi-Klima (1968) and Halliday (1975). Constructivists think of children as the *creators of language* by using an entirely innate set of principles. Therefore, they maintain that language is an active, interactive process. As a child constructs language, he or she usually makes errors that exemplify the rules that he or she knows. Adults and other children must accept errors as a part of a child's learning, especially when he or she is young.

These linguists state that family members, friends, teachers, and tutors must accept each young child's individuality in speech and growth rate. The process of acquiring language is interactive and continuous and takes place in the social context of each child playing with language. Children experiment with new words, construct new words, engage in conversations with themselves, and practice what they have learned. Therefore, oral language development is different for each child, depending on his or her intellectual ability, home environment, and ethnicity/class circumstances. A child does not solely imitate the oral language of others. If that were so, a child never would use such terms as *"seened"* for *"saw"* or *"goed"* for *"went"* or make a statement like *"I seened little pieces of cotton falling from the sky today."*

STAGES OF ORAL LANGUAGE DEVELOPMENT

Most young children develop through the same basic stages of oral language development, at different rates. Usually babies progress from *cooing*, to *babbling*, to *single words*, to *two-word utterances*, sometimes called *telegraphic speech*, to *complex sentence structure*. Most kindergarteners use fairly complex sentence structure. Some children make this progression much more rapidly than others, depending on their intelligence, home environment, or special needs.

The forty-four *phonemes* (sounds) in English are mastered in a predictable way. Oral language development also is related to how *kernel* (basic) sentences can be transformed into *passive form* or *question* or *negative sentences*.

Here is a brief description of the stages of a young child's oral language development:

Two years—Children develop many two-word sentences (telegraphic speech) and may say nursery rhymes over and over.

Three years—Children have about a three-hundred-word vocabulary. At this age a child's vocabulary grows very rapidly.

Three and a half years—The /b/, /m/, /p/, /v/, and /th/ sounds develop.

Four years—Children have about a nine-hundred-word vocabulary.

Four and a half years—The /d/, /t/, /n/, /g/, /k/, /ng/, and /y/ sounds develop.

Five and a half years—The /v/, /sh/, /z/, and /l/ sounds develop.

Seven and a half years—The /s/, /w/, /r/, /th/, and /wh/ sounds develop.

Seven to eight years—Sentence foundation is mastered (pronouns and prepositions).

Eight years—All sounds have been mastered, and speech should be easily understood.

CHECKLIST OF ORAL LANGUAGE SKILLS

	Always	Sometimes	Not Yet
1. Pronounces /b/, /m/, /p/, /v/, and /h/ correctly.	_____	_____	_____
2. Pronounces /d/, /t/, /n/, /g/, /k/, /ng/, and /y/ correctly.	_____	_____	_____
3. Pronounces /v/, /sh/, /zh/, and /l/ correctly.	_____	_____	_____
4. Pronounces /s/, /w/, /r/, /th/, and /wh/ correctly.	_____	_____	_____
5. Pronounces most consonant sounds correctly.	_____	_____	_____
6. Pronounces most long and short vowels correctly.	_____	_____	_____
7. Speaks in sentences of at least four or five words.	_____	_____	_____
8. Speaks in complete sentences.	_____	_____	_____
9. Uses varied syntactic (grammatical) structures.	_____	_____	_____
10. Understands the language of adults when spoken to.	_____	_____	_____
11. Understands the language of classmates when spoken to.	_____	_____	_____
12. Can follow simple oral directions.	_____	_____	_____
13. Has adequate articulation with no stuttering or speech defects.	_____	_____	_____
14. Uses appropriate vocabulary for his/her level of maturity.	_____	_____	_____
15. Can be easily understood by adults.	_____	_____	_____
16. Can be easily understood by classmates.	_____	_____	_____
17. Uses oral language to share personal thoughts and ideas.	_____	_____	_____
18. Is willing and able to participate in class sharing time (show-and-tell).	_____	_____	_____
19. Engages in conversation with classmates.	_____	_____	_____

Name: _____ Grade: _____ **PP**

CHECKLIST OF ORAL LANGUAGE SKILLS *(continued)*

	Always	**Sometimes**	**Not Yet**
20. Enjoys participating in dramatic play.	_____	_____	_____
21. Asks appropriate questions of teacher, tutor, and classmates.	_____	_____	_____
22. Participates effectively in small-group discussions.	_____	_____	_____
23. Participates effectively in large-group discussions.	_____	_____	_____
24. Can read appropriate material aloud.	_____	_____	_____
25. Enjoys playing with language such as rhyming nonsense words.	_____	_____	_____

Developing Oral Language Skills in Early Childhood Programs

Here is a brief summary of several strategies and materials that can improve the oral language skills of young children. Any of these strategies and materials can be modified in the light of the needs, interests, and abilities of specific students.

Dramatic Play

Dramatic play is motivating and helpful for improving oral language skills. Dramatic play consists of acting out and repeating the words and actions of other people. Dramatic play may help children to do the following:

- Improve vocabulary skills;
- Improve ability to engage in conversation with adults and classmates;
- Interact in a positive way with other children;
- Understand the roles and feelings of other people;
- Enhance their creativity, since children imagine, act, and make up events during dramatic play;
- Deal with life situations by acting out different emotions. As an example, two children can pretend to be a mother or father and a child trying to decide if the child should purchase a specific toy; and
- Assume both leadership and group participation roles.

Dramatic play is enriched by using props of various kinds and using learning centers in a classroom. Teachers can encourage dramatic play by providing such props as adult clothing and materials related to activities like a veterinarian's office, a grocery store, a post office, a doctor's or dentist's office, an airport, a drug store, or a travel agency.

The following activities encourage young children to engage in dramatic play:

- School trips to the post office, an airport, an animal hospital, a shopping mall, a grocery store, a drug store, and a pumpkin patch, among countless others;
- Having adults who have interesting occupations, interests, or experiences visit the classroom;
- Reading aloud a variety of narrative trade books, informational books, and poems;
- Second-hand experiences such as viewing videotapes, pictures, simple demonstrations, realia, models, and films;
- Classroom learning centers; and
- Using dramatic play kits (see the next section).

Dramatic Play Kits

Early childhood educators can use *dramatic play kits* to motivate young children to participate in dramatic play. A dramatic play kit consists of items that are related, are boxed together, and are motivational to encourage a prescribed type of dramatic play. Here are some ideas for kits that can be used to encourage dramatic play:

- *Grocery store*—Play money, play cash register, play grocery cart, actual grocery items such as canned vegetables and fruit, an old purse or wallet, wax fruit or vegetables, paper bags, and plastic grocery bags.

- *Animal hospital*—Stuffed animals such as dogs and cats, bandages, empty pill bottles, play thermometer, cotton balls, small bottles filled with water, a white shirt, a play brush and comb, a small empty shampoo bottle, and a small dog collar.

- *Post office*—Used letters and postcards; play stamps such as wildlife, animal, or "love" stamps; large index cards; old shoulder bag purses for mailbags; and mail boxes made of shoe boxes with names and addresses printed on them.

- *Restaurant*—Old order pads, napkins, paper or plastic plates, plastic utensils, an apron, play money, play cash register.

- *Beauty shop*—Plastic brushes, plastic combs, cotton balls, old curlers, colored water in old nail polish bottles, hairpins, and mirror.

Costumes

Costumes of various kinds can help children as they pretend to be various characters. Children can put on costumes with snaps and strong ties independently. Elastic waistbands are also helpful. Cut down the clothing so children don't trip. Here are some clothing items that may motivate different kinds of dramatic play: hats; wigs; accessories such as purses, ties, scarves, old jewelry, aprons, and badges; and shoes and slippers.

Hats and wigs may not be feasible if any of the children have head lice. One way to use hats and wigs in those circumstances is to give each child a shower cap for his or her own repeated use. The child puts on the shower cap before putting on a hat or wig.

Literature Circles

A *literature circle* can improve young children's oral language skills. Have the children read a book related to the thematic unit they have been studying and then sit in a small group with the teacher or tutor and discuss that book. Model appropriate "book talk" and ask questions to facilitate the group discussion. Encourage the children to ask each other questions without the teacher as guide.

Learning Centers

Here are some examples of *learning centers* and appropriate materials in early childhood classrooms:

- *Science center*—aquarium, terrarium, class pets, magnets, thermometer, compass, shells, magnifying glass, simple microscope, prism, plants, informational books on the topic being studied, and blank journals for recording observations of experiments and scientific projects.

- *Social studies center*—maps, globe, simple atlas, traffic signs, artifacts from other countries, flags, informational and narrative books on themes being studied, and writing materials to make class books or the children's own books.

- *Art center*—markers, crayons, watercolors, easels, colored pencils, unlined paper, children's scissors, paste or glue, scrap materials, clay, play dough, and books with directions for constructing various craft items.

- *Rhythm center*—piano, cassette or CD player, tape recorder with musical tapes, rhythm instruments, songbooks, and copies of sheet music for songs sung in class.

- *Reading center*—narrative trade books, information trade books, cassette tape recorder, headsets, taped books and stories, markers, pencils, writing paper, 3-inch × 5-inch cards for recording words for word bank, stapler, construction paper, hole punch, typewriter, computer, envelopes, pictures for different holidays, rhyme games, alphabet cards, words on word cards representing out-of-school environmental print (*STOP, walk, park, Disney,* etc.). The reading center also should include a library corner, oral language materials, and language arts materials.

- *Arithmetic center*—rulers, measuring cups, movable clock, play money, cash register, calculator, height chart, geometric shapes, children's books about numbers and arithmetic, and writing materials for creating stories about mathematics.

- *Block area*—blocks of many different sizes and shapes, toy cars, trucks, items related to the thematic unit, and reading material related to the themes.

Wordless (Textless) Books

Wordless (textless) books have complete story themes, with no words. The story line is entirely carried by the pictures that make up the book. The child reconstructs the story line by interpreting the pictures, some of which may be intricate. Many wordless books are designed for children as young as three. However, some wordless books are useful with intermediate-grade students and even beyond if they have special needs. Some even may appeal to adults (Abrahamson, 1981).

Wordless books can help develop picture interpretation skills, beginning story structure, creativity, and imagination as well as *oral language skills*. They also are very motivating since children can formulate their own story rather than merely listening to or reading the author's words.

Here is a procedure for using wordless books:

1. Introduce the wordless book. Explain how the children will have to use their own creative storytelling skills to interpret the book.

2. Guide the children through the book, encouraging them to interpret each picture and to predict what may happen next. They should try to determine and use the basic story line of the book.

3. Go through the wordless book several times, asking children to tell the story each time.

4. If desired, have the children put a sticky note on each page of the wordless book so that their written text accompanies the picture.

Appendix VI contains examples of contemporary wordless (textless) books.

Games to Improve Oral Language Skills

Who Took the Halloween Candy Bars?

NOTE: If some students have religious prohibitions against discussion of Halloween, the name of the holiday and the phrase "trick or treat" can be removed and the activity can still be used.

Begin this game by saying: "*Just before Halloween there was a bowl of little candy bars for trick or treat on a table by the door. On Halloween night Mom went to get the candy bars and they were all gone. Who took the candy bars from the candy bowl?*"

[Look at one of the children and use his or her name.] "[*Betsy*] *took the candy bars from the candy bowl.*"

Betsy says: "*Who me?*"

The leader says: "*Yes you.*"

Betsy says: "*Couldn't be.*"

The leader says: "*Then who?*"

Betsy repeats the first line, using another child's name: "*LaDonna took the candy bars from the candy bowl.*"

Keep saying the rhyme and name the other members of the class, class pets, and other people the children know.

What Is the Mystery Animal?

This game illustrates the use of barriers to promote oral language as visual clues are eliminated. One child describes a mystery item to another child who cannot see it. The child who is guessing asks questions to learn about the mystery item.

Have children bring a stuffed animal from home. Have a pillowcase ready, along with a large enough box to cover the mystery items. Choose a child to fill the pillowcase with stuffed animals. That child then tells the other children to shut their eyes or turn in the opposite direction. The child takes an animal from the pillowcase and hides it under the box. He or she then tells the other children to open their eyes or turn around. The child uses words to describe the mystery animal. The other children listen and, as descriptions are given, they ask questions that will help identify the stuffed animal. After the stuffed animal is identified, another child takes a turn selecting an animal and describing it to the group.

This Is What I Did Today

Young children may need practice in summarizing what they did on a specific day. This game requires drawing paper, markers, crayons or paints, and a pencil. Words that the teacher or tutor can use in this game are *describe*, *tell*, *draw*, and *picture*.

Model the correct sentence structure by saying, "*I took my puppy Honey for a walk in my neighborhood today. What did you do?*" After the children answer, ask them to draw a picture of one thing that they did. They also can use invented spelling or dictation to describe their activity. If they use dictation, write it on the drawing. Then give the children the opportunity to tell the class about their drawings. Hang the pictures in the room or corridor of the classroom or literacy center. Children enjoy seeing their work and the opportunity to share their art with family members and friends.

How Do You Use It?

This game requires photographs or actual objects to show to children. Examples of words that can be used in this game are *pencil, book, dishes, chair, rug, computer, knife, fork, spoon, dishes.*

Tell the children that they are going to see some items that are used both at home and at school. Use photographs or the actual objects if possible. Show the children an item. Ask *"How do we use these items?"* and let them take turns answering. Begin with items such as *chair, table, rug, easel, paintbrush, clock, pencil, marker,* or *crayon.* Next use items of clothing such as *socks, shoes, dress, coat, pants, T-shirt,* or *raincoat.* Then use pictures of items that are found in the home such as *chair, sofa, bed, stove, refrigerator, television set, knife, spoon, fork,* or *dishes.* Pictures of types of transportation are also useful, such as *airplane, school bus, car, train, motorboat, pontoon boat, sailboat, ferry, dump truck, pick-up truck, tractor-trailer,* or *trolley.*

Letter-Name and Sight-Word Knowledge

Do you think it is necessary for young children to be able to identify all of the letter names before entering kindergarten? Although it may be helpful for children to be able to identify the letters before beginning to read, reading instruction should stress sight-word identification along with letter-name identification. However, since the letters eventually must be called by name, young children must learn to both recognize and identify them.

This chapter opens with a pre-assessment device about letter-name and sight-word knowledge. Next I briefly describe letter-name recognition and identification and then present numerous classroom-tested strategies and materials for improving ability in letter-name recognition and identification. Next I provide a brief description of sight-word recognition and identification and a sampling of strategies and materials for improving ability in sight-word recognition and identification. The chapter closes with several games and reproducibles for improving ability in sight-word recognition and identification. After reading this chapter, any reading teacher or tutor should be well prepared to teach and reinforce both letter-name knowledge and sight-word knowledge to all the children with whom they work, including those with special needs of various types.

Decide whether each statement is *accurate* (true) or *not* (false). Evaluate your answers after you have read the chapter. The answers are on page 320.

_____ 1. A child must learn to identify all of the capital and lowercase letter names before learning to identify any sight words.

_____ 2. Knowledge of letter names in late kindergarten is the single most influential factor in later first-grade reading achievement.

_____ 3. All capital letters should be presented before any of the lowercase letters.

_____ 4. Trade books have been written that emphasize all the letter names in context.

_____ 5. Tactile strategies undoubtedly are most effective for children with learning disabilities to learn difficult letter names.

_____ 6. Young children should learn letter names both in context and in isolation.

_____ 7. Games are an effective way for young children to practice letter names.

_____ 8. Reproducibles are a useful way for young children to practice letter-name recognition and identification if they are not overused.

_____ 9. Sight-word recognition is as important in actual reading as in sight-word identification.

_____ 10. A child's sight vocabulary are all the words that he or she can identify immediately upon seeing them.

_____ 11. Many sight words do not have a regular phoneme-grapheme relationship and therefore cannot effectively be analyzed by phonics.

_____ 12. An ascender is a letter that reaches above the line.

_____ 13. Configuration always is a useful element of sight-word knowledge.

_____ 14. Children with special needs may need ten or more exposures to a sight word before it becomes part of their stock of sight words.

_____ 15. Sight words usually are structure or function words without a referent.

_____ 16. Sight words usually should be presented both in context and in isolation.

_____ 17. Although it is not recent, the *Dolch Basic Sight Word List* is still very useful. (See Appendix VII.)

_____ 18. The language-experience approach (LEA) is a very effective strategy for young children in learning and reviewing important sight words.

_____ 19. Word masking is a variation of the *cloze* procedure.

_____ 20. Children often enjoy completing activity sheets in sight-word knowledge if the activity sheets are not overused.

LETTER-NAME RECOGNITION AND IDENTIFICATION

Letter-name recognition and *letter-name identification* are both important beginning reading skills. However, they are *not* a prerequisite to beginning reading instruction. Instead, most young children learn a sampling of *environmental print* and *sight words* such as *STOP, Wal-Mart, Target, mom, dad, dog, cat* and various can and cereal box labels before they can recognize and identify all the letters. In addition, the language-experience approach (LEA), as explained in Chapter Two, and various types of writing activities should take place before formal instruction in the letter names. Since identification of the alphabet letters traditionally has been important in reading instruction, it probably always will be stressed in homes, preschools, and kindergartens. However, it should not be overemphasized at the expense of other emergent literacy skills.

In homes and preschools, children learn the names of some letters and how to write some of them. By the time they are three years old, a few children can identify as many as ten alphabet letters, while by the age of four, some children can write a few recognizable letters, most often the letters found in their first names. They usually write their first names all in capital letters. However, even children with above average linguistic aptitude who may be able to read and write at a rudimentary level before kindergarten entrance may require several months or more to learn all of the letter names. A few children with special needs may be able to learn only five letter names during twenty or more individual tutoring sessions.

However, all children in kindergarten and beginning first grade should be able to recognize and identify all of the capital and lowercase letter names for several reasons. Family members and friends place great emphasis on this knowledge. *Research has found that the knowledge of letter names in late kindergarten and early first grade is the single most important predictor of subsequent first-grade reading achievement* (Durrell, 1980).

The child who can identify the letter names probably came from a home environment in which literacy activities such as reading regularly to the child, scribbling and writing activities, and developing prior knowledge have been emphasized. The child in such a home learns both letter names and sight words quite rapidly, especially if he or she has good linguistic aptitude.

A child should identify a letter by its actual name; it is not sufficient to call the lowercase "*a*" a little circle and a little stick. The child also should learn and use the terms *capital* and *lowercase* instead of *big* and *little*. A case can be made that a lowercase *b* is actually a big letter, not a little letter. I think the term *capital* instead of *uppercase* is less confusing for children.

Although letter recognition is easier for most young children than is letter identification, it is less important in reading achievement. Here is an example of letter recognition:

Put an X on the lowercase *m.*

t m y a d

Here is an example of letter identification:

What is the name of this letter?

m

Obviously, letter identification, not letter recognition, is needed in reading. Although letter recognition activities similar to the one above probably have some value as a starting point, letter identification should be emphasized.

A child must have *100* percent competency in identification of both capital and lowercase letter names. Merely identifying the majority of the letters is not sufficient. If a child has apparent difficulty learning to recognize and especially to identify the letters, *teach only one letter at a time. Tactile strategies*, discussed later in this chapter, usually are especially helpful. If a child does not seem to have much difficulty, it may be possible to teach two letters at a time. In this case, select two letters that do *not* look similar, such as *y* and *k*. Do not try to teach *m* and *n* in the same lesson.

Research has not discovered any single best order for teaching either the capital or the lowercase letter names. Usually children are taught to first recognize, identify, and write the letters in their own first names. After that, a few teachers or tutors prefer to teach children to recognize and identify all of the lowercase letter names first, followed by the capital letter names. However, most teachers and tutors present matching capital and lowercase letters in pairs, such as *F* and f. A few teachers or tutors teach letter names in terms of their usefulness to young children. In this approach, the letters *s*, *i*, and *b* would be presented before the letters *q* and *v*, since the latter two letters are much less common. However, the letters *X* and *x* are often needed to complete reading tests and workbooks.

Children also need to learn the difference between a letter and a word. Using an experience chart can be very effective for this concept.

Some teachers and tutors present the letter names in D'Nealian script because of the help this may give children in later making the transition to cursive handwriting. However, other teachers and tutors prefer Zaner-Bloser handwriting (block handwriting) because it better matches the print found in the books that children read and it usually is easier for young children to learn.

Strategies, Materials, and Reproducibles for Improving Letter-Name Knowledge

The following classroom-tested strategies, materials, and ready-to-duplicate activity sheets are all helpful in improving letter-name recognition and identification. They should all be modified depending on the needs, interests, and abilities of specific pupils.

Although letter-name knowledge is best presented and reviewed in the context of actual reading materials, some children, especially those with special needs, also require practice with letter names in isolation, such as in games and activity sheets. However, as much as possible, children should learn and practice letter names in the context of meaningful narrative and simple informational trade books, rhymes, and finger plays. (For suitable finger plays, see Chapter Three).

A selection of books that help children learn individual letter names can be found in Appendix VIII.

Tactile or Tracing Strategies

Tactile or tracing strategies (VAK or visual-auditory-kinesthetic) strategies are especially useful with children who have learning disabilities and those children who simply are unable to remember the letter names. Since tactile strategies are time-consuming, they should be used only with children who have real difficulty in recognizing and identifying letter names.

Here are some tactile strategies that have proven very effective.

- *Instant pudding*—This tactile strategy is very motivating and fun for young children. Prepare a package of instant pudding (children usually like chocolate the best) and place it in a flat pan (like a cake pan). Have the child draw the target letter name in the pudding while saying its name aloud. The child should use the terms *capital* and *lowercase*. The child can lick his or her fingers after each letter is drawn.

- *Hair gel*—Place some hair gel in a Zip-Loc® freezer bag. Spread some of the hair gel on a piece of butcher (shiny) paper. Have the child draw the target letter in the hair gel, while saying the letter name. Have the child state whether it is a capital or lowercase letter.

- *Shaving cream*—Have the child draw each target letter in commercially available shaving cream. Shaving cream is quite popular with young children since it is not particularly messy.

- *Colored sand or salt tray*—Place sand or salt in a flat plan such as a cake pan. Grind a piece of colored chalk and add it to the sand or salt to make it colorful (or buy pre-colored sand). Have the child draw the target capital or lowercase letter in the sand while saying its name aloud.

- *Oobleck recipe*—Combine 3 cups water with 2 boxes of cornstarch. Then have the child draw each target letter in the oobleck, which is spread on a sheet of heavy paper such as butcher (shiny) paper. Read the book *Bartholomew and the Oobleck* by Dr. Seuss (1950) either before or after the oobleck is used for letter naming. This is a very popular tactile strategy with young children.

- *Clay*—Have the child form each target capital or lowercase letter out of clay, while saying the letter name aloud. Have the child indicate whether the letter is capital or lowercase.

- *Edible alphabet pretzels*—Forming pretzels in the shape of alphabet letters helps children to remember how to identify them. You need:

1 cup lukewarm water	2 teaspoons sugar
1 cake active yeast or 1 pkg. dry yeast	3/4 teaspoon salt
1 egg yolk beaten with 1 tbs. water	4 cups all-purpose flour
coarse salt	

Preheat an oven to 475 degrees. Grease cookie sheet. Slowly stir yeast into 1 cup lukewarm water, following the package directions. Set aside. Combine flour, sugar, and salt. Add yeast to mixture to form a stiff dough. Turn dough out onto floured counter and knead eight to ten times or until it is smooth and elastic. Oil a large bowl. Turn dough in bowl to oil both sides and then cover with a clean, damp cloth. Let the mixture rise in a warm place until it is double in size. Punch down and shape into letters. Place on a cookie sheet. Baste each pretzel with egg yolk mixture. Sprinkle with salt. Let the mixture rise again until it is almost double. Bake for 10 minutes or until golden brown and firm. Eat and enjoy!

- *Pipe cleaners*—Have the child bend a pipe cleaner into the shape of each target letter. Then the child can trace over the pipe cleaner, while saying the letter name aloud. The child also can state whether the letter is a capital or lowercase.

- *Magnetic letters*—Magnetic letters are a tactile strategy that can be used for presenting and reviewing letter names. They are commercially available through teachers' catalogs, online, and in teacher stores. The child can easily move them around to match capital and lowercase letters or to construct words. Magnetic letters are useful for first-grade and perhaps second-grade children who have special reading needs, with older preschool children, and with kindergarten children.

Activities for Each Letter of the Alphabet

Many activities can be used for presenting and reviewing the alphabet letters. This section presents only one example for each letter of the alphabet. Some suggested cooking and baking projects for the various letters are presented in Appendix IX.

The Letter A

Purchase or construct an ant farm village. An ant farm village from Uncle Milton Toys is available in a number of places, including online at unclemilton.com. Alternatively, it is quite easy to construct one with wood, two pieces of glass, and ants from the neighborhood.

The Letter B

Make bubble paintings. Mix tempera paint and liquid soap to a thin consistency. Pour the mixture into yogurt or cottage cheese containers, one for each child. Give each child a short length of straw. Then let the children blow bubbles in the containers so that bubbles froth. Have them lay a piece of paper lightly over the container and the bubble design will transfer.

The Letter C

Have children do canoe lacing. Cut a double canoe shape and punch holes all around the edges. Tie one end of the yarn to the canoe and stiffen the other end of the yarn with a piece of tape. Have children pull the yarn in and out of the holes. Here is a sample pattern for the canoe lacing.

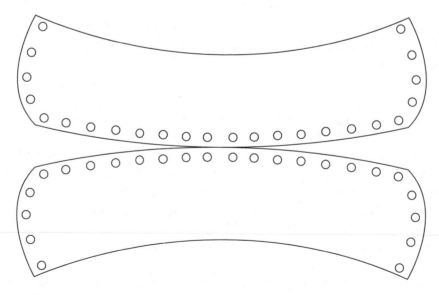

The Letter D

Have children make dogs using a dog pattern and glue dried lima or kidney beans on the dog to form the lowercase letter d. Here is a sample pattern for a dog.

The Letter E

Study evaporation by marking water level in a clear jar. Observe and mark the decreases over time. Then discuss evaporation by having children listen to an appropriate book, a simple encyclopedia article, or simple material found online. One book that can be used for this purpose is by Press (2001).

The Letter F

Have children do feather painting, using feathers instead of brushes to paint pictures.

The Letters G, H, and I

Have children make guitars, horses, and/or igloos and glue dried lima beans or kidney beans onto the object they made to form the first lowercase letter in its name. Here is a sample pattern for each object.

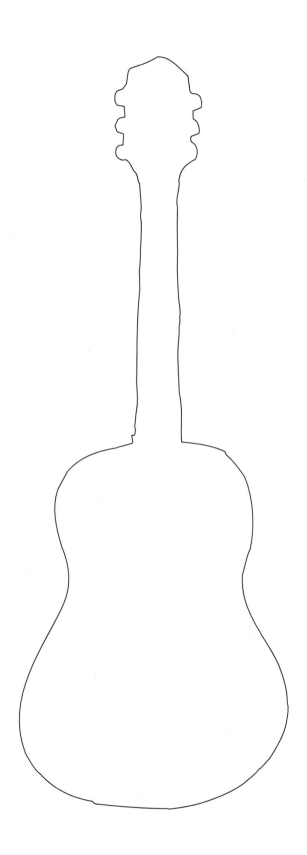

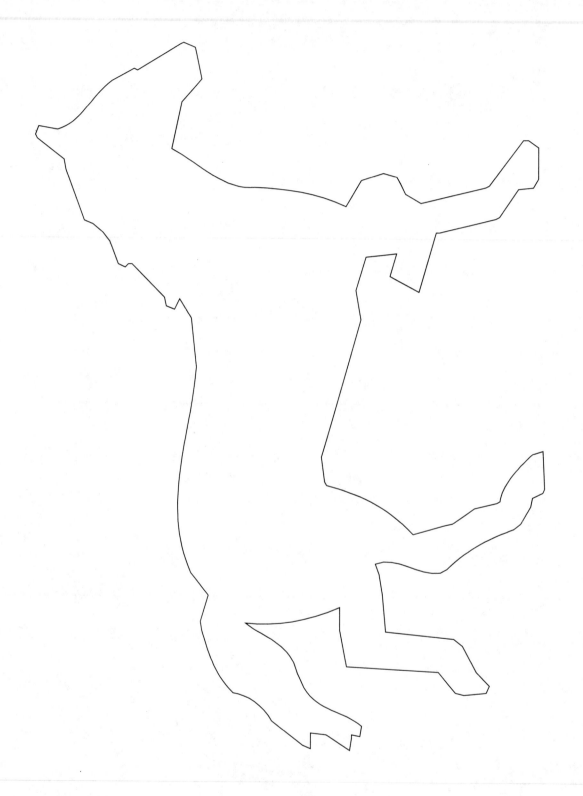

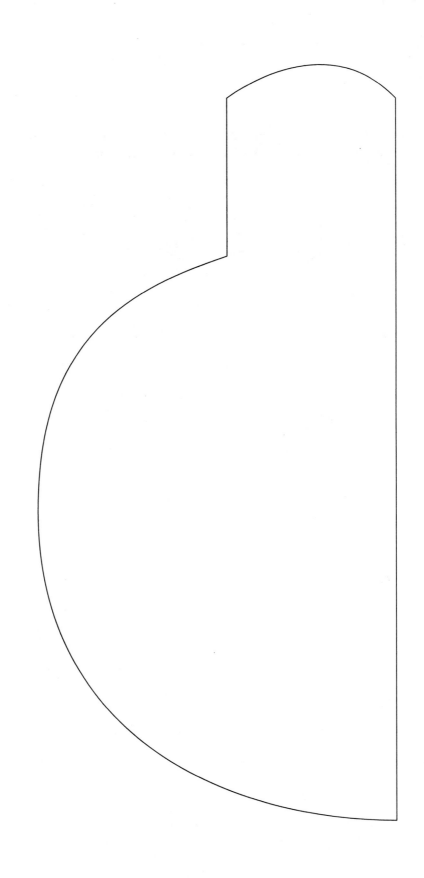

The Letter J

Have children make jungle animals, such as a lion, tiger, zebra, giraffe, cheetah, or antelope from clay or Play-Doh®.

The Letter K

Have children make kangaroos and glue dried lima or kidney beans onto the kangaroo to form the lowercase letter k. Here is a sample pattern for the kangaroo.

The Letter L

Have children make love collages by cutting out pictures of things that they love. They then can dictate or write stories about the items on the collage.

The Letter M

Have children make marble paintings. Put some paper in a large, shallow box. Show children how to dip marbles in paint and tilt the box so that the marbles roll across the paper.

The Letter N

Have each child make his or her own name card. To do so print each child's name on cardboard and cover the name with glue. Have children sprinkle sand on the glue to make a name card with an interesting texture.

The Letter O

Have children string O-shaped cereal for necklaces on string or dental floss.

The Letter P

Have children make pigs and glue dried lima or kidney beans on it to form a lowercase p. Here is a sample pattern for the pig.

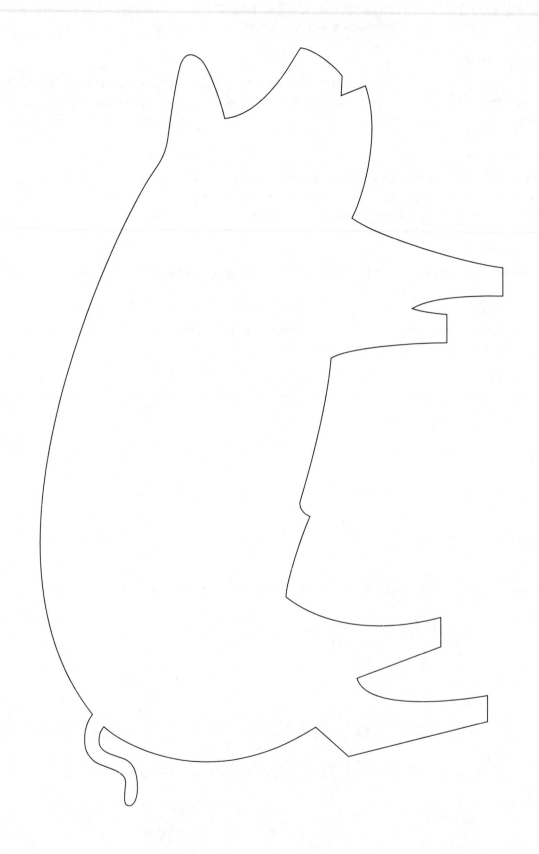

The Letter Q

Have children make paper quilts by drawing lines to divide a sheet of paper into four columns and four rows. In the top row place a circle, square, triangle, and rectangle, each of a different color. Ask children to finish the patterns by pasting the appropriate shapes on their quilts.

The Letter R

Have children make ribbon collages by gluing various colors of ribbons to a sheet of heavy construction paper or cardboard.

The Letter S

Have children make sand paintings. Mix dry sand and dry paint. Have children make a pattern on heavy construction paper or cardboard with glue. Then have them shake the sand/paint mixture on the glue and shake off the excess to make a sand painting.

The Letter T

Have children make telephones out of heavy manila paper. Then have them print their names and phone numbers on their telephones. Here is a sample telephone pattern.

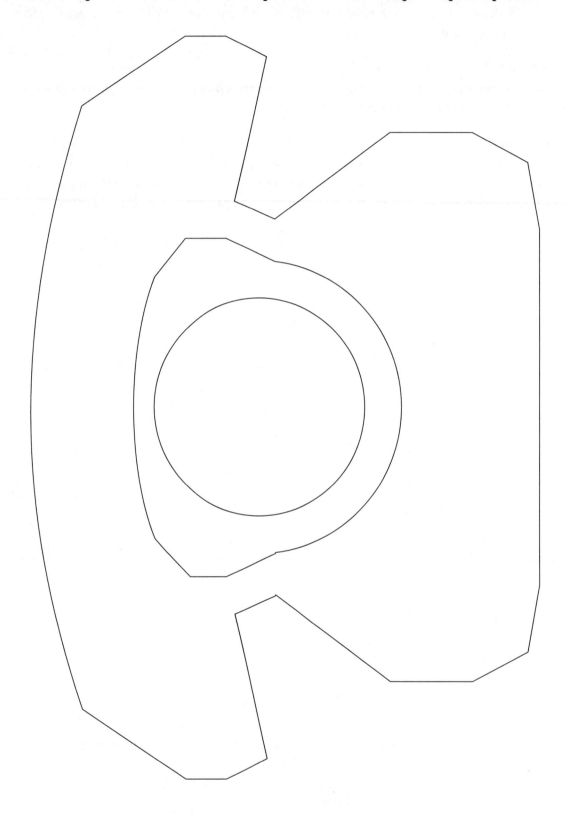

The Letter U

Have children make umbrellas. Then have them glue dried lima beans or kidney beans to form the lowercase letter u on the umbrella.

The Letter V

Make a volcano by building papier-mâché around an open glass jar with its mouth pointing upward. Paint the outside of the volcano. When the volcano is dry, mix 1/4 cup vinegar, 1/4 cup liquid detergent, and red food coloring in the jar, and carefully add 6 tablespoons baking soda that has been dissolved in warm water. The volcano will erupt!

The Letter W

Have children make unique spider webs by using white chalk on black construction paper.

The Letter X

Have each child make his or her own treasure box by painting an egg carton and adding glitter while the paint is still wet.

The Letter Y

Have children make yarn designs, making something out of a piece of yarn without cutting it.

The Letter Z

Have children make zoo pictures by drawing animals that can be found in the zoo.

Games for Reviewing Letter-Name Knowledge

This part of the chapter presents a sampling of classroom-tested games that can be used to review the capital and lowercase letter names. Any game that is used to review a reading skill should primarily emphasize the reading skill to which it is devoted rather than the game. Although games encourage some competition, they are very motivating for most children, especially for children with special needs such as learning disabilities or reading disabilities when no other strategy is very effective.

Research has indicated that children have a *53* percent greater gain in knowledge when playing active games in comparison with practice using activity sheets. Even passive games result in a *30* percent better gain than activity sheets (Dickerson, 1982).

Alphabet Bingo

To Construct the Game

Cut cardboard to make enough 8 -inch × 11-inch sheets for each child (any similar size will work just as effectively). Divide each sheet into nine to twelve sections. Print an alphabet letter on each section. Make certain each sheet contains a different combination of letters. Cover the sheets with clear self-stick vinyl. For markers, use small pieces of paper, bottle caps, poker chips, or anything similar.

To Play the Game

To practice letter-name identification: As the caller says a letter name, have the child place markers of some type on his or her card. When a complete row—either horizontal, vertical, or diagonal—is covered, the child calls out "BINGO." If you wish, children can play "Cover the Card" occasionally. To win the game, the child must be able to identify each letter name as he or she takes off the markers to prove that he or she has won.

To practice letter-name recognition: Hold up a card with a letter name on it and ask whether any child has that letter on his or her sheet. This version of the game ends when the first child playing the game has "covered" his or her sheet.

Letter-Name Basketball

To Construct the Game

Obtain a soft foam basketball and hoop. Hang the hoop at an appropriate place and height for the children. Then divide the group into two teams.

To Play the Game

Hold up a flashcard with a letter printed on it to the first team member in Team A. If the child correctly provides the letter name, he or she should try to shoot a basket. If the child makes the basket, his or her team earns 2 points. If the basketball hits the rim of the basket, the team earns 1 point. This child goes to the end of the team line. Continue this same procedure with Team B. Keep playing until all of the team members have had a chance to shoot at the basket.

Alphabet Race

To Construct the Game

Construct a race track or use an open-ended game board. Construct 1-inch × 3-inch flashcards containing each capital or lowercase letter of the alphabet or each target letter of the alphabet to be learned. You also need a marker and a die.

To Play the Game

Have a child throw the die, identify the letter on the flashcard, and then move the number of spaces on the die. To provide more practice, have the child identify one flashcard for each space that he or she moves.

Newspaper Search

To Construct the Game

Provide a newspaper page and a marker or crayon for each child.

To Play the Game

An adult or child names a letter. Everyone else searches his or her newspaper page to find the letter and circle it. Continue in the same manner. Having the children look for both capital and lowercase examples of the letter named may provide additional practice.

Bang

To Construct the Game

Cover a Pringles® potato chip can with red self-stick vinyl or red construction paper. Attach a piece of heavy string about 1 to 2 inches long to the top of the can and use aluminum foil to make a "firecracker" wick. Then print the capital and lowercase letters with a marker on 1-inch × 2-inch cards made of tag board. In addition, print the word BANG on several cards. During the game, shake the can often to mix up the cards.

To Play the Game

Children take turns drawing a card and saying each letter name. If the child can correctly say the letter name, he or she keeps the card. If a child draws the word BANG, he or she must return all of the cards to the can. The first child to collect ten cards (or any preset number) is the winner of the game.

A Cherry Tree with the Alphabet

To Construct the Game

You need one piece of 12-inch × 7-inch tag board, twenty-six pieces of 2-inch × 1-inch of tag board, a marker, and a pair of scissors. Enlarge and cut out the following tree design using the 12-inch × 7-inch piece of tag board.

A B C D E F G

H I J K L M N O

P Q R S T U V W

X Y Z

Print the capital letter names on the tag board tree. Cut the small pieces of tag board into the shape of cherries. (See the pattern.) Print the lowercase letter names on the small pieces of tag board.

To Play the Game

Put the tag board tree on a flat surface. Have the children match the letter on each cherry with its corresponding capital letter on the tree. If you wish, the game can be made self-checking by placing the appropriate capital letter on the back of each cherry.

Concentration (Memory)

To Construct the Game

Use a marker to make capital and lowercase 1-inch × 2-inch letter cards out of tag board. Construct two sets of identical cards. Make sure that the children cannot see through the cards when they are turned over.

To Play the Game

Place the letter cards face down on a flat surface. Have the children take turns picking up a card in one set and trying to find the card that matches it in the other set. When a match is made, have the child say the letter name and keep the card. Give points or prizes for the number of cards that each child has.

Eating the Alphabet

To Construct the Game

Print the capital and lowercase letter names on small cards about 1-inch × 1-inch. Then collect sturdy boxes on which an animal head and different alphabet strips are glued. Cut holes in the opposite sides of the boxes so children can reach in for the cards.

To Play the Game

Have the children take turns choosing a card and "feeding" it to the animal that has a similar alphabet letter on the strip under its mouth. This illustration should clarify this game.

Letter Chairs

To Construct the Game

Make fifty-two 1-inch × 2-inch letter cards, each of which has a capital or lowercase letter name on it.

To Play the Game

Have children sit on chairs that are lined up behind each other. Begin at the front of the line and show a card with a capital or lowercase letter name printed on it. If the child can give the letter name correctly, he or she stays in that chair. If the child gives an incorrect answer, he or she goes to the end of the line and all of the other children move up. Children try to stay at the front as long as they are able to be the "captain."

Matching Letter Names with Seasonal Themes

To Construct the Game

Print capital and lowercase letter names on hearts and arrows, Pilgrims and turkeys, jack-o'-lanterns and black cats, snowflakes and snowmen, umbrellas and raincoats, fall leaves and rakes, among others.

To Play the Game

In each case, have the child match the capital and lowercase letter names.

Let's Jump Up

To Construct the Game

Place a list of capital or lowercase letter names on the chalkboard or an experience chart. Make two 1-inch × 2-inch cards for each letter on the board.

To Play the Game

Give each child two or four letter cards, each of which should be different. Point to one letter on the chalkboard or experience chart. The children with that letter card jump up and say the letter name. The child who says it first gets the other children's cards. The winner is the child with the most cards at the end of the game.

Can You Match These Letter Cards?

To Construct the Game

Make two decks of both the capital and lowercase letters on construction paper cards. The cards should be about 2 inches × 3 inches. Make a 1/4-inch border on the bottom edge, so the child can place the letters right side up. Cover the cards with clear self-stick vinyl. The dealing deck can be one color, and the drawing deck can be a different color.

To Play the Game

Deal the target letters from the dealing deck to two to four players. The other deck will be the drawing pile. Each child draws from this pile in turn and lays the card down so that all the players can see the letter. The player who has the matching letter card lays down the card, says the letter, and keeps both cards in front of him or her. When one child has used up all the dealt cards, the child with the most letter pairs in front of him or her is the winner.

Reproducibles for Improving Letter-Name Knowledge

Here are four reproducible activity sheets for improving ability in letter-name knowledge. Duplicate them and use them in their present form or modify them in any way that seems appropriate. The four activity sheets are

> *Help the Bear Cub Get Home to Its Den*
> *Match the Shoes*
> *Match the Right Animal Mother and Baby*
> *Letter Dogs*

HELP THE BEAR CUB GET HOME TO ITS DEN

The bear cub is lost! Help him get home by filling in the missing lowercase alphabet letters. If you fill them all in correctly, he will be home.

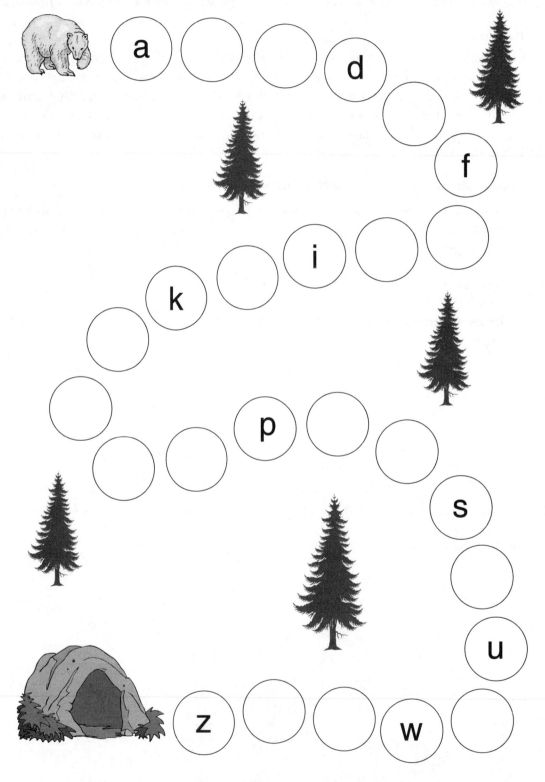

MATCH THE SHOES

The left shoe in each pair is on the left side of the sheet. The right shoe is on the right side of the sheet. Match the capital letters to the lowercase letters. Draw a line from each left shoe to each right shoe.

Left Shoe

Right Shoe

MATCH THE RIGHT ANIMAL MOTHER AND BABY

Help each animal mother find her own baby. Match the capital letters to the lowercase letters.
Draw a line from each animal mother to her correct baby.

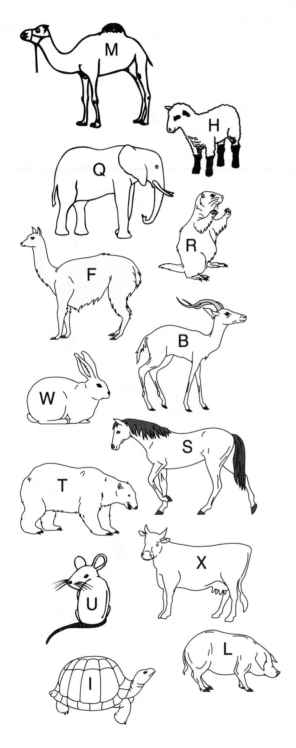

LETTER DOGS

Write the capital letter on each dog.

LETTER DOGS *(continued)*

_____ a

_____ d

_____ n

_____ g

_____ h

_____ w

_____ y

SIGHT-WORD RECOGNITION AND IDENTIFICATION

Sight-word recognition and *sight-word identification* are both elements of *sight-word knowledge*. *Sight-word recognition* is being able to select a target word when it is found with other similar-appearing words. On the other hand, *sight-word identification* is the ability to say a word immediately while reading. Sight-word identification is both more difficult and more important, and thus should receive the most emphasis. Sight-word recognition can be taught and reviewed as a beginning point.

Many sight words have an irregular *phoneme-grapheme (sound-symbol) relationship* and therefore cannot be analyzed by using phonics. Such words usually are most effectively learned as a total unit. Examples include *of, is, said, many, once, were, you, would, who, where,* and *they.*

Sight vocabulary can be defined as all the words that a reader can immediately identify. Although a reader may first have had to analyze these words by phonics, structure, or context, he or she now has them in his or her sight-word bank. A large sight-word bank means that a child does not have to stop and analyze most of the words while reading. A small sight-word bank can slow the reader and therefore interfere with comprehension. All children should master all of the basic sight words by the end of third grade. Reading teachers and tutors often must provide children with special needs with much motivating practice to make that goal. An insufficient sight-word bank is a major reason why a child who has been an adequate reader in the primary grades may begin to have reading difficulties in fourth grade and beyond.

Young children should also be able to identify the basic sight words, since a very small number of these words comprise a large portion of the words found in everyday reading for both children and adults. As an example, the following ten words comprise at least *25 percent* of all the words found in print material: *the, of, and, a, to, in, is, you, that,* and *it.*

The most common twenty-five words in the English language make up about *one-third* of all the words found in print materials (Fry, Kress, & Fountoukidis, 2000).

Sight-word identification consists of examining a word's total shape, its first several letters, its length, or its special characteristics such as *ascenders* (letters that reach above the line, such as *b, f, h, k,* or *l*) and *descenders* (letters that go below the line such as *g, j, p, q,* or *y*). *Configuration* or *drawing a frame around an entire word* is another subskill of sight-word identification. The following illustrates the technique of configuration:

hippopotamus

However, configuration is only an effective word identification technique in words with a unique configuration or shape. A number of common words are not suitable for configuration, such as *one, man,* and *ran.*

Some subskills of sight-word identification are still taught, even though they provide irrelevant or unimportant cues. As an example, the double *o* in *look* is said to be "*two eyes.*" However, consider that all the following words also contain a double *o* in the same position in the word: *book, cook, hook, shook, took, goose, moose, loose, moon, noon,* and *stood.* Another irrelevant cue is looking for the small words in larger words. Although this approach can be correct sometimes, as in the word *snowman,* it is not helpful if a child notices the words *fat* and *her* in *father.*

Some common words found in reading are among the most difficult for young children to learn since they are so irregular. Many reading teachers believe that some children, especially those with learning disabilities, may need *120* to *140* or more meaningful exposures before a word becomes part of the child's sight-word bank.

When choosing words from a sight-word list to present to children, consider *usefulness* and *word difficulty.* As an example, although the sight word *once* is difficult for children to remember, it is fairly common. Therefore, it probably should be taught and practiced fairly early. Sight words often are *structure* or *function* words, meaning that they have no referent and do not represent a concept. Such words can be difficult for young children to remember because the child cannot associate the word with a concrete concept. However, the few content sight words, such as *school* and *mother* often are easier for children to remember.

Sight words should be presented both *in context* and *in isolation,* so that most children can learn them effectively. Seeing sight words in context is beneficial for most children. In addition, children with special needs, including those with learning and reading disabilities, also need much motivated practice with sight words *in isolation.* When words are presented and practiced *in isolation,* children may pay more attention to the general appearance of the word, including its special characteristics. On the other hand, when words are presented *in context,* children may pay more attention to word meanings and the way in which the word is used. Teaching *structure* or *function* words such as articles, prepositions, and conjunctions *in context* is very important because the most effective way to understand such words is to notice how they are actually used in reading. Presenting sight words in context and isolation helps children to learn both their meanings and pronunciation. If children already know the meaning of a sight word, a reading teacher or tutor should spend most of his or her time presenting its unique features, including how it is spelled and its pronounceable word parts. Knowing how to spell and/or sound out a word partially or entirely helps children to learn and remember new words.

Immediate recognition and *accuracy* of a word are both important in identifying sight words. Children need different amounts of time to reach a high level of sight-word identification. When they have reached an acceptable level of accuracy in identifying words, they gain *automaticity* or *immediate recognition* of sight words. A golfer, for example, may remember trying to keep track of and successfully perform all of the tasks involved in learning to golf well. However, a competent golfer probably performs all of those tasks automatically. This automaticity is what children need to achieve when they are identifying sight words.

Good readers may be able to learn *four times* as many sight words in a specified period of time as children with special needs. Children with special needs require numerous meaningful opportunities to learn sight words: easy trade book reading, motivating games, and interesting, challenging activity sheets. Suggestions and resources later in this chapter will help all children, including those with special needs, achieve the automaticity and accuracy in sight-word identification that will enable them to become efficient readers in the primary grades and beyond.

Strategies for Improving Ability in Sight-Word Knowledge

This section contains classroom-tested strategies, materials, games, and reproducible activity sheets that help improve children's abilities in sight-word recognition and identification. Although much of the material in this section works best with young children, a number of the strategies can easily be adapted for older children who have limited sight-word knowledge.

Reading Materials

All kinds of reading materials undoubtedly are the most effective way of teaching and reviewing sight words for most children. Although sight words can be presented and practiced in isolation occasionally, children should learn and practice sight words in the context of real reading materials as much as possible, including meaningful narrative and information trade books, poetry, and nursery rhymes, among other genre. (Also see Appendix X for a list of books that reinforce basic sight words.)

Extensive reading of all kinds of materials certainly is the most effective way for children to practice sight-word identification. However, some children apparently do not enjoy reading any type of material. Therefore, reading teachers or tutors should provide all students with a wide variety of easy, highly interesting narrative and informational books to read for pleasure and information. Children always should be given choices about the books they are going to read.

Predictable books (as discussed in Chapter Two) usually help children learn sight words in individual, partner, or small-group reading settings.

Here is a strategy that reading teachers and tutors can use for teaching sight words:

1. Select a book that children will enjoy and that contains the sight words you want to review. If possible, use an oversized version of the book so that children will be able to easily follow along while you read.

2. Preview the book with children, read it aloud to them, and then discuss it.

3. Point to each word as you read it aloud.

4. Reread the book. Ask children to read the repeated parts or other easy parts.

5. After several rereadings of the book, copy the text onto chart paper or cover the illustrations in the big book. With the pictures covered up, have children focus on identifying the words, helping the children only if necessary.

6. Duplicate the book and cut the duplicated version into sentence strips. Have children match the individual sentence strips to those contained in that version. Then have children reassemble the book, sentence by sentence. Sentences can also be cut up into individual words. Have children reconstruct each individual sentence by placing the cut-out words in the proper order.

Tracing Activities

The *tracing strategies* that were described in detail earlier in this chapter for helping children remember difficult letter names are equally useful in helping children remember difficult sight words. Since tracing is time-consuming, it should be used only with children who are having trouble, on sight words that are especially difficult, and only as long as necessary. Even children with special needs should be able to remember sight words using conventional methods after using tracing for a fairly short time.

Several tracing strategies that were described earlier in this chapter can be used to help children remember difficult sight words, including: *instant pudding, hair gel, shaving cream, colored chalk sand or salt trays, shaving cream, oobleck, Play-Doh or clay, edible alphabet pretzels, pipe cleaners,* and *magnetic letters.*

When using instant pudding, hair gel, colored chalk sand or salt trays, or shaving cream, have the child print the target sight word in the material, saying it aloud as he or she makes it. Have the child trace the word in the material as many times as necessary to remember the word. When using Play-Doh, modeling clay, pipe cleaners, or magnetic letters, the child can form the target sight word out of the material. In each case, have the child form the word enough times to ensure mastery and then use each word in a sentence.

Puffed Word Cards

Puffed word cards provide a unique tracing strategy for children who have difficulty remembering words. These three-dimensional, textured cards help children remember difficult sight words.

Making these cards requires:

- Paint Puffer™ (a nontoxic chemical formula that, when added to acrylic paint and heated, causes the paint to expand to fifty times its original volume; it can be ordered from most school supply companies)

- Acrylic paint (red, green, or blue)

- Half-inch paintbrush

- White tag board or poster board

Cut tag or poster board into flashcards about 3 inches by 5 inches (3 by 8 if the sight word is long, such as *hippopotamus*). Mix Paint Puffer with acrylic paint, about two parts of paint to one part of Paint Puffer. Using an art paintbrush, print sight words on the flashcards with the paint/Paint Puffer mixture. The thickness of the paint film will determine the height of the "puffed" word: the thicker the film, the higher the puffed word. For a very "tall" word, build up several layers. Apply several heavy coats of paint mixture, letting each coat dry several minutes before adding the next coat.

"Puff" the words by applying heat. The paint may be puffed either wet or dry. Heat a convection oven to about 230 degrees. Lay the flashcards on a cookie sheet in a single layer and put the cookie sheet into the oven. Dry paint will puff within seconds, while wet paint will take two or three minutes. The puff will flatten out if the flashcards are left in the oven too long or if the oven temperature is above 250 degrees.

NOTE: The mixture of paint and Paint Puffer will keep indefinitely in a closed container. There is no time limit between paint and puffing. Do not apply the Paint Puffer to thin paper, as the edges will curl.

Here is the basic procedure for using the *"puffed"* flashcards.

1. Show a word card to a child.

2. Ask the child to say the word.

3. Have the child say the word.

4. Have the child trace over the raised letters of the word with the index (pointer) finger of the hand with which he or she writes.

5. Have the child say the word again.

6. Have the child use the target word in a sentence.

7. Have the child write the word on a piece of paper, looking at the "puffed" word only as needed. Repeat this procedure until the child can say the word immediately.

The Language-Experience Approach (LEA)

The *language-experience approach (LEA)* that was described in Chapter Two is effective in helping all young children, including those with special needs, learn to identify difficult sight words. The child's *word bank* (see page 24) should be stressed when *sight-word identification* is emphasized in LEA. A child's word bank also can be an easy-to-find source for the spelling of some commonly used and meaningful sight words.

Screen Board

A *screen board* is a tracing device that helps children learn difficult sight words. Construct a screen board by attaching wire screening to a frame made out of four boards and fastening the screen with masking tape to cover the rough edges. Have the child put lightweight blank paper on top of the screen board. Have the child write the target sight word on the paper with a dark crayon. Writing with crayon on top of the screen provides a raised texture that a child can trace with his or her index finger while saying the sight word. Here is an illustration of a screen board.

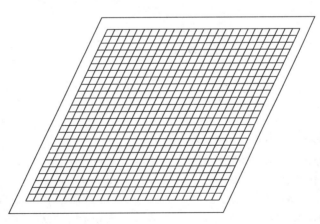

Breaking and Making Sight Words

Write five sample cards of each target sight word on 3-inch × 5-inch index cards. Use large letters and add cutting lines on each card. Make one model card for each word card. Place each set of cards in a large brown envelope. Have the pupils cut the word cards on each cutting line and then rebuild the words below the model cards. Have children continue practicing each sight word until it is learned. Here is an illustration of this activity.

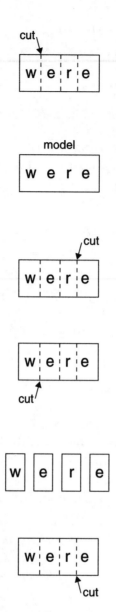

Recognizing Function (Structure) Words

In the humorous trade book *Who Sank the Boat?* (Allen, 1982), the opening sentence contains a total of twenty-two words, ten (or 45 percent) of which are function words. Here is the opening sentence: *"Beside the sea on Mr. Peffer's place, there lived a cow, a donkey, a sheep, a pig, and a tiny little mouse."* The pupil who can immediately recognize function words is well on the way to becoming a fluent, effective reader.

Macaroni Sight Words

With a marking pen, write the alphabet letters on dried macaroni. Make ten of each letter. Write the target sight words on word cards about 3 by 5 inches. Then give each child some heavy, stiff twine to string the letters in the proper order to spell the words on the cards. Here is an illustration of this activity.

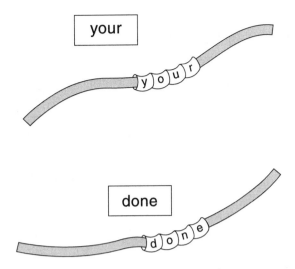

Word Masking

Have children follow along as a big book is being read aloud. During the second reading of the big book, cover some words with masking tape or sticky notes. When the teacher or tutor reaches one of them, he or she pauses, and the children try to predict what the word might be. After they answer, uncover the word and ask the children if they were correct or not. In the word-masking procedure, sight-word identification, context clues, and comprehension are stressed.

Key Vocabulary

Silvia Ashton-Warner (1963) described *key vocabulary words* as *"organic"* or words that come from within the child and his or her own experiences. Ashton-Warner wrote that key vocabulary words act as captions for important life events that a child has experienced. Have the child meet with the teacher or tutor so the teacher or tutor may ask, *"What words would you like to learn today?"* The child answers with a word such as *pizza, bicycle,* or *computer.*

Ashton-Warner found that the most common categories of key vocabulary words for children were *fear words (murder, storm, fire, die), affection words (love, kiss, darling, hug), locomotion words (car, bus, jet, truck),* and a *miscellaneous category* that reflected cultural and other considerations (*Disneyland, football, holiday, piñata, soccer*).

Ashton-Warner called key vocabulary *"one-look words"* because one look was often all a child needed to learn the word permanently. The main reason that key vocabulary words seemed so easy for children to learn is that they usually carried a strong emotional significance for the children. Once the child has told the teacher or tutor a word he or she would like to learn, the teacher or tutor writes the word on an index card or a small piece of tag board using a dark marker. Have the child share the word with as many people as possible during the day. After the child has done so, the child can add the word to his or her word bank.

Word Window

Cut a window either in a 3-inch × 5-inch index card or a small piece of poster board so that the child can hold it directly over words in dictated or written language-experience charts to frame or isolate a target sight word. A similar window also can be made to frame target sight words in children's trade books if you wish, although a word window in a book may not be as effective unless the print is quite large. Here is an illustration of a word window:

another

Word Wheels

Construct a word wheel to provide practice in learning difficult sight words. Cut one circular disk about 6 inches by 8 inches in diameter and a somewhat larger disk. Print target sight words with a marker on the larger of the two disks. Cut a sight-word window on the smaller disk so that each sight word on the larger disk is visible as the smaller disk is turned. Fasten the two disks with a brad so that the smaller disk can be turned easily, exposing each of the sight words. The child is to immediately say each sight word as it appears in the window.

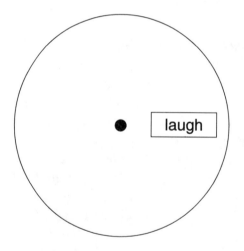

Learning Function (Structure) Words

Function (structure) words are very difficult for some children to learn because they have no referent. Examples of function words are *were, been, with, what, that,* and *who.* They also can be called *glue words.* They are difficult to teach because they cannot be made concrete for children.

Here is one strategy for teaching the most difficult function (structure) words (Cunningham, 1980).

Step One: Choose a function word and write it on a vocabulary card for each child. Locate or create a story in which you use the word many times. Before beginning the story, tell the children to hold up the card they have every time they hear the word that is printed on the card. As you tell the story, briefly pause each time you come to the target function word.

Step Two: Ask children to volunteer to make up a story using the target function word. Children should hold up their cards each time they hear a classmate use the function word.

Step Three: Ask the children to study the words on their cards. Then go to each child and cut the word into letters (or have the children do it themselves). Have the children try to arrange the letters to make the word. Check each child's attempt for accuracy. Then have them mix up the letters and attempt to make the word again several times. Each child should be able to do this before going to the next step. Encourage children to practice making the word during their free time.

Step Four: Write the word on the chalkboard and ask children to pretend their eyes are like a camera and to take a picture of the word and put it into their minds. Have them close their eyes and visualize the word in their minds. Then they should open their eyes and check the chalkboard to see if they have correctly visualized the word. Have them do this three times. Finally, have the children write the word from memory after the chalkboard has been erased, and then check their spelling when it is rewritten on the chalkboard. They should do this three times.

Step Five: Write several sentences on the chalkboard, each containing a blank in place of the word that is being studied. As you come to the missing word in the sentences, have a child come to the chalkboard and write the correct word in the blank space.

Step Six: Provide the children with actual books or print material in which the target function word appears. Ask them to read through the story and whenever they find the word to underline it lightly with pencil. When they have done this, read the material to them one more time, pausing each time you come to the word so the children can read it together.

Animal Tachistoscope

Using a *hand tachistoscope* is a motivating way for children to practice important sight words. Although a tachistoscope can be constructed without using an animal theme, many young children find it more motivating if it is made in the shape of an animal. However, it also can be made to reflect a holiday theme.

Constructing a Tachistoscope in the Shape of a Bear

Trace a bear pattern, such as the one on the next page, on a sheet of tracing paper. Place the tracing paper on top of a sheet of carbon paper. Place these on top of a piece of white poster board. Trace over the tracing to transfer the pattern onto the poster board. Remove the tracing paper and carbon paper. Color the bear with marking pens and then cut out the bear and laminate it. Trim the laminating film from the cut-out bear. Using an art knife, cut two horizontal slots about 2 inches long and 1 inch apart on the bear's body. Cut a piece of white poster board into strips about 2 inches by 12 inches and laminate them.

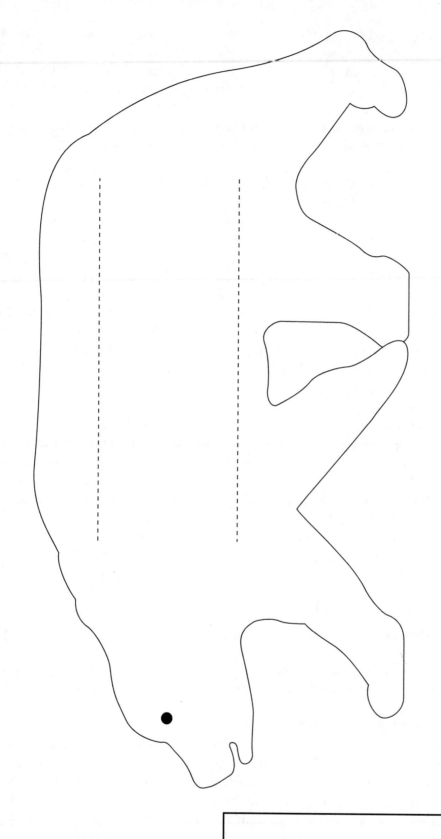

do
some
they
her
you
said
was
as
down
were

How to Use the Tachistoscope

Select target sight words with which the child needs practice. Using a marking pen, print the sight words on the laminated paper strips, one under the other and about 1 inch apart. Place the word strip behind the tachistoscope and thread it through the bottom slot and then back through the top slot. To use it, slide the word strip up to expose a word. Have the child identify the word. Then pull the word strip up to expose the next word and ask another child to identify that word. Continue in this way. When you are finished with the sight-word practice, remove the word strip and wipe off the words with a damp paper towel. New words then can be printed on the word strip. After a little practice, a child can use the tachistoscope for independent practice or for practice with a reading buddy.

Three-Step Strategy for Teaching Difficult Sight Words

Here is a useful strategy for teaching difficult sight words to young children.

1. *Seeing*—Write the target sight word on the chalkboard and pronounce it. Call attention to features of the word, such as the initial consonant and word endings, that might be similar to words that were presented earlier. Use each word in a sentence so its meaning can be deduced. (When children are better readers, they will not need such detailed introduction to new words.)

2. *Discussing and defining*—When the children don't know the meaning of the new word, discuss the word in detail. Children need to use their prior knowledge to determine the meaning of the word, and they should consult a simplified dictionary or a classmate if they are not certain of its meaning.

3. *Using and writing*—Encourage the children to use the new word in their speaking and writing. Have one or more children make up a sentence containing the word. Write each of the sentences on the chalkboard, chart paper, or an overhead transparency. Beginning readers can place the words in their word banks. New words become completely known in two ways: (1) through repeated exposure when they occur often in material that the children read and (2) when they are often used in children's writing.

Games for Improving Sight-Word Knowledge

Here are several games that reading teachers and tutors can use to improve sight-word knowledge. As stated earlier, research has found that children make excellent gains in reading skills, including sight-word knowledge, when they are playing active games in comparison with practice using activity sheets (Dickerson, 1983). However, all such games should emphasize the target reading skill, not just playing the game.

Memory (Concentration)

To Construct the Game

Print target sight words on pieces of white poster board 1 inch by 3 inches. Make two sets of identical word cards that children cannot see through.

To Play the Game

Shuffle the two sets of cards and place them separately on a table or desk. Have a child turn up a card in one set and try to find the card that matches in the other set. When he or she has made a match, have the child pronounce the word. If the word is pronounced correctly, the child keeps the card. Then another player has a turn. The winner is the player who has made the most matches and pronounced the words correctly. If you wish, have the children use each matched word in a sentence.

Match the Picture to Its Name

To Construct the Game

Gather large brown envelopes, construction paper, marking pens, and scissors. Cut 3-inch × 3-inch cards from construction paper. Draw a picture on each card and write the picture name on the back. Square off the envelope and print a picture word in each square. Store loose picture cards in the envelope. Here is an illustration.

front of card

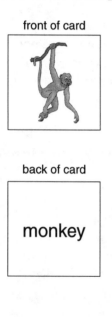

back of card

monkey

doll	girl	horse	monkey
duck	ball	man	chicken
apple	cow	dog	banana
school	cat	pig	desk

To Play the Game

Have the child match each picture card to the square containing the same word. The back of each picture may be used for self-checking.

Throwing a Die for Words

To Construct the Game

Three colors of construction paper, a die, and three small boxes are needed for this game. Cut the colored construction paper into 1-inch squares. Print a target sight word on each square. Put the squares into separate boxes according to the color of the paper.

To Play the Game

The players throw the die to see who begins the game. The child with the highest number starts by choosing the number of words on the die from any one box. In other words, if the die roll was a 4, the child chooses four words. If a child cannot pronounce any one of the words, he or she loses all the words from that turn. After being reminded about the missed word by the adult, the child returns the words to the appropriate box. Play continues to the first player's left. The winner is the child with the most words when all three boxes are empty.

Matching Words

To Construct the Game

Construct two sets of identical word cards about 1 inch by 2 inches. The number of cards will depend on the number of players involved.

To Play the Game

Four cards are placed face up in front of each player. Five cards then are placed face up in the middle of the table. The rest of the pack is placed face down in the middle of the table. If the first player has a card that matches any of the five face-up cards in the middle of the table, he or she picks it up, pronounces the word, uses it in a sentence, and keeps the pair, placing them face down in front of himself or herself, and continues playing until he or she can make no more pairs. The child then draws to fill his or her hand to four cards and replaces any missing face-up cards to leave five on the table. If, during this process, cards that match are drawn and placed on the table, they are left for the individual who has the next turn. Play continues to the first player on the left. If a player can match a card in the middle of the table but cannot pronounce the word and use it in a sentence, he or she must place the card in the middle and leave it. If the following player can pronounce the word and use it in a sentence, he or she receives the pair. The winner is the child with the most pairs when all of the cards have been played.

Sight Word Tic-Tac-Toe

To Prepare the Game

Arrange nine chairs in the middle of the classroom in a tic-tac-toe formation. Then divide the children in a group or the class into two teams—the X's and the O's. Write target sight words on word cards that are large enough for all the children to see easily.

To Play the Game

Flash a target sight word. The child whose turn it is must pronounce the word correctly and use it in a sentence. If the sight word is pronounced and used in a sentence correctly, the child takes the card with an X or O, depending on his or her team, and selects a chair to sit in. The first team to have three X's or O's in a row is the winner.

What Is the Word?

To Prepare the Game

Print easily confused and difficult basic sight words on an overhead transparency, large flashcards, or sentence strips or place them in a pocket chart as shown in the illustration.

jump	sit	two	two
one	who	like	who
ran	dog	bet	dog
time	once	laugh	once
put	not	three	put
friend	why	came	friend

To Play the Game

Have four sight-word cards in a row. The three on the left should be different from one another and the fourth should match one of the three. Show only the three different words to the children. Have children pronounce each exposed word while you point to it, one at a time. Then give the children a minute to guess which one of the three words will appear when you reveal the word on the right. Then uncover the "mystery word" so that the children can see whether they guessed it correctly. Before going on to the next set of words, have the children again pronounce all four words while you point to them in varying orders.

What Word Goes in the Box?

To Prepare the Game

For this game you need a large box and word cards about 1 inches by 2 inches with target sight words printed on them.

To Play the Game

Have children sit in a circle around the large box. Give each child a card with a difficult sight word from a story or trade book. Either read or play a tape recording of that story or book. When the child's word is read in the story, the child says. "*. . . goes in the box*" and throws the card into the box. The child then is given another word card from the book or story.

The Sight-Word Ladder

To Construct the Game

Construct a number of card packs of ten words each out of 1-inch × 2-inch white poster board. Print target sight words or sight-word phrases on each of the cards. Construct a small ladder that will hold ten cards. The rungs of the ladder can be made from wooden dowels 3/4 inch around and three vertical poles can be made from wood 1 inch by 2 inches wide. This illustration may clarify the sight-word ladder.

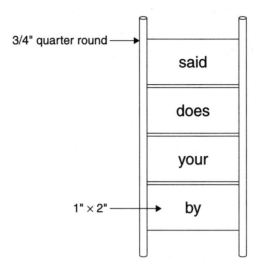

To Play the Game

Each child is given a pack of cards and tries to use them to "climb" the ladder. Cards are laid on each rung of the ladder. The child then tries to climb it by pronouncing the sight words or sight-word phrases. After the child has mastered the first ten words, he or she exchanges packs and begins again with new words and phrases.

Reproducibles for Improving Sight-Word Knowledge

Here are four reproducible activity sheets for improving sight-word knowledge. They can be duplicated and used in their present form or modified as appropriate for particular children. The activity sheets that follow are

Can You Find the Lost Animals?
Winter Fun
Find and Write These Sight Words
Locate the Target Sight Word As Quickly As You Can

CAN YOU FIND THE LOST ANIMALS?

Circle all the animal names that you can find. They might go across, backward, or up and down. If you can find all of the lost animals, they will all be able to get home. When you're done, check the bottom of this sheet to see if you missed any.

```
r t a n t e l o p e x y w t m n o d o g g h i n i o l
y s r a e b c j f r y b d a b c x z o p y s t m o r r
w x o f e g c r t m n y u g h t t u v x y z z o e r e
o s s h o r s e j j a b b x c d e e e e r o o y y v
l r e h s i f c o w r a c c x y o u u a b c f g g h o
f d r g g p i g o t u x r o j l k k m n o p q q q r r
l o p g u s k u n k m o n y p q r s s t o r e e d o
g g t i g e r s u r r p q z e o a a r r s s e e o f x
t n a h p e l e o x r f e r r e t t u a s e i m o y o
```

fox ferret fisher cow pig wolf skunk antelope horse lion tiger elephant bear

WINTER FUN

Use the words in the box to solve this puzzle about *winter fun.*

HOCKEY	**SKIING**
SNOWMAN	**SKATING**
TOBOGGANNING	**WALKING**
VISITING	**SLEDDING**

V _ _ _ _ _ _ _

_ _ A _ _ _ _

_ _ C _ _ _

_ A _ _ _ _ _

T _ _ _ _ _ _ _ _ _ _

_ _ _ I _ _

_ _ O _ _ _ _

_ _ _ _ _ _ N _

FIND AND WRITE THESE SIGHT WORDS

Look at the word on each line. Then put a *circle* around each letter you need to make the word. *Then write the word on the line.* The first one is done for you.

1. there   f t o p h e y r x e p r   _____*there*_____

2. down   d r b d o u w v r s t n   _____

3. they   b k l t h o i x p e r s y   _____

4. said   r s o a y u i f k d r t u   _____

5. have   o c h e d a s v l k e u p   _____

6. would   w y o s z u r l d t v a a   _____

7. very   b c v o e r t m n y o p q   _____

8. one   o r u t v n x p q e s t c o   _____

9. laugh   x l r d a o m l u w g t t h   _____

10. some   t s r o m t u e l p p r b b u   _____

11. yes   d f y w q a e o s p m b n o   _____

12. over   d o b v w e p k r t y c w o   _____

13. out   l o t y e u v m b v o t x r s   _____

14. do   e r y w q d p u q p r y o s l   _____

15. for   f w y q e v n o p u c x c c r   _____

Name: _____ Grade: _____

LOCATE THE TARGET WORD AS QUICKLY AS YOU CAN

The word *which* appears *24* times on this activity sheet. Move your eyes from left to right as quickly as you can and *circle the word* "which" each time you see it.

carry which many what why sing made warm those whose

which white myself again know drink kind because wash

while which paper thought soon father below which earth

young state once which through food wish own wash which

best clean far both which wore seven once which know

which again when write wonder which ride would shoe

said wish which there cold today where every four one

much which off been went ever goes start does always two

play may which never sleep please because which wall own

done three pick hurt which pull us buy which head city

plant which might weight wonder which whale last most

young hear which being second late paper group along

while white face enough almost above chose which got

often watch which read grow show whip which maybe

just brown which again after eight around new must too

whip six myself again play way which ride will not long

5

Improving Competency in Phonics

Many family members and friends of young children apparently believe that children's reading problems are the result of the public schools not teaching phonics. Do you believe that this is true? Not only is it untrue, but North American public schools always have taught phonics to a greater or lesser degree. Many children have learned some basic phonic skills. Although a lack of competency in phonic skills certainly may contribute to a child's reading difficulties, it is only one possible cause.

This chapter is designed to help reading teachers, tutors, family members, and friends present phonic skills effectively to all children, including those with learning and reading disabilities. It opens with a pre-assessment device about the content of phonics and how to teach it. Next is a brief but comprehensive description of phonics, common phonic elements, and common phonic rules. This is followed by a number of classroom-tested strategies for improving ability in phonics, including developing phonemic awareness, cross-checking word identification strategies, and using Elkonin boxes, a word wall, word sorts, tongue twisters, Hinks Pinks. Appendix XI suggests various trade books that reinforce the various phonic elements. Finally, the chapter describes several games and provides several classroom-tested reproducibles for improving ability in phonics.

After reading this chapter, any reading teacher, tutor, family member, or friend should be well prepared to teach and reinforce phonics to all the children with whom they work, including those with special needs.

Decide whether each statement is *accurate* (true) or *not* (false). Evaluate your answers after you have read the chapter. The answers are on page 322.

_____ 1. Phonemic awareness is an important emergent reading skill in which all young children should be competent before beginning a phonic program.

_____ 2. Phonics is the study of speech sounds and their relation to decoding or "breaking the code" in reading.

_____ 3. Synthetic phonic analysis is more useful than analytic phonic analysis.

_____ 4. Analogy is a technique in which words are taught using onsets and rimes.

_____ 5. A consonant digraph consists of two or three consonant letters that appear together, each of which retains some element of its own sound while blending with that of the others.

_____ 6. A vowel digraph occurs when two adjacent vowels together have a sound that is different from the sound that either of them would record separately.

_____ 7. The schwa sound (ə) is the unstressed vowel sound in a word of more than one syllable.

_____ 8. The commonly taught phonic generalization "*When two vowels go walking, the first one does the talking*" is accurate *100 percent* of the time.

_____ 9. The phonic rule "*Words having the double e usually record the long /e/ sound*" is accurate most of the time.

_____ 10. The *VC (short vowel) pattern* is consistent most of the time.

_____ 11. Mass market trade books can be very useful in teaching or reviewing the various phonic elements in the context of actual reading.

_____ 12. All of the systematic phonic programs that are advertised in the media are helpful to children who lack phonic competency.

_____ 13. A word wall is a very useful strategy for reviewing word patterns and high-frequency words.

_____ 14. It is important for young children to cross-check word identification by using more than one cueing system.

_____ 15. Action phonics is a motivating way for children to learn consonant blends and consonant digraphs.

_____ 16. Hinks Pinks are rhyming pairs that children enjoy making up and illustrating.

_____ 17. Most children are able to read a short passage correctly even when all of the vowels are omitted.

_____ 18. Nonsense words can be used in rhyming activities.

_____ 19. Word wheels can be used to practice attaching an initial consonant, consonant blend, or consonant digraph to various rimes.

_____ 20. All computer software available is equally useful in reviewing phonic elements.

PHONEMIC AWARENESS

Phonemic awareness is an important skill in which a child must be competent before being exposed to phonics instruction. Children who lack phonemic awareness will not learn phonics successfully.

Phonemic awareness consists of the following skills:

- *Discriminating among objects*, some of which begin with the target sound and some of which do not. For example, some objects for the phoneme /b/ are as follows (the ones in italics are the correct ones): *ball, bib, bell,* doll, cake, *boat.*

- *Discriminating between pictures that represent minimal pairs of words.* Place each pair of pictures on a table or desk and ask the child to point to the picture whose name you say. As an example, for the word pairs *mouse* and *house* ask the child to point to the picture of the *mouse.*

- *Being able to rhyme words.* The child must understand the concept of rhyming words and be able to provide several rhyming words for the target words. Some of these can be nonsense words. Here are some rhyming words for the target word bat: *cat, dat, fat, hat, lat, mat, nat, pat, rat, sat, tat, vat, wat,* and *zat.*

- *Listening to predictable books and then "reading"* them along with the teacher, tutor, family member, or friend.

- *Being able to discriminate between pairs of words* that are pronounced orally, on cassette tape, or on a computer. Some word pairs should be alike, while others should be different. The child should state whether the pairs are alike or different. Here are several word pairs that can be used for this purpose: *hill—hall, can—come, pan—pin, bit—bit, men—men, cub—cube, boy—toy, last—last, wish—wash, head—head.*

PHONICS

Phonics (also known as *graphophonics* or *graphonics*) is the study of speech sounds and their relation to decoding or "breaking the code" in reading. I agree with many reading specialists that competency in phonics is very important in ensuring a child's success in reading. However, a few children with limited phonic knowledge can learn to read at least to an extent. *However, all children who are able should at least learn the most basic phonic elements of consonant sounds, consonant blends, and short and long vowel sounds.*

Stahl, Osborne, and Lehr (1990) have written the following about phonics:

> *Insufficient familiarity with the spellings and spelling-to-sound correspondence of frequent words and syllables may be the single most common source of reading difficulties. (p. 115)*

However, reading teachers, tutors, and family members should understand that *phonics is only a means to effective reading and not an end in itself.*

Phonic analysis is only one technique that children should use in identifying words. Indeed it is most effective when combined with another word identification technique such as use of context. This is illustrated by the following example:

Sadie would like a _____ for her birthday on March 8.
Sadie would like a p_____ for her birthday on March 8.

The addition of the consonant *p* helps the reader determine that *puppy* is one likely answer.

There is no value in having a child know that the /*i*/ in *bib* is short unless the child can decode the word successfully and has it in his or her meaning vocabulary.

Any student reading on the fourth-grade level or above probably has all of the phonic skills that he or she ever will need and does not need phonics practice. In addition, children always should be given opportunities to *use* the phonic skills that they learn. Research has found that children do not use phonic information unless the skills that have been taught are applicable to their current reading instruction (Adams, 1990).

Phonics instruction always should be *systematic*, but *meaningful*, *functional*, and *contextual*. Phonics instruction should be especially systematic with much meaningful practice for many children with special needs.

The two main approaches to teaching phonics are *analytic* and *synthetic*. In analytic phonic analysis (implicit phonics), consonants are not taught in isolation because the consonant sounds are distorted in isolation. The sound /*d*/ is not pronounced in isolation as "*duh.*" Instead, consonants are taught within the context of an *entire word*. As an example, the sound /*d*/ is referred to as the sound that is heard at the beginning of the words *dog*, *dad*, *duck*, *doll*, *dig*, *dish*. The reader begins with an entire word and then decodes it using word structure and phonics.

On the other hand, in *synthetic phonic analysis* (explicit phonics) each word is decoded sound by sound, and the word is "put together" using individual sounds. Both the consonant and vowel sounds are pronounced in isolation. For example, in saying the word *bat*, the child would say "*buh-a-tuh.*" Many children have difficulty determining how a word is pronounced using synthetic phonic analysis since they are not proficient in *auditory blending*. Since the consonant sounds are distorted, these children cannot determine what the word is supposed to be after they have blended it sound by sound.

I recommend using a combination of analytic and synthetic phonics. Some children, especially those with special needs, cannot discriminate between the individual sounds unless they are presented and practiced in isolation. This is especially true of short vowel sounds, and may also be the case to some extent with consonant sounds. I believe that *the single most effective way of teaching young children to decode words is by using analogy* (word families). *Analogy* involves using *onsets* (beginning consonants, consonant blends, or consonant digraphs) and *rimes* (word families). These terms are explained later in this chapter.

Analogy is a technique in which words are taught in rimes, such as the following:

b-at, c-at, f-at, h-at, m-at, p-at, s-at, v-at

Usually the first word in the group is called the *header.* Often first an onset composed of an initial consonant is attached to the rest of the word (the rime). Consonant blends or consonant digraphs usually are added later. Here are the most common rimes to which initial consonants, consonant blends, or consonant digraphs can be added:

-ay, -ill, -ip, -at, -am, -ag, -ack, -ank, -ick, -ell, -ot, -ing, -ap, -unk, -ail, -ain, -eed, -y, -out, -ug, -op, -in, -an, -est, -ink, -ow, -ew, -ore, -ed, -ab, -ob, -ock, -ake, -ine, -ight, -im, -uck, -um

THE MOST COMMON PHONIC ELEMENTS

Phonics is a very complex topic, and this book provides only a very brief introduction. For more information, refer to one or more of the resource books on this topic that are listed in Appendix XI.

Phonemes are the sounds that occur in a language. There are *forty-four or forty-five phonemes* in English, depending on what source is used. A phoneme is usually written as a phonetic symbol between two forward slash marks */f/*. A *grapheme* is the written symbol for a phoneme or word. A grapheme is composed of one or more letters. As an example, it takes the two letters *c* and *h* to represent the single phoneme */ch/*. There are about 251 graphemes in written English. English does not have a completely regular phoneme-grapheme relationship as do some other languages such as Finnish and Spanish.

Consonants

A *consonant* is created when the outgoing breath stream is blocked by an organ of speech. The organs of speech are the *hard palate*, the *soft palate*, the *larynx*, the *tongue*, the *teeth*, the *lips*, and the *vocal chords*. When the blockage is complete, the resulting sounds are known as *plosives* or *stops*. When the blockage is only partial, the resulting sounds are called *continuants*. Continuants are also classified as *voiced* or *voiceless* depending on whether or not the vocal chords vibrate while producing the sound.

Here are some examples of *plosives:*

/g/	gate	/k/	kitten
/b/	bit	/p/	pig
/d/	dish	/t/	top

The following nasal sounds are one type of *continuants:*

/m/	mouse	/n/	night

Fricatives are continuants that are made when the outgoing breath escapes with audible friction.

/v/	vase	/f/	fan
/z/	zoo	/s/	see
/h/	hand		
/th/	those (voiced)	/th/	thank (voiceless)
/j/	jump	/ch/	choose
/sh/	ship		

The *liquid sounds* are the following:

/l/	lamp		/r/	run

The *glide sounds* are the following:

/w/	water		/y/	yes

Consonant Blends

A *consonant blend* consists of two or three consonants that are adjacent to each other. Each consonant retains some element of its own sound while blending with that of the others. Although most consonant blends occur at the beginning of words, they also can be found at the end.

Here are examples of consonant blends:

/bl/	bloom	/br/	brush	/cl/	climb
/cr/	crack	/dr/	drink	/fl/	flower
/fr/	frog	/gl/	glide	/gr/	grass
/pl/	plant	/pr/	press	/sc/	score
/sk/	sky	/sm/	smell	/sn/	sneak
/sp/	spill	/spl/	splash	/spr/	spread
/st/	still	/str/	strap	/sw/	swim
/tr/	trip	/tw/	twist		

Consonant Digraphs

A *consonant digraph* is composed of two consonants that record a single sound that is different from the sound that either one would record separately. Here are examples of consonant digraphs:

/ch/	chip	/gh/	rough	/ng/	sing
/ph/	phase	/sh/	shoe	/th/	thick (voiceless)
/th/	that (voiced)	/wh/	when		

Vowels

A *vowel* results when the organs of speech modify the resonance chamber without stopping the flow of the outgoing breath. All vowels are voiced; there are no nasal vowels in English. One vowel is distinguished from another by the quality of its sound. Here are examples of the vowels:

/a/	ate	/a/	and	/a/	air
/a/	talk	/a/	car		
/e/	he	/e/	end	/e/	learn
/e/	her	/e/	pear	/e/	sergeant
/i/	ice	/i/	igloo	/i/	shirt
/o/	hope	/o/	ostrich	/o/	often
/o/	for	/o/	worth		
/u/	use	/u/	tube	/u/	umbrella
/u/	turn				

/y/	fly	/y/	lady	/y/	hymn
/w/	how (diphthong)				
/y/	boy (diphthong)				

Diphthongs

A *diphthong* is composed of two vowel sounds that together record one sound that is different from the sound that either of them would have recorded separately. Here are several examples of words that contain a diphthong:

/ow/	how	/ou/	out	/oi/	soil
/oy/	boy	/ew/	few		

The Schwa Sound

The *schwa sound* (ə) is the unstressed vowel sound in a word of more than one syllable. Any one of the five vowel letters can be the schwa sound when it is found in an unaccented syllable. The schwa sound has a sound that is similar to that of the short /u/. Here are several words that contain the schwa sound:

/a/	comma	/e/	elephant	/i/	pencil
/o/	lion	/u/	minus		

Vowel Digraphs

A *vowel digraph* occurs when two adjacent vowels record one sound. Here are some words that contain a vowel digraph:

/ai/	brain	/ay/	day		
/ee/	meet	/ea/	seat, bread, great		
/ie/	tie				
/oa/	goat	/oe/	toe	/ow/	blow
/oo/	book	/oo/	moose	/oo/	flood
/ui/	suit				

Rimes

A *rime (word family, phonogram,* or *graphemic base)* is a group of vowels and consonants that are pronounced and learned as a unit. (See examples on page 169.) These are used in teaching phonics with the use of analogies. A comprehensive listing of rimes can be found in Fry, Kress, & Fountoukidis (2000).

Some Common Phonic Rules

There are a myriad of phonic rules that sometimes are taught to young children. Although some of them are consistent enough to be useful, others are not. Clymer's forty-two-year-old research into the usefulness and consistency of phonics rules remains very useful and valid. Clymer (1963) conducted a classic research study in which he attempted to determine the reliability or consistency of forty-five commonly presented phonic rules. His results suggested that only *eighteen* phonic rules are consistent enough to warrant teaching to primary-grade children. He used sets of basal readers to ascertain the phonic rules commonly presented in the primary grades at that time.

Clymer drew his conclusions based on the arbitrary decision that a phonic rule should be at least 75 percent consistent to be presented to young children. Some more common rules such as *"When two vowels go walking, the first one does the talking"* (when two vowels are found next to each other, the first one is usually long and the second is usually silent) were not found to be consistent. However, it may be useful to teach a few of these anyway, since they are commonly contained in the materials that young children are reading.

The rules that Clymer found to be consistent enough to be presented to young children are the following:

- The *r* gives the preceding vowel a sound that is neither long nor short. (*car, her, skirt, care, pear, Myrtle*)

- Words having a double /*e*/ usually have the long /*e*/ sound. (*beet*)

- In /*ay*/ the /*y*/ is silent and gives /*a*/ its long sound. (*play*)

- When *y* is the final letter in a word, it usually has a vowel sound. (*fly, baby*)

- When *c* and *h* are next to each other, they make only one sound. (*church*)

- /*Ch*/ is usually pronounced as it is in *check, match,* and *kitchen,* not like /*sh*/.

- When *c* is followed by *e, i,* or *y,* it is likely to record the sound of /*s*/. (*cent, civil, bicycle*)

- When *c* is followed by *a, o,* or *u,* it is likely to record the sound of /*k*/. (*cake, coat, cub*)

- When *ght* is found in a word, /*gh*/ is silent. (*sight*)

- When two of the same consonants are found side by side, only one is heard. (*ladder*)

- When a word ends in /*ck*/, it has the same last sound as in *book.* (*pack*)

- In most two-syllable words, the first syllable is accented. (*paper*)

- If *a, in, be, ex,* or *de* is the first syllable in a word, it is usually unaccented. (*about, inside, belong, export, decide*)

- In most two-syllable words that end in a consonant followed by *y,* the first syllable is accented and the last is unaccented. (*´turkey*)

- If the last syllable of a word ends in *le,* the consonant preceding the *le* usually begins the last syllable. (*tur/tle*)

- When the first vowel element in a word is followed by *th, ch,* or *sh,* these symbols are not broken when the word is divided into syllables and may go with either the first or second syllable. (*bachelor, witchcraft, synthetic, fashion*)

- When there is one *e* in a word that ends with a consonant, the *e* usually has the short sound. (*bed*)

- When the last syllable is the sound *r,* it is unaccented. (*farmer*)

Resources for additional information about phonics can be found in Appendix XI. In addition, a list of trade books that are useful to practice phonics in context with children can be found in Appendix XII.

Strategies and Materials for Improving Ability in Phonics

Here are a number of classroom-tested strategies and materials for teaching and/or reviewing phonics. All of these suggestions can be adapted in light of the needs, abilities, and interests of particular pupils.

Presenting the Vowel Patterns

Vowels are difficult to decode because vowel sounds can be spelled in many different ways. The long /e/ sound can be spelled in *seventeen* different ways. Most children who are taught to recognize *vowel patterns* do better in identifying words than those who do not know how.

Here are the main *vowel patterns* and their prediction success (May, 1998):

- VC (short vowel) pattern (*hat*); 86 percent regular
- VCC (short vowel) pattern (*back*); 89 percent regular
- VCE (long vowel—silent /e/) pattern (*bake*); 81 percent regular
- VVC (long vowel) pattern (only /ai/, /ea/, /ee/, /oa/); 77 percent regular
- CV (long vowel) pattern (*go, be, cry*); 77 percent regular

According to May, teaching these patterns to children can make a significant difference in their reading fluency and comprehension.

Here is a brief list with examples of each pattern. Many more can be added to each list.

Short VC	Short VCC	Long VCE	Long VVC	Long CV
hat	band	take	sail	he
bet	best	same	heat	hi
sit	lick	mine	pail	by
mop	block	rope	boat	so
hut	jump	tube	seen	be
cap	sang	rake	brain	go
get	sand	bite	road	we
top	well	cone	meet	cry
run	hill	take	toad	me

Use these steps to teach these vowel patterns:

1. Use the term *CV pattern*, for example, instead of the term *Consonant Vowel Pattern*, which is harder for children to say and remember.

2. Print words from each of the five vowel pattern groups on separate cards so that children can use them to practice.

3. Choose eight *VC* words and read them aloud, pointing out that each word ends with a vowel followed by a consonant. Tell them that these are all *VC* words.

4. Hand each of the children five cards, so they have a word from each of the five vowel pattern groups. As an example, Maria might have *get, land, rake, hail,* and

go. Ask the children to hold up the word card that illustrates the vowel pattern that you put on the chalkboard. Help the children who have held up the wrong card to find the right one.

5. When all the children are holding up the correct pattern, have each of them read his or her word (with your help if required) and put it on the chalkboard railing. As each child comes to the chalkboard, ask him or her what kind of word he or she has (such as the *VC pattern*) and have the child point to the vowel letter and the consonant letter.

6. If desired, divide the class into pairs to play a game of *Concentration.* Have the partners make two cards for each of the ten words in the *VC column.* Use more of the words for a more difficult game.

Variability Strategy

Children should learn to be very *flexible* in their approach to decoding unknown words. They can be taught the *variability strategy* as part of this approach.

1. First try the most common pronunciation of the letter—the one that the letter typically has.

2. If the common pronunciation gives a word that is not an actual word or a word that does not make sense in the sentence, try another pronunciation.

3. If you still decode a word that is not a real word or does not seem to make sense in the sentence, ask for help from the teacher, tutor, or classmates.

Cross-Checking Word Identification Strategies

Young children must learn to *cross-check* word identification by using more than one cueing system. Children can identify many words by thinking about what word would make sense in that sentence and noticing whether the initial consonant, consonant blend, or consonant digraph in that word matches what they are thinking of. The ability to use *initial letters* in a word along with the *context* is the most important decoding strategy.

The child should learn to do two things together—think about what word would make sense in sentence context and think about the letters and sounds. Many children like to use one or the other but not both. Therefore, some children may guess an unknown word by supplying a word that makes sense in context, while others predict with a word that begins with the correct consonant but makes no sense in the sentence. In order to help children cross-check meaning with sound, first have them guess the word revealing no letters. Then show some of the letters and finally show the entire word. Help them confirm which guess makes sense and contains the correct letters.

To teach cross-checking different cueing systems, write the sentences here on the chalkboard or a transparency. Then cover the word to be guessed with two pieces of paper, one of which only covers the first letter. Use magnets to hold the pieces of paper on the board. Use the children's own names to make this activity more interesting for them.

Rylee likes to visit the *zoo*.
Muhammad likes to see the *monkeys* play.
Eve likes to watch the *tigers*.
Ross likes to look at the *lions*.
Luisa likes to watch the *seals* swim.

Ask the children to read each sentence and try to predict what word is covered up. In the first sentence, they may predict such words as *park*, *zoo*, *museum*, *playground*, *circus*, *carnival*, or *fair*. Next to each sentence write each guess that makes sense. When they have made several guesses, uncover the letter *z*. Erase any guesses that do not begin with this letter and still make sense. If there are any new guesses that begin with *z* and make sense, write them down. If a child begins guessing anything that begins with a *z*, say "*Zebra does begin with a z, but I can't write down that word because people don't go to the 'zebra.'*"

When you have written down all the appropriate guesses, uncover the word. If the word that you have uncovered is one that the children guessed, praise them; if it is not, tell them that this was hard and you are sure that they will be able to do it the next time. Continue with each sentence by going through these same steps:

1. Read each sentence and write down any guesses that make sense.

2. Uncover the first letter and erase any guesses that do not begin with that letter.

3. Have the children make more guesses; write down only those that make sense and begin with the correct letter.

4. Uncover the entire word and determine whether any of the guesses were correct.

Changing a Pig to a Bug

In this activity, children change one animal, a *pig*, into a *bug* (adapted from Cunningham, 1999) by changing one letter at a time. As they change that letter, they listen for where they hear the change and review the consonants and vowels. To begin the activity, write the names of these five living creatures on the chalkboard—each of which has a short vowel sound:

pig   cat   bug   bat   fox

Then say the words together with the children, stretching out each word and talking about the beginning, middle, and ending sounds. Pay particular attention to the middle sound, that is, the short vowel sound in each of these words. Next ask the children: "*Can you change a pig into a bug?*"

Tell the children that if they follow the directions and think about letters and sounds, they will be able to do this. Give them sheets of paper and then give these directions:

1. Write "*pig*." (Point to the word *pig* on the chalkboard. Everyone copies it onto their papers.)

2. Now change the *pig* into *pit*. (The children decide they have to change just the last letter from a *g* to a *t* and write *pit* under *pig*.)

3. Now change the *pit* into *fit.* (The children decide they have to change just the first letter from a *p* to an *f.*)

4. Now change the *fit* to *fat.*

5. Then change the *fat* to *sat.*

6. Next change the *sat* to *sag.*

7. Then change the *sag* to *rag.*

8. Next change the *rag* to *rug.*

9. Finally change the *rug* to *bug.*

Say: *"Now you have finally changed the pig into a bug. Wasn't that a lot of fun?"*

Action Phonics

An interesting approach to beginning letter-sound phonics, called *action phonics*, teaches the beginning letter- and letter-combination-sound associations through physical actions or movements that begin with the targeted sound (Cunningham, 1987). The actions are found below.

Teaching beginning letter-sound relationships using action phonics requires children to move their bodies, which tends to reinforce their memories of the letters and sounds. Children connect the graphic letter with the physical action and subsequently with the associated sound. The physical movement acts like a *"conceptual glue"* that holds the sound and the symbol together.

One or two initial consonants and their sounds can be taught each week. Begin by reviewing all of the previously learned consonants, actions, and sounds, and then present the new initial consonant with its accompanying movement and sound. Review initial consonants by assigning one to each child. As a student comes forward and demonstrates the movement associated with his or her consonant, children should guess the letter and sound. In another variation, children form a circle, with one child or the teacher acting as a leader. The leader has all the letters printed on individual cards. The leader picks one letter, shows it to the group, and the entire group demonstrates the accompanying action. The activity progresses from one action to another as the leader moves from one letter card to another. This activity can also be used by a physical education teacher to review children's phonic learning.

Teachers and tutors who teach beginning letter-sound relationships often find children making the action at their seats when they try to read or spell words on their own. Action phonics is a motivating way to teach phonics even at those times when children want to get out of their seats and move around the classroom.

b	bounce	t	talk	fl	fly
c	catch	v	vacuum	fr	frown
d	dance	w	walk, wiggle	gl	glare, glue
f	fall	y	yawn, yell	gr	grab
g	gallop	z	zip	pl	plant
h	hop, hum	ch	cheer	pr	pray

j	jump	sh	shiver, shout	sw	swallow
k	kick	th	think	sk	skate, skip
l	lick	wh	whistle	sl	sleep, slide
m	march	br	breathe	sm	smile
n	nod	bl	blow, blink	sp	spin
p	paint, pat	cr	crawl, cry	st	stand still, stop
q	quiet	cl	climb	tr	track, trip
r	run, rip	dr	drive	tw	twist
s	sit, sip				

Rhyming Activities

The following activities provide practice in working with *rhyming elements*. In addition, these activities focus on listening, following directions, and noticing stress and intonation patterns.

Number Rhymes

Pronounce and emphasize two words that rhyme with a *number word*. Have the children supply the *rhyming number word* that finishes each sentence.

Late and *gate* rhyme with _____ (*eight*).
Fun and *sun* rhyme with _____ (*one*).
Mix and *fix* rhyme with _____ (*six*).
See and *tree* rhyme with _____ (*three*).
Heaven and *eleven* rhyme with _____ (*seven*).
Threw and *blue* rhyme with _____ (*two*).
Men and *then* rhyme with _____ (*ten*).
Pour and *sore* rhyme with _____ (*four*).
Alive and *drive* rhyme with _____ (*five*).
Line and *mine* rhyme with _____ (*nine*).

Rhyming Animal Names

Have the children name an animal that rhymes with each of the following words: *pear (bear), box (fox), weep (sheep), fig (pig), mitten (kitten), fog (dog, hog, frog), coat (goat), loose (goose, moose), house (mouse), fear (deer), trunk (skunk), cantaloupe (antelope), rake (snake), mat (cat, rat).*

Providing Rhyming Words

Read some sentences. Have children listen carefully so they can provide words that rhyme with the last word in each sentence. The last word in the sentence should be stressed. Here are some examples of this activity.

My puppy Honey has to take a *pill.* (*bill, dill, fill, gill, hill, Jill, mill, quill, till, will*)
I spend the summer at my house by Birch *Lake.* (*bake, cake, fake, Jake, make, rake, sake, wake*)
Yesterday Sammie fed his neighbor's *cat.* (*bat, fat, hat, mat, rat, sat, vat*)
In the summer Julie likes to play in the *sand.* (*band, hand, land*)
Today is a beautiful sunny *day.* (*bay, hay, jay, may, pay, say, stay, way*)

Today Tyrone found a baby bird's *nest.* (*best, chest, pest, rest, vest, west*)
Last week Ben caught a big *frog.* (*bog, dog, fog, hog, log*)
Are you able to count to *ten?* (*Ben, den, hen, men, pen, when*)
When I was in the West last summer I saw a *moose.* (*goose, noose*)
My dog has a purple *ball.* (*call, fall, hall, mall, stall, wall*)

Hinks Pinks

Hinks pinks are rhyming pairs that children enjoy making up, illustrating, and then using to solve riddles. Teachers and tutors also like them because they emphasize the spelling pattern-rhyme relationships and provide children with a real purpose for looking for and manipulating rhyming words.

Here are several illustrations of hinks pinks, followed by examples of hinks pinks that you can use in your own classroom. Children also will be eager to construct some of their own.

black tack	pale whale	mean Jean	spread bread
beast feast	red bed	weed seed	trim Jim
nice lice	big wig	rob Bob	white kite
miss kiss	plump grump	stuck buck	mouse house
bum plum	thin chin	crush brush	rule mule
plug jug	punk trunk	rose nose	goof proof
late Kate	bad Brad	grab cab	make cake
scrub tub	nurse purse	turn churn	clown crown

To use these hinks pinks in a classroom, offer them to the children as a pair of definitions. For example, *black tack* could be "dark pushpin" and *beast feast* could be "animal special dinner."

Word Walls

A *word wall* is useful for reviewing *word patterns* and *high-frequency (sight) words.* Place words on a wall in alphabetical order; add about five new words a week. A variation of a word wall can be made on large chart paper. Words can be selected from experience charts and stories, basal readers, narrative and informational trade books, and elsewhere. They should be very *functional words* that children need to use often in their reading and writing. Because these words are located on the wall, they can be used as a type of practical dictionary. As an example, a child can find out how to spell the words *talk, scream,* or *friend* by looking at the proper place on the wall. Difficult-to-remember words also can be reviewed by using the word wall regularly.

For example, after a *rime* such as *–ell* has been presented, place several *–ell* pattern words on the wall. You can place all the pattern words on the wall alphabetically by rime. For example, the *–ab* pattern should be first, followed by the *–ack* and *–ad* patterns, and so forth. The first word in each column should be the *model* (header) word, accompanied by an illustration that children can refer to if they forget how to identify the model word. When children have difficulty with a pattern word and cannot use a pronounceable word part to unlock the word's pronunciation, they can consult the word wall. Help them identify the model word and then use the analogy strategy to identify the unknown word.

Here are some strategies using a word wall.

Mind Reader

In trying to be a *"Mind Reader"* the teacher or tutor thinks of a word on the wall and then provides five clues to that word. Select a word and write it on a piece of scratch paper, but do not let the children see it. Have children number their scratch paper from 1 to 5. Tell them that they should try to figure out which of the words on the word wall is written on the scratch paper. Tell them to expect five clues. By the fifth clue everyone should be able to guess, but mind readers may guess it sooner. The first clue should always be: *"It's one of the words on the wall."*

Next to the number 1 children should write the word they think it might be. Each succeeding clue should narrow down what it can be until by the fifth clue, there is only one possible word.

Here is an example of this activity.

1. *It's one of the words on the wall.*

2. *It has six letters.*

3. *It begins with the consonant blend /str/.*

4. *It contains the vowel /ea/.*

5. *It means about the same as the word* creek. (*stream*)

Ruler Tap

In *"Ruler Tap,"* the adult pronounces a word and then taps out several letters in that word without saying those letters. When the tapping stops, ask a child to finish spelling that word out loud, using the word wall if necessary. If the child correctly finishes spelling the word, he or she gets to call out a word and tap some of the letters.

Pantomime

Pantomime an action (*jump, fish, run, throw, wash*) or use gestures to indicate an object or other item (*dog, cat, bell, lamp*) and then have the children write the appropriate rime on an *every-pupil response card* and hold it up. Have the child point to that word on the word wall and identify it. Before pantomiming the word, tell children the *model (header) word* of that rime.

Several Additional Strategies

Write a number of simple words that have been spelled phonetically. Have children pronounce each of these words by interpreting the phonetic spellings.

Make five decorated boxes and label each box with a short vowel. Have children locate pictures or objects whose names contain the short vowel sounds and place them in the appropriate boxes. Each day take out the pictures and objects and review the vowel sounds.

Use color names to complete a rhyme. Say "Name the color that rhymes with. . . ." Here are some examples:

mean and queen (*green*)	hay and say (*gray*)
threw and you (*blue*)	sack and tack (*black*)
bed and thread (*red*)	light and kite (*white*)
mink and stink (*pink*)	down and frown (*brown*)

Games for Improving Ability in Phonics

This part of the chapter contains several games that improve ability in phonics. All reading games should stress the target reading skill, not merely playing the game. The games suggested in this section should be very interesting to young children, including those with special needs.

Phonic Rummy

To Construct the Game

Make a deck of cards with the target phonic elements that you want to review. On each card write one phonic element and four words that use the target phonic element. Underline one of the four words (target phonic element). The deck may consist of 36, 40, 44, 48, or 52 cards. For each phonic element there will be *four* cards, each of which has a different word underlined. A deck of 36 cards would teach *nine* phonic elements, and 40 cards would teach *ten* phonic elements.

Here are examples of words and phonic elements for the cards:

a	**br**	**sh**
bat	bring	shoe
can	break	ship
sat	broke	shore
fan	bridge	shape

To Play the Game

The dealer shuffles the cards and then deals eight cards face down to each player. The rest of the cards are then placed face down in the middle of the table. The first player to the left of the dealer asks for a word using a certain phonic element on which he or she wants to build. For example, a child might say, "I want Erin to give me *sat* from the /a/" group, pronouncing the short /a/ sound. If Erin has that card, she gives it to the caller. The player (caller) then continues to call for certain cards from different people. If the person called on does not have the card, the caller takes a card from the center pile, and the next player to his or her left has a turn. When a player completes a "book" (that is, when he or she has all four cards from a certain phonic pattern), the player lays it down. Players only can lay down "books" when it is their turn to draw. The player who gets the most "books" before someone else empties his or her hand is the winner.

Match a Pair of Pictures

To Construct the Game

This game is an adaptation of *Concentration*. It can be played with one child or several children. Select pairs of pictures so that two picture-naming words begin with the same letter-sound: *ball—boy; cat—candle; dog—duck; fox—fan; gate—goat; horse—hand;*

kite—kitten; lion—lamp; mouse—moose; pail—pig; rake—rabbit; sun—snake; tiger—table; woman—window. Shuffle the cards and lay them face down on the table.

To Play the Game

The first player turns up two cards, trying to match a pair of initial letter-sounds. If the player is successful, he or she picks up both cards. If the child does not match initial letter-sounds, both cards are again turned face down. Other players continue taking turns. Each player tries to notice and remember the location of pictures that have been turned up but not matched. The winner is the player or team with the most pictures at the end of the game.

Go Fish

To Construct the Game

Construct a deck of word cards in which the words match in some way: rhyming words; words that begin with the same consonant, consonant blend, or consonant digraph; words that have the same short vowel sound; words that have the same long vowel sound, and so forth.

To Play the Game

This game should be played with four or five players. Deal each child five cards, and spread the rest of the cards out in the middle as the "*card pond.*" The object of the game is to find matches to the words in the child's hand. A turn begins when a player looks at his or her cards and asks a second player for a card that matches the criterion, for example, "*Do you have a word that rhymes with bat?*" If the second player has such a card, he or she gives it to the first player, who matches it and lays the card down face up. The first player then makes another request for a card. If the second player does not have the requested card, the first player must "*Go Fish.*" This means laying a card down, face up, and taking a card from the "pond." If the drawn card doesn't match the face-up card, the player keeps one, throws the other back into the pond, and the next player's turn begins. Play continues until one player matches all the cards in his or her hand.

Normally players receive one point for each card matched but must subtract a point for each card that remains in their hands at the end of a round. The game continues until a prescribed point limit is reached, usually 50 to 100 points.

Using Cups to Make Words

To Construct the Game

Obtain some large foam coffee cups. Usually a hundred can be purchased for several dollars or less. When two of these cups are stacked, their lips fit together well, and they also can be easily rotated. Print beginning consonants, consonant blends, or consonant digraphs on the lips of some cups with a black marking pen. Usually *eight* to *ten* per cup is practical. Print the target *rimes* on the lips of the other set of cups. *Two* to *four* rimes seem to be the most effective. (See the accompanying illustration.)

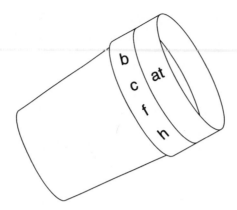

To Play the Game

Have children take one beginning consonant, consonant blend, or consonant digraph cup and one rime cup, fit them together, and rotate them so that all the combinations of consonants, consonant blends, consonant digraphs, and rimes can be formulated. If you want, have children write down all the words that can be made from the various combinations. Although this technically may not be called a "game," it is interesting practice in using rimes to decode and spell words.

Pick-Up Sticks

To Construct the Game

Obtain a set of Popsicle® sticks with words to be practiced written on one end of each stick. Each of the target words should contain a phonic element that the child needs to practice. One stick should have the word *ZAP!* written at the end. All sticks should be placed word-end down into a Pringles® can, another type of can, a cup, or some other opaque container.

To Play the Game

One child begins by pulling a stick up from the container. If the player can pronounce the word with the target phonic element, he or she keeps the stick. If he or she cannot pronounce the word quickly, it must be returned to the container. Each player pulls one stick at a time, followed by the next player. Play continues until the *ZAP!* stick is pulled. At this point, the players count the sticks that they have, and the player with the most sticks is the winner.

A variation of this game requires each player to pronounce the target word as it is pulled out. If he or she is unable to pronounce the word, the player continues to pull word sticks until one can be pronounced. The player who pulls the *ZAP!* stick is the instant loser (or winner if you want another variation). Children enjoy watching the number of sticks left in the can become smaller and smaller.

Phonic Bingo

To Construct the Game

Make cards that look like Bingo cards out of cardboard. (See the accompanying illustration.) Print initial consonants, consonant blends, and consonant digraphs on the cards in random order. Have children make tokens out of small squares of colored construction paper or have them use any other appropriate markers.

f	sh	sl	b
gr	t	s	r
ch	fl	dr	wh
scr	p	m	l
sp	v	gl	j

g	b	dr	d
pl	r	spl	tr
y	z	w	s
n	tw	sl	bl
m	str	v	fr

To Play the Game

Pronounce a word beginning with one of the consonants, consonant blends, or consonant digraphs. Tell the children to look at their cards for the letter or letter combination that represents the word's initial sound. Tell those children who have a word beginning with that letter or letter combination to cover it up with a token of some kind. Continue to pronounce words until one child has covered his or her entire card. The first child who does this is the winner, or the game may be continued until all the cards are covered.

War of the Words

To Construct the Game

This game should be played by two to four children in a group. You need to have a deck of word cards. Give each group of children a deck of 3-inch by 5-inch cards, asking them to divide them up among themselves and having them write a word on each card so that it fills a large portion of the card. New cards can be added to the deck as needed over time.

To Play the Game

Place all the word cards together, shuffle them, and distribute them to each player face down. Set an agreed-on time limit of about five to ten minutes, start the timer, and the game begins. Each player plays one card face up from his or her deck. The player must be able to pronounce the word to continue playing. Once each player presents a card and pronounces it, the player with the longest word wins the round and all the cards that were played. These words go to the bottom of the player's pile.

Then a new round is begun in the same manner. If the longest word is shared by two or more players, then a "*war*" begins. Each of the players involved in the tie plays another card face down and then one face up and pronounces it. The player with the longer of the second face-up cards wins all the cards played in that round. Another tie brings on another war with two more cards played by each tied player, one face down and one face up. Play continues in this way until the timer bell goes off. At this point players count the cards they have. The player with the largest number of cards is the winner.

Reproducibles for Improving Ability in Phonics

The following five reproducible activity sheets for improving ability in phonics can be duplicated and used in their present form or modified in any way in the light of the needs, interests, and abilities of specific pupils. The activity sheets include:

Use the Clue to Write the Correct Consonant Blend
Use the Clue to Write the Correct Consonant Digraph
Print the Correct Vowel in Each Word
A Vowel Word Puzzle
Hinks Pinks

USE THE CLUE TO WRITE THE CORRECT CONSONANT BLEND

Read the clue. Use one of the consonant blends *sn, sp, st, scr, spr,* or *str* to make a word that completes the clue. The first one has been done for you.

Clue	**Word**	
1. loud sound	**scr**	eam
2. another name for creek	_____	eam
3. a reptile	_____	ake
4. another name for twig	_____	ick
5. a season of the year	_____	ing
6. a hard metal	_____	eel
7. the opposite of go	_____	op
8. to injure one's ankle	_____	ain
9. to cut with scissors	_____	ip
10. these are worn on legs	_____	ockings
11. something a child can throw in the winter	_____	owball
12. seen in the sky at night	_____	ars
13. a child may do this when he or she has a cold	_____	eeze
14. a person eats with this	_____	oon
15. this creature moves very slowly	_____	ail
16. football is an example of this	_____	ort
17. to hit	_____	ike
18. to clean a kitchen floor	_____	ub
19. where an astronaut travels	_____	ace
20. get ready for schoolwork	_____	udy

USE THE CLUE TO WRITE THE CORRECT CONSONANT DIGRAPH

Read the clue. Use one of the consonant digraphs *ch, sh, voiceless th,* or *voiced th* to make a word that completes the clue. The first one has been done for you.

Clue	**Word**
1. boat	_____**sh**_____ ip
2. meal	lun _____
3. this is worn on a foot	_____ oe
4. worship	chur _____
5. used to sit on	_____ air
6. slim	_____ in
7. an animal	_____ eep
8. a barnyard bird	_____ icken
9. an item of clothing	_____ irt
10. opposite of tall	_____ ort
11. used to write on a blackboard	_____ alk
12. part of a person's hand	_____ umb
13. another name for boy or girl	_____ ild
14. opposite of freeze	_____ aw
15. word that often is used at the beginning of a sentence	_____ e
16. opposite of dull	_____ arp
17. part of a house	_____ imney
18. part of a person's face	_____ eek
19. opposite of here	_____ ere
20. word that comes before "fourth"	_____ ird
21. opposite of warm	_____ illy
22. something used in sewing	_____ imble
23. what people do in a mall	_____ op
24. leader of a tribe	_____ ief
25. found at the seashore	_____ ell

PRINT THE CORRECT VOWEL IN EACH WORD

Print either *a*, *o*, or *i* in each of the words in these sentences. When you are finished, reread all of the sentences to be sure that they are all correct. The first one has been done for you.

1. That m__**a**__n had to sleep on a c__**o**__t last night.

2. Is a d____g a better pet than a c____t for a child?

3. Rylee has g____t to take a n____p this afternoon.

4. That paper b____g is very b____g.

5. My m____p and p____n are in the hall closet.

6. A b____t is n____t a mean creature.

7. The water in the t____p is always very h____t.

8. I saw s____x r____ts in the old house I visited.

9. A rabbit can h____p, while a c____t can't.

10. Susie saw a b____g p____g at the farm today.

11. J____m likes to j____g every day.

12. Jake b____d on a p____g at a farm sale today.

13. Mack's house is in t____p t____p shape and should sell quickly.

14. That p____t of soup is very h____t.

15. A c____t is a kind of b____d that can be used in camping.

16. I will l____t a l____t of children come to my house.

17. My place at the lake has both a d____ck on the house and a d____ck in the lake.

18. P____t has a f____n in his bedroom.

19. D____nald wants a h____m sandwich for lunch.

20. Salli has a b____g r____d hat that she wears at the beach.

A VOWEL WORD PUZZLE

Read each clue. Write the vowel (*a, e, i, o, u*) that completes each word that fits the clue. The first one has been done for you.

Clue

1. to sleep on   b**_e_**d

   opposite of good   b**_a_**d

   to try to buy   b**_i_**d

   part of a flower   b**_u_**d

Clue

2. to stay behind   l____g

   part of the body   l____g

   part of a tree   l____g

   to carry   l____g

Clue

3. to gamble   b____t

   this word connects two parts of a sentence   b____t

   used in baseball   b____t

   used with a carpenter's drill   b____t

Clue

4. an insect   b____g

   large   b____g

   used to carry   b____g

   to ask for something   b____g

Clue

5. this is thrown   b____ll

   male cow   b____ll

   this rings   b____ll

   this asks for money   b____ll

A VOWEL WORD PUZZLE (Continued)

Clue

6. used to write with   p____n

    used in sewing   p____n

    used in cooking   p____n

    a clever saying   p____n

Clue

7. a boy's name   D____ck

    this says "quack"   d____ck

    tie a boat to this   d____ck

    part of a house   d____ck

Clue

8. a unit of measure   p____ck

    to place in a suitcase   p____ck

    used in ice hockey   p____ck

    to lift up   p____ck

Clue

9. a vehicle   tr____ck

    a railroad car travels on this   tr____ck

    play a joke on someone   tr____ck

Clue

10. an animal kept as a "friend"   p____t

    to place   p____t

    a deep hole   p____t

    to touch lightly   p____t

HINKS PINKS

A hink pink is made up of two rhyming spelling patterns that make a funny description. Read each definition and see if you can make up a hink pink for it. You can work with a buddy if you want. The first one has been done for you.

1. dark old house   _____ black shack _____

2. young lady's hair   _____

3. make-believe reptile   _____

4. courageous man's name   _____

5. early morning young deer   _____

6. slim woman's name   _____

7. marry a man's name   _____

8. unusual wild animal living in the woods   _____

9. hire a canvas dwelling   _____

10. good falsehood (lie)   _____

11. pleasant insects   _____

12. large branch   _____

13. caught deer   _____

14. embrace insect   _____

15. make butter   _____

16. attractive musical instrument   _____

17. eating utensil for meat   _____

18. burn front part of a house   _____

19. appealing monarch   _____

20. heavy rodent   _____

Improving Ability in Word Structure and Context

What do you believe is the most important technique of word identification? Although a number of lay people may believe that the answer to that question is *phonics*, the correct answer is *context*. The use of context is especially powerful when it is combined with phonics. This statement may be illustrated by the following example:

Emilio wants a ⎯⎯⎯⎯⎯ for his birthday.

Emilio wants a p⎯⎯⎯⎯⎯ for his birthday.

The addition of the consonant *p* greatly narrows the possibilities. With the addition of the letter *p* some probable answers are as follows: *puppy, parakeet, pony,* or *parrot.* Of those answers, *puppy* probably is the most likely. Context clues always should be taught using meaningful reading materials with young children.

This chapter will help reading teachers, tutors, family members, and friends present word structure skills and context effectively to all children, including those with learning and reading disabilities. The chapter opens with a pre-assessment device on the content of both word structure and context and how to effectively teach these word identification skills to young children. Then I present a brief description of word structure, including the most useful prefixes and suffixes.

Next, I present classroom-tested strategies for improving ability in word structure, followed by several motivating games and four reproducible activity sheets.

After a brief description of context clues, I suggest a number of strategies for improving ability in this important word identification technique, including wide reading of motivating materials, listening for reading miscues, the use of rebuses, simple variations of the cloze procedure, and understanding that context clues are not always effective. The chapter closes with four reproducible activity sheets for improving ability in the use of context.

Decide whether each statement is *accurate* (true) or *not* (false). Evaluate your answers after you have read the chapter. The answers are on page 325.

_____ 1. Word structure is using word parts to determine the meaning and pronunciation of unknown words.

_____ 2. A derivational suffix indicates grammatical items and plurals.

_____ 3. A morpheme is the smallest unit of meaning in a language.

_____ 4. Learning morphemes is a *constructive process* that children begin as early as the age of about four.

_____ 5. In first grade, about *50 percent* of the words students should be able to read contain more than one syllable.

_____ 6. *Un-* (meaning *not*) is one of the first prefixes that is taught young children.

_____ 7. Using the analogy strategy and rimes helps young children to effectively pronounce words of more than one syllable.

_____ 8. "Tying words together" is a useful strategy for helping young children review such compound words as *playground, cupcake, blackbird, sunset,* and *grandmother.*

_____ 9. A *magnet* can be a useful tool in teaching about the formation of compound words.

_____ 10. "*Grayhair*" is an example of an actual compound word.

_____ 11. The use of context clues is a word identification technique in which the reader determines the meaning and perhaps the pronunciation of unknown words by examining the context in which they are located.

_____ 12. Young children instinctively understand the value of using context clues while they are reading.

_____ 13. In "*experience clues*" the reader uses his or her prior knowledge to determine the meaning of an unknown word.

_____ 14. Simple variations of the cloze procedure cannot be used with young children before the third-grade level.

_____ 15. Most students can identify words more effectively in isolation than in sentence context.

_____ 16. Wide reading of a variety of motivating materials is the single most effective way to improve ability in the use of context.

_____ 17. Poor readers generally are effective in monitoring their silent and oral reading.

_____ 18. Children can be helped to become aware of miscues that interfere with their comprehension by listening to tape-recorded material.

_____ 19. A *rebus* is a picture that is used in place of a difficult, but important, word.

_____ 20. Context clues are effective nearly *100 percent* of the time while reading fairly difficult material.

WORD STRUCTURE

Word structure (structural analysis) is using *word parts* to determine the meaning and pronunciation of unknown words. This word identification technique can be useful in enlarging a child's meaning vocabulary, especially if it is used in combination with context clues and phonics.

Word structure is composed of a number of different skills. One subskill is attaching an *affix* (a *prefix* or *suffix*) to a *base* or *root word* to form a *derivative*. *Derivational suffixes* alter the part of speech of a word or its function in some way. Common derivational suffixes can form *nouns*, as in the words *voyage* or *lemonade*, while others form *adjectives*, such as *smaller* or *motherly*. Still others change the function of a verb so that it indicates a *person*, as in the words *teacher* or *painter*. Several of the most common derivational suffixes taught in the primary grades are *-er*, *-less*, *-y*, and *-ness*.

Inflectional suffixes indicate grammatical items and include the plural *-s*, as in *cats*; third-person singular, as in *plays*; present participle *-ing*, as in *laughing*; past tense *-ed*, as in *landed*; past participle *-en*, as in *fasten*; comparison *-er* and *-est*, as in *quicker* and *quickest*; and the adverbial *-ly*, as in *rapidly*. In addition, *-s*, *-ed*, and *-ing* are commonly found in all beginning reading materials and therefore are taught in first grade. The suffixes *-er*, *-est*, and *-ly* may be taught in second grade.

Word structure also is related to the term *morpheme*, which is the smallest unit of meaning in a language. A morpheme can be either *free* or *bound*. A *free morpheme* is a group of letters that make up a meaningful word, such as *zebra*, *ski*, *center*, *woman*, or *mall*. A *bound morpheme* is composed of one or more letters that cannot function alone, as does a real word. Examples of bound morphemes include the prefix *-un* in the word *unhappy* and the suffix *-ing* in the word *walking*.

Several other subskills of word structure are understanding the use of *compound words*, *syllabication*, *accent (stress)*, and *word origins*. *Contractions* also usually are considered a part of word structure, although they should be learned as *sight words*, especially in beginning reading instruction. It usually is more helpful for a child to learn a contraction as a sight word than for a child to determine which letters are omitted in a contraction.

Fairly simple compound words such as *bluebird*, *snowman*, *playground*, *blackberry*, or *bulldog* are learned in the primary grades. *Rudimentary syllabication* skills are presented in the upper primary grades, while *beginning accent* often is presented in third grade. Word origins are not taught until the intermediate grades, and then only to students with above average reading skills.

Discussing prefixes, suffixes, base words, and compounds may remind you of memorizing lists of word elements. However, learning morphemes is a *constructive process* that children begin as early as age two. As an example, a young child around the age of four may say the following: "*My father goed to work this morning.*" This is an example of over-generalizing a new grammatical concept. The child has constructed a rule for the past tense of the verb *go*. Later the child will better understand the specific situation and say *went*.

Clymer's list of phonic generalizations was included in Chapter Five. Because some of these rules also deal with word structure, refer to this list when needed. However, since there is a direct link between suffix generalizations and the reader's mental ability to separate suffixes from word roots in order to identify the total word, it is helpful to teach older primary-grade children the following rules:

- When adding a suffix beginning with a *vowel* to a word that ends with an *e*, the *e* is often dropped (i.e., *rose* to *rosy* and *escape* to *escapade*). However, in a word such as *changeable*, the *e* is *not* dropped because to do so would give the *g* a *hard sound*.

- When adding a suffix beginning with a *vowel* to a word that ends in a *single* consonant with a short vowel before it, the final consonant often is doubled (i.e., *hop* + *ing* = *hopping* and *tap* + *ing* = *tapping*). This enables the reader to differentiate between the words *tapping* and *taping*. However, *y* is not changed to *i* when adding *ing* as in the words *fry/frying*. English does not allow two *i*'s together, and without the *y* the word would be spelling *friing*.

- When adding a *suffix* to a word that ends with *y* preceded by a *vowel*, the *y* is not changed (i.e., *monkey* + *s* = *monkeys* and *turkey* + *s* = *turkeys*).

Awareness of oral and written grammar increases through the primary grades as children better understand the concepts of past tense and third-person plural. The use of word structure as a word identification skill should build on these *constructive elements*. The instruction provided for children should be *functional* rather than mechanical and isolated. For example, primary-grade children can use their knowledge of the prefix *un-* meaning *"not"* to construct meaning for such words as *unkind, unhappy, unable,* or *uncertain.*

If a child reads for meaning and uses grammatical clues as well as meaning clues, translating letters into sounds should happen automatically. For example, children usually can pronounce the *-ed* suffix correctly in the following words, although three different pronunciations are possible: *walked, played,* and *landed.* That also is true with the suffix *-s* that is represented by the /z/ sound in such common words as *boys, girls, painters, tails,* and *toes.*

Compound words receive considerable emphasis beginning in first grade. The English language is constantly expanding by the addition of new compound words such as *spacecraft* and *website.*

Compound words can be difficult for children to identify since they appear long and complex. A child who knows the words *butter* and *milk* may still have a difficult time identifying the word *buttermilk* because it looks difficult. Children should learn to identify each word in a compound word separately, and then pronounce them together. They also should learn that the meaning of the compound word usually is a composite meaning of the words in it. However, they should understand that the meanings of the individual words that compose a compound word do not always give a clue to the meaning of the compound word, as in the words *dragonfly, copperhead,* and *cattail.*

See the bibliography section on Additional Reading for Chapter Six for books that can be used to review compound words.

Some reading specialists, including this author, do not believe that traditional syllabication is particularly useful in either word identification or spelling since computer word-processing programs are so common today. Instead, dividing a word into "chunks of meaning" may be more useful in analyzing a word structurally. As an example, the word "butter" can be chunked as *butt/er* instead of the dictionary division *but/ter*, which is the more common one.

On the primer (beginning) reading level only 15 percent of the words have more than one syllable; in first grade about 25 percent of the words are polysyllabic; and by sixth grade 80 percent of the words have two or more syllables. That is the reason primary-grade children should begin to understand how to divide words either into *"chunks of meaning"* or traditional syllables.

In summary, word structure is usually most *functional* when it is used along with context clues and phonics. If a child attacks a word of more than one syllable using word structure, he or she first should decode each "chunk of meaning" or syllable phonetically and then blend them into a recognizable word that is in his or her meaning vocabulary. After the word has been analyzed both structurally and phonetically, the child should use meaning clues to determine whether or not it makes sense.

Here are the most common prefixes that children in the upper primary grades may encounter in their reading materials.

Prefix	Meaning	Example
im-, in-	not	impossible
micro-	short, small	microwave
mis-	wrong, not	mistake
non-	not	nonstop
post-	after	postpone
pre-	before	prefix
re-	again	reheat
sub-	under, below	subzero
un-	not	unhappy

Here are the most common suffixes that children in the primary grades will encounter.

Prefix	Meaning	Example
-able, -ible	is, can be	comfortable
-ar, -er, -or	one who	farmer
-en	to make	fasten
-en	made of	golden
-er	more	quicker
-est	most	quickest
-ful	full of	joyful
-ing	present participle	jumping
-less	without	careless
-like	resembling	homelike
-ly	resembling	fatherly
-ness	state or quality of	kindness
-s	plural, third-person singular	dogs, runs

Strategies for Improving Ability in Word Structure

Here are several classroom-tested strategies for improving word structure in the primary grades. Any of them can be used in their present form if they are applicable or modified in the light of the needs, abilities, and interests of specific pupils.

The Analogy Strategy and Rimes

Using the *analogy strategy and rimes (phonograms)* can help children attack words of more than one syllable. Many children with special needs feel simply unable to decode large words and will not attempt to do so or else guess wildly.

Using the analogy strategy and rimes may help children combine vowel patterns (phonics) and syllabication (word structure). As an example, examine the two following words and the two different ways that each word theoretically could be pronounced.

CV Pattern: tig/er   VC Pattern: ti/ger

CV Pattern: mod/el   VC Pattern: mo/del

The child should learn to read such words aloud or silently in context and then select the pronunciation that makes sense. The analogy approach with rimes should be used *thoughtfully* and *flexibly*—not just drawing lines between syllables with no regard for context.

A Generalization Strategy for Teaching Syllabication

Gunning (1996) suggested the following syllabication strategy using the generalization approach.

Step One: Auditory Perception of Syllables

Tell the children that many words have parts called *syllables*. Pronounce a group of words and have the children clap once for each syllable that they are able to hear: *li-on, let-ter (lett-er), ga-rage, win-dow, fer-ret (ferr-et), chalk-board, fur-nace, shel-tie, wom-an, thun-der, Mon-day*, and so on. *When children understand this concept, they can join in.*

Step Two: Perception of Printed Syllables

Present one- and two-syllable words that contrast with each other so that children can understand printed syllables.

be	*quick*	*walk*	*butter*	*foot*
below	*quicker*	*walking*	*buttermilk*	*footprint*

Step Three: Perception of a Syllable Generalization

When children understand what syllables are, present target words that demonstrate a syllable generalization. Here are several words that illustrate the suffix *-ing* generalization:

jump	*laugh*	*wash*	*scream*	*fry*
jumping	*laughing*	*washing*	*screaming*	*frying*

Have the children read each word in the "pair" and contrast them. Help them to determine that the words on the top have only one syllable while the words on the bottom are composed of two syllables. Read each word on the bottom and have the children clap as they hear the separate syllables in the word. Help children to discover that the *-ing* at the end of each word makes up a separate syllable. In later lessons help them determine other prefixes and suffixes and widen the generalization.

Step Four: Guided Practice

Have the children read signs, poems, and short selections and sing songs that contain words illustrating the target generalization. Have them then complete review exercises in which they use syllabication clues and sentence context to choose the word that correctly completes a sentence. The following may illustrate this activity:

Elena can *jump, jumping* rope very well.
I couldn't stop *laugh, laughing* after I heard the joke.
Patti does not like to *wash, washing* dishes very well.
At the Halloween fun house Pauli heard a lady *scream, screaming.*
My father likes to *fry, frying* eggs for breakfast.

Step Five: Application

Have children read all types of narrative and content selections that contain words with more than one syllable. Help them to apply generalization(s) that they have learned.

Tying Words Together

Obtain a sheet of 8-inch by 10-inch poster board, a marker, scissors, and ten pairs of 16-inch shoelaces. Select ten compound words and print the first half of each compound word on the left of the poster board and the second half of each compound word on the right side of the poster board in scrambled order. Punch holes by each of the word halves. Have each child thread a shoelace through the holes beside half of each compound word to the other part to make a complete compound word. Have the child continue until he or she has made all of the correct compound words.

Here are some compound words that can be used in the following activities. For a comprehensive list of compound words, consult Fry, Kress, and Fountoukidis (2000).

afternoon	grandfather	sandpaper
airline	grandmother	seashell
airplane	haircut	shoelace
airport	hilltop	snowman
applesauce	homework	snowplow
backbone	jellyfish	spotlight
ballpark	lifeboat	starfish
baseball	lighthouse	strawberry
basketball	lipstick	sunflower
birdhouse	moonlight	sunshine
birthday	newspaper	suntan
bulldog	notebook	thunderstorm
buttermilk	oatmeal	tiptoe
chalkboard	outfield	toothbrush
cookbook	outfit	touchdown
cupcake	pancake	upstairs
doorbell	paperback	wastebasket
earring	playground	watermelon
earthquake	popcorn	wheelchair
firefighter	postcard	windmill
fireplace	railroad	woodland
flashlight	rainbow	woodpecker
football	raincoat	wristwatch
goldfish	sailboat	

Magnetic Compound Words

To practice in forming compound words, print each part of a number of compound words on small word cards. Then attach a paper clip to each word card. Have the child pick up two word cards that form an actual compound word with a horseshoe magnet. Have the child pronounce the word and write all of the formed compound words on a sheet of paper.

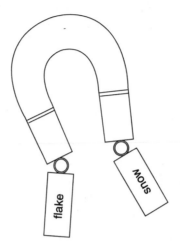

Are These Real or Make-Believe Compound Words?

The reading teacher or tutor can write a number of compound words on the chalkboard, a transparency, or a duplicated sheet of paper. Some of these compound words should be actual, while others should be make-believe. Have the child write all the words in two columns on a sheet of paper—those that are true compound words and those that are not, as shown in the example below.

Real Compound Words	Make-Believe Compound Words
headache	dogears
nightgown	slipperyice
skateboard	pizzaslice
snowflake	hospitalroom
lifeguard	snowday
firewood	shinyfloor
cockpit	prettygirl
skyscraper	chesthair
driveway	cateyes
classmate	bankcheck

Illustrated Compound Words

Have the child choose several compound words that can be illustrated in a humorous way. Have the child write each compound word and then illustrate it. Some compound words that can be illustrated in this way are *anchorperson, blueprint, bulldog, carpool, cupcake, dragonfly, earthworm, eyeball, homesick, jellyfish, keyboard, lightheaded, pancake, ponytail, quicksand, rattlesnake, shortstop, starfish, sunflower, turtleneck,* and *windpipe.*

What Are These Compound Words?

Construct a large wall chart with five headings, such as Living Creatures, People, Things, Places, and Time, written on the top. Then ask the children to locate compound words that fit under the headings. Here is an example:

Living Creatures	People	Things	Places	Time
bluebird	boyfriend	fireplace	highway	today
bulldog	girlfriend	doorknob	driveway	sunrise
earthworm	anchorperson	football	sidewalk	sunset
sailfish	landlord	baseball	showroom	Thanksgiving
starfish	teammate	basketball	underground	weekend
woodpecker	roommate	tugboat	expressway	someday
goldfish	lifeguard	motorcycle	overpass	afternoon
blackbird	grandfather	cookbook	crosswalk	everyday
grasshopper	grandmother	grapefruit	playground	sometime
rattlesnake	frogman	lighthouse	ballpark	breakfast

Animal Suffixes

Obtain large sheets of construction paper or poster board. Draw various animals—such as a *fox, dog, cat, monkey, donkey, tiger, elephant, deer, mouse,* or *rat*—without their tails on each sheet. On the body of each animal print a base or root word. Make various tails and print a suffix on each tail. Have the child pin a suffix to an animal in the correct position and read the derived word aloud as well as using it in a sentence.

Find Them in the Newspaper

Make three columns on a large sheet of paper and label them *Prefixes, Suffixes,* and *Base (Root) Words.* Have children cut words out of a newspaper and paste them into the correct columns.

Structural Puzzles

Review prefixes, suffixes, and compound words with *puzzles.* Print a derivative or compound word on a piece of poster board with a marker. Cut each piece apart between the base (root) word and affix or between the two small words in the compound word using a different type of cut for each. The puzzles can be laminated for durability. Have the child reassemble each of the puzzles and pronounce the completed word. Here are illustrations of this activity.

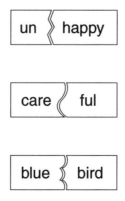

Games for Improving Ability in Word Structure

Here are several games that improve ability in word structure. Any reading game should stress the target reading skill, not just playing the game. The games included in this part of the chapter should be motivating to all young children, whether or not they have special needs.

Automobile Prefixes and Suffixes

To Construct the Game

This game provides practice with common prefixes and suffixes. You need poster board, a marking pen, and a pair of scissors. Draw the outline of an automobile wheel on a sheet of poster board. Cut out several door forms and wheel forms. Write base (root) words on the door cutouts and prefixes and suffixes on the wheel cutouts. Leave one wheel cutout blank.

To Play the Game

Allow two children or two teams to take turns constructing words with prefixes and suffixes by using the wheel and door cutouts. Each child or team receives one point for a word made with a base word and either a prefix or suffix and two points for a word made with a root word and both a prefix and suffix. If a child makes a non-word, he or she loses one point.

Compound Concentration

To Construct the Game

Use compound words to play a variation of Concentration. Print one-half of a compound word (for example, *blue* of *bluebird* or *blueberry*) on each card. Then number the cards consecutively on the back. Place the cards in order with the *number side showing*.

To Play the Game

Five to ten children can play this game. The first child says two numbers, and the appropriate cards are turned over so that the words are visible. If the two cards form a compound word and the child can pronounce it and can correctly use it in a sentence, he or she keeps the cards and takes another turn. If not, another child has a turn. The child who has the greatest number of cards at the end wins the game.

Making Words

To Construct the Game

This game is most appropriate for children in third grade who do not have special needs. Select three objects such as *shoe boxes*, *file boxes*, or *coffee cans* and label each set of objects in the following way: *prefixes*, *base (root) words*, and *suffixes*. Make a number of cards out of poster board, each of which contains an appropriate prefix, base (root) word, or suffix.

To Play the Game

Have each child select a card from each group and try to make a word from all three word parts. An additional point can be given if the child can correctly use the word in a sentence. After a specified period of time, the child who has made the most correct *derivatives* and used them in a sentence is declared to be the winner.

Can You Spin an Ending?

To Construct the Game

This game provides practice with common inflectional endings. Construct a spinner out of poster board with inflectional endings written around using a marker. Write base (root) words on word cards with a marker. The accompanying illustration should clarify the construction of this game.

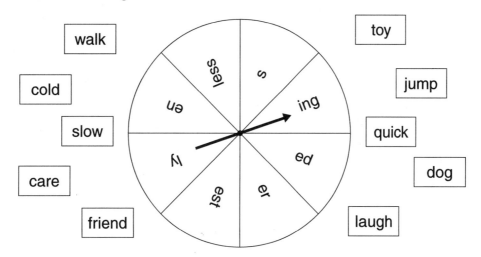

To Play the Game

Give each player a stack of base (root) word cards. The children take turns spinning the spinner. The player who spins tries to make a word by combining the inflectional ending that he or she spins with one of his or her base (root) word cards. If the child does so successfully, he or she earns one point. Otherwise, he or she loses one point. After a child has used a base (root) word card to form a word, that card is out of play for the rest of the game. The game ends when one player runs out of cards.

Butterfly Match-Up

To Construct the Game

Using poster board, a marker, and a pair of scissors, cut out butterfly shapes from the poster board. Write the two parts of compound words on the wings. Cut the butterflies in two parts. (See the accompanying illustrations.)

To Play the Game

Place all of the butterfly wings in a large brown envelope. Let one or more children reconstruct the butterflies to form compound words. If you wish, the child or children can use each newly constructed compound word in a sentence.

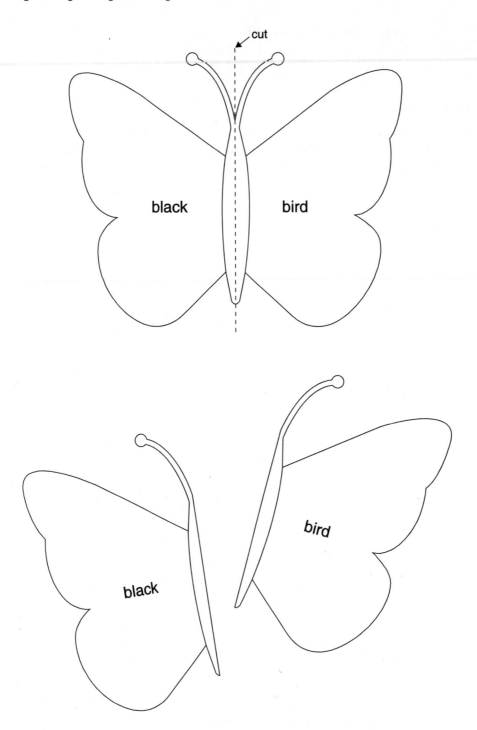

Reproducibles for Improving Ability in Word Structure

These four reproducible activity sheets for improving ability in word structure can be duplicated and used in their present form or modified in light of the needs, abilities, and interests of specific pupils. The activity sheets are

Illustrating Common Compound Words
Locating Incorrect Verb Suffixes in Story Context
Attaching a Correct Suffix to a Base (Root) Word
Deducing Compound Words from Two Clues

ILLUSTRATING COMMON COMPOUND WORDS

Draw a picture for each word on this sheet. The first one is done for you.

1. snowman

2. goldfish

3. doghouse

ILLUSTRATING COMMON COMPOUND WORDS *(continued)*

4. starfish

5. sailboat

6. airplane

ILLUSTRATING COMMON COMPOUND WORDS *(continued)*

7. bluebird

8. newspaper

9. snowflake

10. football

LOCATING INCORRECT VERB SUFFIXES IN STORY CONTEXT

Read this story to yourself. Some of the words in the story have an *incorrect suffix (ending).* *Cross each of these words out,* and *write each word* with its *correct ending* above the word that you crossed out.

My Puppy Goes to School

I have a black cocker spaniel puppy name *Honey* who is now seven months old. She starting puppy school when she was three months old and went every Monday evening for eight weeks. *Honey* never miss a lesson and received a certificate when she was finished saying that she *passed!*

In puppy school *Honey* first learned to "*sit*" when I told her. I gave her a treat when she sat on command. She also learning to be *handled.* This means that I first held her in my arms with her stomach up and then made her stand still as I held her while she stood up on her two hind legs. These "*social exercises*" made her easier to train.

Next *Honey* learned the "*down*" command, and she receiving a treat when she lay down. She also learned the "*stay*" command, both when she was sit and was lying down. Then *Honey* learned to "*heel,*" which means that she walking right along my left side without pulling ahead of me or lagging behind. She received a treat every time she did a command correctly.

Honey will start school again in two weeks. This class is calls the *beginner class* and is for older puppies like *Honey.* She will be in this class with about ten other young dogs, many of whom were in the puppy class with her.

Honey loving her puppy school, and I know that she also will enjoy this next class. She especially enjoys the treats she gets when she obeys a command!

ATTACHING A CORRECT SUFFIX TO A BASE (ROOT) WORD

In each group of words *draw a line* from the *base (root) word* on the left to the *suffix* on the right to make the *correct word*.

Group 1

brush	hood
child	en
gold	es
care	ful

Group 2

quick	less
girl	ing
walk	hood
life	ly

Group 3

land	ly
sleep	ed
rapid	ness
good	y

Group 4

watch	ly
rain	en
wood	y
slow	ful

Group 5

mother	er
quick	hood
fast	less
tooth	en

DEDUCING COMPOUND WORDS FROM TWO CLUES

Read each two clues. Try to figure out the compound word. Write your answers on the lines. The first one has been done for you.

1. A male (boy) cow and the animal who is said to be "man's best friend": ____*bulldog*____

2. What coffee is usually poured into and a dessert that a child may eat on his or her birthday: _____

3. A very dark color and a creature that flies in the air: _____

4. Another name for automobile and a body of water for swimming: _____

5. Something to write with and a piece of lumber: _____

6. Found on a person's head and a piece of jewelry: _____

7. The color of the sky on a sunny day and a small piece of fruit: _____

8. Something to put on a slice of bread and a creature that swims in water: _____

9. This shines in the night sky and the opposite of "dark": _____

10. Something a person reads from and a creature that can be used to bait a fishing hook: _____

11. A creature with a shell and the part of the body directly under the head: _____

12. The part of a bicycle that "turns" and a piece of furniture to sit on: _____

13. This can ache in a person's mouth and something very much like glue: _____

14. Something to put food on and what is found in a lake: _____

15. This shines in the sky and a light brown color: _____

16. This means "pull" and a vehicle that travels on water: _____

17. The opposite of "go" and something that helps a person to see better in the dark: _____

18. What a dog may do if it is angry and a make-believe creature that breathes fire: _____

19. A group of musicians and the opposite of "sit": _____

20. What cars and trucks travel on and another word for automobile: _____

CONTEXT CLUES

Context clues are a word identification technique in which a reader figures out the meaning and sometimes the pronunciation of unknown words by looking at the context in which they are found. The context can be the sentence, the adjacent sentences, the paragraph, or the entire passage. It also can involve grammar clues.

Context clues are not always helpful, especially if there are a number of unknown words in the material. The average reader is only able to use context clues an estimated *5 to 20 percent* of the time. However, children often become more adept in using context clues as they progress through the elementary grades. Children must be given considerable direct instruction and practice in the use of context if they are going to be able to use it effectively. Do not tell children to use context clues without giving them direct instruction and much motivated practice. In addition, they must receive encouraging feedback when they are using context clues effectively.

Context clues can be classified in several ways. Here is one useful classification scheme (Rinsky, 1997).

- *Direct explanation clue*—Often authors know that a reader will not know a word and therefore place it in an explanation to clarify it.

  Example: The uncommon term *carcinoma* is another term for the more common term cancer.

- *Experience clue*—A reader's own experiences and prior knowledge can help determine an unknown word.

  Example: All of the members of our class like to work in cooperation to finish an important job.

- *Words in a series*—Often unknown words in a series can be determined from clues.

  Example: The digestive system consists of the esophagus, the stomach, the large and small intestines, and the colon.

- *Restatement*—To clarify authors may repeat what they have stated.

  Example: An English cocker spaniel can try to be dominant if it is not properly trained. In other words, an English cocker spaniel can try to "run the household."

- *Contrast and comparison*—Words such as "but" may give clues to word meaning.

  Example: Geri smiled at me, but showed her disapproval by what she said to me.

- *Inference*—Nearby words or sentences provide clues.

  Example: Jamie is a very talkative and opinionated person. His loquaciousness can be very aggravating at times.

Context clues are the single most useful technique of word identification. However, context is most helpful when it is used along with word structure and phonics and when there are not many unknown words in the reading material. Usually there should be *no more than one in fifty* unknown words in the material if context clues are to be used effectively.

Context clues should be presented as early as the beginning reading level when an adult reads a sentence with an omitted word and asks the children to suggest a word that makes sense in that sentence. At the primary-grade level, explain the importance of context clues to the pupils and encourage them to use context clues to determine the meaning of unknown words that they meet while reading. In addition, ask children to read simple sentences and select the omitted word that makes sense in each sentence from the options that are supplied. As an example:

Tyler lost his _____ on the way home from school yesterday. (moose, mittens, mend)

Children in the primary grades and beyond should be able to supply words that make sense while reading both silently and orally, even if the provided words are not the actual words found in the reading material. All children should be taught that using context clues is not just guessing, but instead is a calculated estimate of the meaning of unknown words that requires interpretive thinking.

Children in the primary grades are often discouraged from risk taking, which may hinder their reading progress. However, the practice of word substitution can be carried to an extreme, such as when children mispronounce half or more of the words in the reading material. Such children should continue to receive practice and/or reinforcement in sight word identification, word structure, or phonics depending on their weaknesses.

Here are the main advantages of using context clues:

- Most children can identify words in context that they cannot identify in isolation.

- Words that do not have a consistent sound-symbol relationship, such as *laugh*, *through*, *father*, *should*, or *rough*, may be more easily identified by using context clues.

- Readers who can use context clues effectively become independent decoders more quickly than children who cannot. They learn to be effective predictors of words. They then are able to confirm or reject their predictions based on context. Then they quickly read on.

- Children who have difficulty with phonic skills that require closer attention to visual features may identify unknown words more easily.

Here are the major limitations of using context clues:

- Since beginning readers have a very limited reading vocabulary, they often have difficulty in using context clues effectively.

- The surrounding context may not be enough to provide accurate word identification or may provide misleading information.

- Since many synonyms in English could make sense in different contexts, context clues may not be enough for accurate word identification.

To summarize, context is the technique that best represents the concept of reading as a language-based process emphasizing comprehension. Therefore, it normally should receive the most emphasis as a word identification technique, although children with learning disabilities may need more emphasis placed on other word identification techniques, such as phonics. However, these children also need to understand the importance of context clues and use them when applicable.

Strategies for Improving Ability in Context Clues

Here are several strategies for improving context clue usage in young children. They can be used in their present form or modified in any way in the light of the needs, interests, and abilities of specific pupils.

Wide Reading

Wide reading of different kinds of materials is the single most effective way of improving context clue usage in the primary grades. This reading can take the form of predictable books and other easy-to-read books. Lists of contemporary books that are useful for this purpose are found in the appendices to this book. Wide reading also can use dictated and written language-experience booklets and stories, all types of trade books including picture storybooks and informational books, chapter books, and simple children's magazines and newspapers designed for the primary grades.

Since reading improves most effectively when the teacher or tutor is using materials that children can read easily, reading often should be on the independent (easy) or low instructional reading level. Children with special needs usually read as little as possible, since they find reading difficult and unrewarding. Although it may be difficult to motivate such children, having them read very easy, highly motivating materials that are especially chosen for them often helps. Encouraging these children to read self-selected, easy material that specifically reflects their interests, including their own dictated materials, often leads to success.

Self-Monitoring of Reading Materials

Children must learn to monitor their own silent and oral reading. If they do not do so, they are not concerned about whether or not the reading material is making sense. *Self-monitoring* is a mindset in which a child consistently thinks about what he or she is reading and whether or not he or she understands it. If a child does not comprehend what he or she is reading, he or she should learn how to apply such fix-up strategies as rereading the entire passage, rereading just the sentence or sentences that were not understood, using the dictionary, or asking a study buddy or the teacher (tutor) for help.

Listening for Reading Miscues

Children should be helped to become cognizant of miscues (errors) that interfere with comprehension by having them listen to teacher (tutor-read or tape-recorded) material that contains some miscues. They should indicate when miscues occur and tell why that miscue is incorrect. When a child meets a word in context that he or she does not know or is unaware that a miscue has occurred that interferes with comprehension, he or she usually should finish reading the entire sentence because it may provide additional needed information.

Most often the words after the unknown word provide more help than the words before it. The child can use a placeholder (a word that makes sense and is grammatically correct) until he or she locates new information that enables him or her to try another word. The child also can examine the unknown word by using phonic cues along with context clues and then rereading the entire sentence. If none of these strategies is effective, the child should try reading the sentence before or after the sentence containing the unknown word.

Rebuses

An interesting strategy for young children to use for improving ability in context clues is to have the child dictate (or the teacher construct) a chart that uses rebuses (pictures) in place of several difficult, but interesting, vocabulary words. One effective way of using rebuses is to place them in recipes for actual cooking or baking activities in which the child will participate. The recipe then is written on chart paper, read, and subsequently followed. Making deviled eggs, bread, cookies, candy, or salads are all appropriate recipes for using rebuses.

Omitting Words That Can Be Deduced from Context

Construct sentences or short paragraphs, omitting target words that children should be able to deduce from their context. In place of each target word, insert an initial consonant and then x's for the remainder of the letters in the word. Here is an example:

> My dog Honey and I wxxx by a dog park almost every day where dogs are running free. (walk)

When children are able to deduce most of the deleted words by replacing the x's with the actual letters, the next step is to replace target words with x's for each letter, as in:

> Rylee really enjoys coming to my house after school on Wednesday to learn to xxxx books of all kinds. (read)

After children are able to deduce omitted words by replacing the x's with letters, leave blank lines to replace entire omitted words.

> My friend Rich very much enjoys trying to catch _____ in Birch Lake on a warm _____ day in July. (fish; summer or sunny)

Contextual Antonyms

The reading teacher or tutor can construct a number of descriptive sentences that contain antonyms. Then read each sentence containing the antonyms and have members of the class or a group act out the sentence at the same time, demonstrating opposite actions. For example:

> Sally jumped *up* as she threw the blue ball *down.*
> Matt was *laughing* so hard that he ended up almost *crying.*
> Although Tara was *sleeping* very soundly, she *woke* with a start when she heard the ambulance siren.
> When the traffic light changed from *go* to *stop,* my mother braked her car as hard as she could.
> Although I had been very *sad,* when I bought a puppy I was *happy* again.

Drawing Similes

This activity is most appropriate for grades two and three. Divide large pieces of drawing paper into sections. Construct a group of sentences using similes with one word omitted. Here are several examples:

Matt is always sly like a . . . . (fox)
I am usually as busy as a . . . . (bee)
Joanne always acts like a bump on a . . . in school. (log)
That doctor is as hard as . . . . (nails)
My sister usually is as quiet as a . . . . (mouse)

Here are several similes that can be used with children in the upper primary grades. Fry, Kress, and Fountoukidis (2000) have a complete list of similes.

Sample Similes

as cute as a button	as deep as the ocean	as green as grass
as happy as a lark	as hungry as a bear	as light as a feather
as quick as a wink	as stiff as a board	as stubborn as a mule
cries like a baby	eats like it's going out of style	eats like a bird
fits like a glove		as old as the hills
works like a dog	fought like cats and dogs	runs around like a chicken with its head cut off
	stood out like a sore thumb	

Crossword Puzzles

Crossword puzzles can be used to improve ability in context clues with children who are in third grade and above. Construct a crossword puzzle in which children must select a word from a list to complete a sentence. The selected word is to be defined within the context of a sentence. Have the child complete each sentence and then write the correct letters in the appropriate puzzle boxes.

Shanker and Ekwall's Strategy for Teaching Context Clues

Shanker and Ekwall (2002) proposed an effective strategy to teach children to use context clues while they are reading independently. Briefly, here is that strategy.

When you come to a word that you don't know:

1. Say the beginning sound.

2. Read the rest of the sentence. THINK

3. Say the parts that you don't know. GUESS

4. Ask someone to help you and then go on reading.

Step 1 stresses phonics and is helpful because beginning sounds often are the most useful in identifying an unknown word. Step 2 requires the child to use context clues before using additional phonic or structural clues. It is helpful because the words that come after the unknown word are helpful more often than are words that come before an unknown word. The third step requires the child to use other word attack clues, such as ending sounds, medial vowel sounds, and word structure. The final step suggests that children ask for help or continue reading if there is no other alternative. If children must use Step 4, the material is probably too difficult for them, and they should be given easier material to read at least most of the time.

Shanker and Ekwall suggest using the following procedure:

1. Present the steps using a written chart that children can remember and refer to.

2. Model and use the steps yourself with simple sentences.

3. Tell children that this strategy actually works very well.

4. Give children sentences that they can use to apply the steps as you provide help.

5. Ensure that children use the steps as they practice reading.

Here are sample sentences to present and provide children with practice in this identification strategy:

- I heard a *lion* with a beautiful mane roaring in his cage at the zoo. (1, 2)
- Sandpaper is very *rough* and scratchy, but it works well in smoothing wood. (1, 2)
- I am going on a vacation to *Alaska* next summer, where I hope I'll see humpback whales. (1, 2, 3)
- A *porcupine* always tries to protect itself with its quills when it is threatened. (1, 2, 3, 4?)
- All of the *candidates* for president must be able to speak effectively at all times. (1, 2, 3, 4)

Linked Cards

Attach three word cards together with a ring in the upper left corner. Write a sentence with one word missing on the first card. Have the child predict the missing word. After he or she makes the first prediction, have the child flip to the second card, which has the first letter of the missing word written on it. Have the child then confirm the prediction or make another one. Last, have the child flip to the third card that shows the correct word.

Draw a Picture

Divide a large piece of 12-inch by 18-inch manila paper or newsprint into fourths. Print four sentences on the chalkboard. In each sentence one word (that can be illustrated by a primary-grade child) is omitted. Have the child read each sentence silently and draw the illustration of the omitted word on the sheet of paper. Each sentence should allow for a creative answer. Here are several sample sentences:

My favorite food to eat is . . . .
The animal that I would most like to visit at the zoo is a . . . .
In the summer the thing that I like best to do is . . . .
Morgan was as hungry as a . . . .

Magazine Pictures

Give the child pictures from magazines or catalogs. Then read several sentences aloud or record them on tape, omitting one word in each sentence that can be completed by using one of the pictures. Have the child show the picture from the group of pictures that takes the place of the omitted word.

Riddles

Write riddles on cards with only the initial letter(s) of the answer. Laminate the cards. Here are several examples:

Children build me in the winter, but I melt when the weather gets warmer.
    I am a sn_____.
I am called "man's (and woman's) best friend." I am a d_____.
I am found in the kitchen, and I cook foods very quickly. I am a m_____.
I am found in many offices and homes. Children can play games on me.
    I am a c_____.

Word Cards

Print several structure or function words such as *a, an, and, but,* and *the* on individual word cards. Cut out pictures from old magazines or catalogs that can be used along with the word cards to form phrases. Have the child select pictures and word cards to form phrases, as shown in the accompanying illustrations.

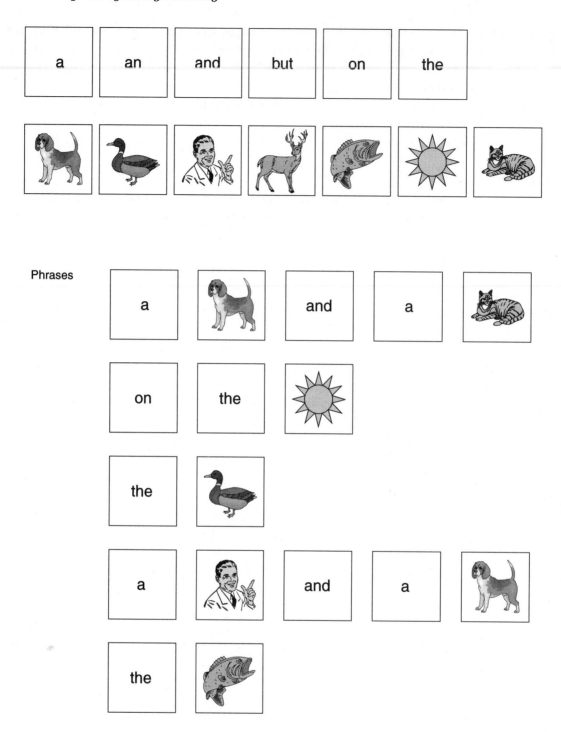

Easy Variations of the Cloze Procedure

The *cloze procedure* was formulated by Wilson L. Taylor (1953) and is based on the *psychological theory of closure*, which indicates that a person wants to complete any unfinished pattern. The cloze procedure is based on the *prediction aspect of reading*, which indicates that a reader attempts to predict the unknown words he or she may encounter in a passage. Therefore, the cloze procedure uses both context clues and grammar clues to help identify unknown words.

The cloze procedure has a number of variations, some of which are relevant in the primary grades. A cloze procedure always is constructed in about the same way from a narrative or informational trade book, a basal reader, or some other type of supplementary reading material. Select a passage of about *250* words (or somewhat less with beginning readers) at what is thought to be the child's high instructional or independent reading level. Then type the first and last sentences with no deletions. Omit every tenth word from the rest of the primary-grade reading material unless the selected word is a proper noun or a very difficult word. When a cloze procedure is used to improve ability in context clues, *count as correct any word that makes sense in the passage.*

A young child should have a number of *"readiness activities"* before being exposed to actual cloze procedures. As one such activity, choose sentences from experience stories and print each sentence on a strip of poster board, omitting one word from each. Then print each omitted word on a word card. Have the child place the proper word card in each sentence strip. Then have the child read each sentence aloud.

As another example, print a short passage on the appropriate reading level and place masking tape over the words to be omitted. Have the children guess each omitted word. After each guess is made, remove the masking tape and have the children compare the actual word with their predictions.

As a final example, *zipper cloze* involves printing some sentences on an overhead projector transparency with one word covered by a small piece of poster board. Place a piece of tape across the poster board to fasten it to the transparency so that the tape serves as a hinge. To show the word to children after having them guess, lift the poster board flap. In the upper primary grades children should be able to discuss why various answers may or may not be acceptable in terms of context or grammar clues.

A simple version of cloze for use in the primary grades has all the deleted words printed in random order in columns at the bottom of the sheet containing the passage. Then the child selects the correct word to complete each blank and prints it in the blank. Another simple version for use in the primary grades has each deletion with two or three options placed under it or after it. Most children enjoy this version of cloze very much. One other fairly simple version for use in second and third grades combines phonic cues and context cues. In this version the beginning letter or several letters (consonant blend or digraph) are written at the beginning of the omission. This variation is called a partial word deletion. As another modification only consonants are provided and the vowels are deleted in every tenth word. One other fairly easy version has random deletions with the omitted words easy to determine. In all of the versions of the cloze procedure, the length of each blank space should be about fifteen typewritten spaces. The cloze procedure is successful with young children if the reading material from which it has been constructed is fairly easy for them to read.

Reproducibles for Improving Ability in Context Clues

Here are four reproducible activity sheets for improving ability in context clues. Duplicate and use any of them in their present form or modify them in any way in the light of the needs, interests, and abilities of specific pupils. The activity sheets that are included in this part of the chapter are

> *What Words Don't Belong?*
> *Cloze Procedure (Omitted Words at the End)*
> *What Is the Mystery Word?*
> *Determining Actual Words from Context*

WHAT WORDS DON'T BELONG?

Read each sentence to yourself and *cross out* each word in that sentence that doesn't make sense.

1. Today is a cloudy cold couch day in the winter.

2. Most children like to drive eat pizza for lunch.

3. My young puppy really likes to go snow to dog school on Tuesday evenings.

4. Most schools have someone to dark help children cross busy streets house near the school.

5. Maria is going on a cruise with her teach parents in a few weeks.

6. Ben enjoys swimming in the heavy Turtle Lake in the summer.

7. Have you ever run seen a fawn in the spring?

8. In the summer I like to kitchen go swimming, boating, and fishing.

9. My mother car bought a new brown leather sofa for our clothes family room.

10. How old is been your brother Raul?

11. A dog should have its eyes teeth brushed every day.

12. Our class visited Miller Park Zoo yesterday painting and saw the lions and tigers, among other animals.

13. A fisher is a vicious animal that lives in the North Woods and is sometimes table seen there.

14. My friend Jamie now lives in church an apartment.

15. I think that a house is not a truck home without a dog.

16. Our family has a washer and grass dryer in the basement.

17. Susie's puppy Jazz likes to cupcake play ball.

18. Ashley likes to eat bicycle pancakes on Sunday morning.

19. My friends have two dishes cats that are named Fluffy and Chugger.

20. In March I plan to have my pencil kitchen and hall painted.

CLOZE PROCEDURE
(OMITTED WORDS AT THE END)

Read this story about a dog obedience school. As you read it, pick a word from the "Answers" at the end to fit in the blank space. Print the word in the blank space. When you are finished, read the story again to be sure that it is all correct.

Dog Obedience School

My black cocker spaniel Honey started beginner dog obedience school last week. There were

twelve young _____ in the school. Honey was the smallest

of all _____ dogs. The dogs looked very different. One was

a huge white _____, and there were several

other very big dogs in the school.

   Since my dog Honey had gone to puppy obedience school last

_____, she already knew the commands of "sit," "stay,"

"come," "stand," and "heel." That is why _____ was chosen

by the dog trainer to show all of the other dogs and

_____ how to do some of the commands. As she was

showing them how to do the commands, she seemed

_____ proud. I think that she was "showing off."

   However, she _____ not completely well behaved at the

school last _____. She tried to smell the noses of the two

dogs who were sitting near her. Then she _____ twice too.

She was supposed to be completely quiet.

   I wonder if she _____ do well in the next seven lessons

at the _____. I hope that she does, but I will

_____ her even if she doesn't. Honey is my dog and my

very best friend!

ANSWERS	
was	barked
love	dogs
the	will
week	owners
she	fall
really	dog
	school

WHAT IS THE MYSTERY WORD?

Read this entire story to yourself. As you read it, try to figure out ONE WORD that has been omitted from the whole story. After you have read the entire story, *write the mystery word in each blank* in the story so it will make sense.

Third Grade

Tanya is in third grade at Martin Luther King School. She usually likes to go to school, but she enjoys some things about school better than others.

Tanya really likes recess when she can play with her friends. However, she always does very well in the subject of _____. In fact, she is one of the best in her entire class.

Tanya does not like arithmetic very well. She thinks that word problems are especially difficult. In fact, although she is good in _____, she has trouble understanding some word problems.

She likes science in third grade since she enjoys conducting and watching scientific experiments. They are often fascinating to her.

Social studies are very interesting to Tanya since she enjoys participating in projects such as constructing a model rain forest or veterinarian's office. She always enjoys _____ social science materials since they are interesting to her.

Is _____ your favorite subject in school? I hope so because a child can learn many, many interesting things from _____.

Copyright © 2005 by John Wiley & Sons, Inc.

DETERMINING ACTUAL WORDS FROM CONTEXT

Read each sentence silently. ONE WORD in each sentence has been replaced by X's. Write the word that makes the sentence correct on the line underneath it.

1. Mari saw several beautiful XXXXX flying when she went to King Zoo.

   _____

2. My baby brother seems to XXX many times during each day.

   _____

3. My puppy Holly wears a blue sweat XXXXX when she goes for a walk in the morning.

   _____

4. Most children like to eat hamburgers and French XXXXX.

   _____

5. Today is a beautiful, warm, sunny XXX.

   _____

6. Donny likes to go to the swimming XXXX every day in the summer.

   _____

7. A child should have XXXX with cereal.

   _____

8. Jill saw a black and white XXXXX walking in the woods yesterday.

   _____

9. My older brother Josh has a new girl XXXXXX.

   _____

10. When a kitten grows up, it will be a XXX.

   _____

DETERMINING ACTUAL WORDS FROM CONTEXT *(continued)*

11. Lynn had a chocolate cake for her XXXXXXXX.

_____

12. My father bought a brown braided XXX for the floor of his office.

_____

13. During the rainstorm, Ross got his shoes and XXXXX wet.

_____

14. My dog is fourteen years XXX.

_____

15. Since it is sunny today, the sky is XXXX.

_____

16. My neighbors, the Gray family, have four girls and one XXX.

_____

17. I like to walk with my XXX every morning.

_____

18. My mother drinks one cup of XXXXXX each morning.

_____

19. Fred drives a big XXXXX for a living.

_____

20. My grandmother had an operation in the XXXXXXXX on Monday.

_____

7

Improving Ability in Vocabulary and Comprehension

Comprehension is the true goal of all reading instruction. Consider that a good reader probably would be able to accurately decode a completely phonetic language such as Finnish, but would be unable to understand it without a thorough understanding of the vocabulary and concepts contained in it.

This chapter is designed to help you effectively present vocabulary and comprehension skills to young children. It opens with a pre-assessment device on comprehension. I then provide a very brief description of meaning vocabularies and their relation to reading achievement and suggest several strategies for improving ability in meaning vocabulary (such as direct and second-hand experiences, word play, semantic mapping, and scaffolding), along with several ready-to-duplicate activity sheets.

The major portion of the chapter is devoted to helping improve the comprehension skills of young children. That part of the chapter briefly describes comprehension and presents a number of classroom-tested strategies and materials, along with four reproducible activity sheets.

Decide whether each statement is *accurate* (true) or *not* (false). Evaluate your answers after you have read the chapter. The answers are on page 326.

_____ 1. The *speaking vocabulary* is the first type of vocabulary that a young child learns in the home.

_____ 2. Vocabulary knowledge is highly related to reading comprehension.

_____ 3. *Direct experiences* are the most effective ways of developing children's meaning vocabulary and knowledge of concepts.

_____ 4. *Semantic mapping (webbing)* is effective in improving a young child's vocabulary knowledge, comprehension ability, and writing skills.

_____ 5. *"Word play"* is an interesting strategy for children to use in motivating vocabulary development.

_____ 6. *Scaffolding* is a strategy that only is effective with young children who have special needs.

_____ 7. Reading comprehension is an interactive process that requires using prior knowledge and print material.

_____ 8. Good readers and poor readers are about equal in their ability in *metacognition (self-monitoring)* of reading material.

_____ 9. Answering *"think and search"* questions is a component of textually implicit (interpretive or inferential) comprehension.

_____ 10. Children in the primary grades can begin to read critically.

_____ 11. *Prediction strategies* are one of the most effective ways of improving reading comprehension.

_____ 12. *Visual imagery* is too difficult a skill for children in the primary grades to use in improving comprehension.

_____ 13. *Puppetry* is an excellent strategy to use in improving the comprehension skills of young children, including those with special needs.

_____ 14. Children in the upper primary grades can make a beginning in discriminating between *real and make-believe.*

_____ 15. *Sequential ability* is a very difficult skill for young children to learn.

_____ 16. The *herringbone technique* can be used for improving ability in textually explicit (literal or factual) comprehension.

_____ 17. *Reading to follow directions* is an element of textually explicit (literal or factual) comprehension.

_____ 18. *Disregarding punctuation* is unimportant in reading comprehension.

_____ 19. Participating in *creative dramatics* can improve comprehension.

_____ 20. *Games* are an excellent way of improving reading comprehension in the primary grades.

TYPES OF MEANING VOCABULARIES AND THEIR RELATION TO READING ACHIEVEMENT

There are a number of different conceptual (meaning) vocabularies. The *listening vocabulary* is the first kind of vocabulary that a young child learns. It is primarily learned in the home by hearing family members (and others with whom the young child comes in contact) speak. A young child next acquires a *speaking vocabulary* by imitating the oral language of family members, other adults, and older children. That is why it is important that young children hear correct grammar and varied, precise vocabulary. It also is the reason that a child learns to speak in a dialect such as the African American or Latino dialect.

Next the child usually learns the *reading vocabulary*, although he or she may learn some elements of the *writing vocabulary* first, or may learn the reading and writing vocabulary at about the same time. The reading vocabulary is mainly learned in school, although early readers learn it in the home or a child-care facility. The writing vocabulary also is mainly learned in school, although a start can be made before school entrance, especially if the child is allowed to use *invented spelling*.

The *potential* or *marginal vocabulary* consists of all the words that a child may be able to determine the meaning of by using context clues; by knowing the meaning of prefixes, suffixes, or word roots; or by understanding the derivatives of words. It often is impossible to determine the size of a child's potential vocabulary because the context in which the word is located may determine whether or nor the child will know its meaning.

Research has found that reading comprehension is composed of two major skills—word meaning (vocabulary) and *reasoning ability*, which probably is the same as reading comprehension. This conclusion also can be made by logical analysis.

Chall (1987) estimated that the average child begins first grade knowing about 5,000 to 6,000 words and that during twelve years of school, he or she learns about 36,000 more. Young children today know many more words than they did in the past because of the influence of television, the World Wide Web, movies, computer software (including computer games), and radio. However, you should remember that whether children "*know*" a word or are just able to repeat it without understanding should be determined by each reading teacher, tutor, or family member.

It is important to note that the size of a child's meaning vocabulary always correlates positively with success in school. Meaning vocabulary consists of such elements as knowledge of synonyms and antonyms, multiple meanings of words, homonyms and homographs, and understanding of relational terms such as *bottom, top, under, over,* and so on.

Graves (1987) expanded the stages of learning words to include the following:

- *Task 1:* Learning to read known words.
- *Task 2:* Learning new meanings for known words.
- *Task 3:* Learning new words that represent known concepts.
- *Task 4:* Learning new words that represent new concepts.
- *Task 5:* Classifying and enriching the meaning of known words.
- *Task 6:* Moving words from *receptive* (listening and reading) to *expressive* (speaking and writing) *vocabulary.*

As can be noted from these six tasks, even when a child apparently "*knows*" a vocabulary term, it may be rather incomplete knowledge. As an example, a person who has done scuba diving much better understands what is involved than a person who has not.

At any grade level, vocabulary development is not a process of listing vocabulary terms and having children look up the definitions. Instead, it should be a part of living. As children grow and continue to have many rich, varied experiences, their meaning vocabularies continue to develop. As an example, by playing or watching football, they can learn such terms as *touchdown, touchback, first down, quarterback, fullback, halfback, guard, pigskin, field goal,* and *goalpost.*

A word is not usually known in isolation. Instead, it usually is known in the context of a phrase, a sentence, a paragraph, or an entire passage. That is why it generally is more effective to learn new vocabulary terms in context than in isolated word lists. As an example, the word *"can"* has many different meanings depending on the *context* in which it is located. Here are a few of the uses for this somewhat abstract word:

I hope that I *can* go to the circus.
My mom opened a *can* of soup for lunch.
The mayor's statement really opened up a *can* of worms.
When I was growing up, my mother always would *can* peaches in the summer.
That new film is now in the *can.*
I hope that the new boss will not *can* me.

Meaning vocabulary development can take many years of direct and incidental experiences. However, even children in the primary grades can make a beginning in this important aspect of the comprehension process.

Strategies for Improving Ability in Meaning Vocabulary

Here is a sampling of strategies than can be used to improve meaning vocabulary with young children. Modify any of these strategies in the light of the needs, interests, and abilities of specific pupils.

Direct and Second-Hand Experiences

Direct experiences probably are the best way of developing the meaning vocabulary and conceptual knowledge of young children. However, since it is not always practical to use direct experiences, *second-hand experiences* often can be used in their place.

When using direct experiences of any type for vocabulary and conceptual development, reading teachers, tutors, or family members should try to build vocabulary and concepts before, during, and after the experience. As an example, before a second-grade class takes a trip to a local children's discovery museum, the teacher should discuss with the children the demonstrations and exhibits they are likely to see there. He or she also should teach some of the most important vocabulary terms related to that museum. During the experience, the teacher can point out the concepts and vocabulary terms that were discussed in school. After the trip, the children as a large group, a small group, or individually (with a teacher's aide or volunteer) can review the vocabulary and concepts.

Several places that are interesting to young children for school or family trips are a pet store, veterinary hospital, zoo, wildlife preserve, forest preserve, museum, planetarium, hospital, aquarium, park, playground, train station, train trip, greenhouse, nursery, nursing home, police station, fire station, post office, dairy farm, grain farm, cattle farm, pig farm, local library, college library, and children's theater, among many others.

Since not all experiences for young children can be direct, second-hand experiences often can be a valuable alternative. As an example, when a third-grade class is studying the *solar system*, they obviously cannot visit the various planets. However, researching and constructing a model of the planets can teach them a great deal about it.

Second-hand experiences that can be used for vocabulary and concept development include using the World Wide Web, interacting with computer software, watching a videotape or DVD, watching films, looking at slides, watching scientific experiments or demonstrations, examining models and realia, looking at pictures, examining actual objects, looking at dioramas, listening to CDs, or listening to cassette tape recordings. As in the case of direct experiences, a reading teacher, tutor, or family member must stress conceptual and vocabulary development while using any kind of second-hand experience.

Wide Reading

Wide reading both to children and by children is one of the most effective ways of improving meaning vocabulary and conceptual knowledge. For example, by listening to a book about visiting a wildlife preserve in Australia, children could learn about such animals as kangaroos, koala bears, wombats, dingoes, fairy penguins, and Tasmanian devils, among others.

Nagy and Herman (1987) found that the number of vocabulary terms children learn through context during periods of *sustained silent reading* (which can occur as early as the second semester of first grade) is far greater than the words they learn through direct instruction. Anderson, Wilson, and Fielding (1988) also found that the amount of independent reading done by a child was the best predictor of his or her vocabulary growth in grades 2 and 3. Therefore, encouraging children to read for pleasure and information in the primary grades is extremely important.

Promoting the Enjoyment of Words

Appendix XIII contains a brief list of mass market books that can be used in the primary grades to promote the *enjoyment of words*. Riddles, jokes, limericks, poems, puns, and finger plays can be used to encourage word play and word enjoyment (see Chapter Three). There are many other books in your school library and local library that also can be used for this purpose.

Word Play

Word play can provide numerous exposures in different contexts that are important to pupils for word meaning knowledge. Children who play with words in interesting ways often show a stronger grasp of meaning than those who do not. Here are several ways to motivate children to engage in word play.

- Ask children *silly questions* about the new words that they have been learning. For example, "Would you like to play with a *wombat*?"

- *Riddles* are extremely motivating to children. To use riddles, children should interact with each other. To construct riddles of their own, children must organize information and decide how this information can be presented in the form of a riddle. Riddles encourage children to use both context clues and interesting material, which can motivate vocabulary development. A brief list of riddle books that can be used with young children is included in Appendix XIII.

- Have children in second and third grades write words in ways that show their meanings. For example, they can write the word *round* in a circle, *up* slanting upward, and down slanting *downward*. Here are examples of this strategy:

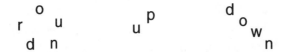

- Have children solve and construct *Hinks Pinks* (see Chapter Five).
- Have children in the upper primary and intermediate grades complete crossword puzzles, word search puzzles, acrostics, and anagrams. These also improve sight word identification.

Semantic Mapping (Webbing)

Semantic maps are a useful strategy for improving meaning vocabulary as well as reading comprehension and for motivating writing. Semantic maps for vocabulary or concept development can be used both *before* and *after* reading. Semantic maps also can be called *semantic webs*, *story webs*, *advance organizers*, *graphic organizers*, or *think-links*. However, they all are very similar in purpose and format. Most children prefer semantic maps to semantic webs since with webs they have to write the vocabulary terms inside the circles on the web, which may be difficult to do.

To construct a map or web, first show a completed map using the target vocabulary terms. With young children the map should be fairly simple to construct and complete. Demonstrate to the children that a map shows the relationships between the vocabulary terms. Then place a partially completed simple semantic map on the chalkboard, transparency, or chart paper and help the children to complete it.

Only after they have had numerous opportunities to work with semantic maps should children be asked to construct or complete a map with a buddy. If semantic mapping is not presented and practiced carefully, a child may become frustrated and never want to use this strategy independently or with a partner again.

Here is a simple semantic map for children in the upper primary grades that has been constructed about "*Animals of the Forest.*"

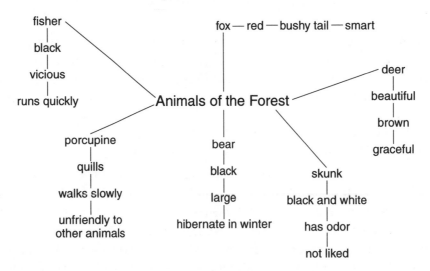

A simple *synonym* or *antonym semantic web* can be used in second or third grade with children of average or above average reading ability. It probably would be too difficult for most children with special needs. Provide the child with a target word for the middle of the web and have him or her either independently or with a partner(s) add as many synonyms or antonyms as possible. Each web should consist of only antonyms or synonyms. This strategy may encourage children to use less-common vocabulary terms in their writing or speaking. Here are examples of a synonym web and an antonym web.

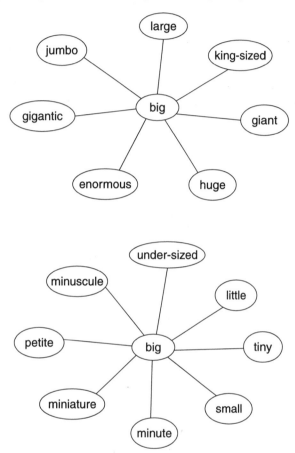

Scaffolding

Scaffolding is effective in encouraging the development of vocabulary and concepts. Scaffolding in reading is partially based on the technique that house painters or carpenters use in their work. Typically, house painters or carpenters do not stand on a ladder. Instead they construct a scaffold of some type by placing a wooden plank between two sawhorses or similar objects. Standing on the scaffold is easier and safer.

In a similar way scaffolding benefits children by providing help instead of asking them to complete a task on their own. In scaffolding an adult may provide a verbal response for a young child who is not able to make that response him/herself. When the baby says *"doggie,"* an adult can say, *"Do you see that doggie walking on a leash? It looks friendly and happy, doesn't it? It looks as if its black fur is very soft and shiny."* In addition to improving the child's vocabulary knowledge, the adult can ask the child to do something that extends his or her knowledge and indicates his or her understanding. Questions that consist of several words are preferable, such as, *"What does that doggie look like?"* or *"Why do you think that the doggie has to walk on a leash?"*

Questions that begin with *what, who, when,* and *where* usually call for one-word answers, while *why* questions often result in more complete answers that have required some thinking. As a child's vocabulary knowledge develops, the adult usually needs to provide less scaffolding.

Reproducibles for Improving Ability in Meaning Vocabulary

Here are two reproducible activity sheets for improving ability in meaning vocabulary. Duplicate and use them in their present form or modify them in any way in which you would like in the light of the abilities, needs, and interests of specific pupils. The activity sheets are

Think of a Synonym
Vocabulary Word Puzzles About Animals

THINK OF A SYNONYM

A *synonym* is a word that means about the same as another word. Read each sentence to yourself and *write a synonym to the underlined word* on the line below the sentence. You can work with a partner(s) or use the thesaurus if you want. The first one has been done for you.

1. Most people are very *glad* when the sun is shining.

   happy, joyful, upbeat, radiant _____

2. A young puppy is often very *naughty*.

   _____

3. The old man fell and *injured* his hip last week.

   _____

4. My mother is the *nicest* person whom I have ever met.

   _____

5. Jackie's sister Beth is very *pretty*.

   _____

6. Pizza is very *good* to eat.

   _____

7. February 5, 2004, was a *cold* and snowy day.

   _____

8. My dog Honey has a *red* tennis ball that she likes to fetch.

   _____

9. Ramon ran as *fast* as he could in the race.

   _____

10. Making a snowman can be *hard* to do if it is very cold outside.

    _____

11. A dog obedience class is *fun* for a young dog.

    _____

THINK OF A SYNONYM *(continued)*

12. Fred's running shoes are really *old*.

_____

13. Ms. Goldman is a very *good* third-grade teacher.

_____

14. I am sailing on a *large* cruise ship in two weeks.

_____

15. Evie would be very *glad* if her family could go to Walt Disney World this year.

_____

16. Mr. Washington seems to be a *rich* man.

_____

17. Mexico is an *interesting* country to visit.

_____

18. Sandi's shirt is *dirty*.

_____

19. Who is the *cutest* girl you know?

_____

20. Davie is the *smartest* boy in our class.

_____

3

VOCABULARY WORD PUZZLES ABOUT ANIMALS

Here are some *vocabulary words about animals. Fill in the missing letters* of each word. When you are finished, check each word to be sure it is correct. You can work with a partner or partners if you would like.

1. c h ___ ___ t a ___

2. t i ___ ___ ___

3. ___ a m b

4. ___ ___ x

5. p o r ___ ___ ___ i n e

6. r a ___ ___ ___ ___ ___ n a k ___

7. g o ___ ___ ___ ___ a

8. w o m ___ ___ t

9. h i ___ ___ o p ___ t ___ m u ___

10. k ___ ___ g a ___ ___ ___

11. f ___ ___ ___ e r

12. ___ ___ i n ___ ___ e r o s

13. w i l d ___ b ___ ___ s t

14. ___ ___ t e ___ ___ ___ e

15. s q ___ ___ r r ___ ___

16. t ___ ___ b ___ ___ w ___ ___ f

17. f ___ ___ ___ ___ t

18. g a ___ ___ ___ ___ e

19. ___ ___ b r a

20. c ___ ___ ___ ___ e

READING COMPREHENSION

Since *reading comprehension* is a complex process closely related to the thought process, it is difficult to summarize in simple terms. Comprehension can be defined as *constructing meaning from the printed material*. It is an interactive process that requires using *prior knowledge* along with *print material*. Therefore, a reading teacher or tutor should consider the characteristics of both the reader and the print material. In the case of the reader, his or her prior knowledge about the material, interest in reading the material, purpose for reading the material, and ability to pronounce the words found in the material should be considered. In the case of the printed material, the *number of difficult words*, the *sentence length*, and the *format* must be considered.

The more prior knowledge a reader has, the less use he or she has to make of the printed material. That is why a specialist in a content area (biology, anthropology, geology, history, economics) normally is able to read material in that area much more rapidly with excellent comprehension than can a person who has less prior knowledge.

Comprehension also can be described as *making connections* between what the reader knows and does not know or between the old and the new material. Comprehension is an *evolving process* that starts even before the reader opens a book, changes as the material is read, and continues to be modified after the book is finished. The developmental nature of comprehension is increased as the reader interacts with others about the material after it has been read. Therefore, whole-class or small-group discussion about mutually read material should occur on a regular basis.

An important recently emphasized aspect of comprehension is *metacognition (self-monitoring)*, a reader's awareness of his or her own thinking while attempting to understand the material. Research has found that *good readers are significantly better at monitoring their comprehension than are poor readers*.

Research also has found close relationships between *comprehension* and *word identification* (Adams, 1991). Therefore, developing word identification (decoding) strategies is very important. However, remember that the use of word identification strategies is only a means of determining the meaning of print material, not an end in itself. When good decoders have problems with comprehension, they need help in developing language proficiency and listening comprehension.

Different Levels of Comprehension

In theory, comprehension can only be divided into two main categories—*vocabulary knowledge (word meaning)* and *understanding the reading material*. However, in this book I have categorized comprehension into four main levels, as I believe that it is important to try to teach the most important aspects of comprehension separately to most children, especially those with special needs such as learning or reading disabilities.

Here are the various levels of comprehension and the most important subskills that comprise them (Miller, 2001).

Textually Explicit (Literal or Factual—"Right There") Comprehension

- Answering "right there" questions that are directly found in the material;
- Placing items in correct sequence or order;
- Locating directly stated main ideas;

- Locating significant and irrelevant details; and
- Reading and following directions.

Textually Implicit (Interpretive or Inferential—"Think and Search") Comprehension

- Answering "think and search" questions (the reader has to deduce the answers from reading the material—they are merely inferred);
- Answering questions that call for interpretation (the answer is not directly found in the material);
- Predicting outcomes;
- Drawing conclusions and generalizations;
- Locating implied main ideas;
- Sensing the author's mood and purpose; and
- Summarizing what was read.

Critical (Textually Implicit or Evaluative—"Think and Search") Comprehension

- Answering questions in which the reader must evaluate or judge the reading material;
- Discriminating between real and make-believe (fact and fantasy);
- Evaluating the accuracy or truthfulness of the material;
- Determining an author's biases; and
- Recognizing propaganda techniques such as the bandwagon effect, testimonials, the halo effect, emotionally toned words, and card stacking.

Scriptally Implicit (Script Implicit, Schema Implicit, Applied or Creative—"On My Own") Comprehension

- Answering "on my own" questions (the reader has to combine his or her prior knowledge with the print material to arrive at new knowledge or actions);
- Application of knowledge to one's own life for problem solving;
- Using *bibliotherapy* (solving a problem through reading about a similar problem);
- Participating in art and construction activities as a follow-up to reading;
- Cooking and baking activities after reading recipes (including those with rebuses);
- Participating in rhythm and music activities as a follow-up to reading;
- Creative writing of prose and poetry (using invented spelling if necessary);
- Creative dramatics and sociodrama;
- Puppetry;
- Conducting scientific experiments and demonstrations;
- Creative book reports; and
- Reading material that greatly appeals to the emotions (the affective aspects of reading).

Some subskills of reading comprehension mentioned earlier are not applicable with young children, while others are. However, all children, including those with special needs, can make a start in all four levels of comprehension and should be provided with many opportunities to do so in preschool, kindergarten, and the primary grades.

Strategies for Improving Ability in Comprehension Skills

Here are several classroom-tested strategies for improving ability in the various elements of reading comprehension. Modify any of them in the light of the needs, abilities, and interests of specific pupils. Most of them are applicable for all young children, including those with special needs, with some modifications.

Prediction Strategies

Prediction strategies are very effective in improving the reading comprehension of young children. In addition, they are very easy to implement. If children make predictions about the content of reading material before and during reading, their comprehension improves significantly. Predictions can begin as early as the preschool level, by asking young children to make simple predictions about story content from hearing the title of a book and during the reading aloud of the book. Before listening to or reading a book, children can answer such prediction questions as these:

- What do you think this book (story) will be about?
- What do you think will happen in this book (story)?
- What would you like to have happen in this book (story)?

During the reading of a book or story, the following questions can be posed:

- What do you think will happen next in this book (story)?
- What would you like to have happen next in this book (story)?
- What do you think (story character) will do next in this book (story)?
- What do you think (story character) should do next in this book (story)?

Two other effective prediction strategies that are applicable for use in kindergarten and/or the primary grades are the *Directed Listening-Thinking Activity (DL-TA)* and the *Directed Reading-Thinking Activity (DR-TA)*. These two prediction strategies follow the same general format except that in DL-TA the children *listen* to the material, while in DR-TA they *read* it for themselves. Both were developed in some form by the late Russell G. Stauffer of the University of Delaware (1975, 1980). Both are useful since they involve prediction and listening (reading) with precise purposes. Both encourage *active involvement* with the reading material by having children make predictions about the material content and then checking the accuracy of their predictions to confirm or disconfirm them.

Here are the basic steps of both DL-TA and DR-TA:

1. Have children listen to (read) the title of the narrative or informational book or story and then, considering this title and their prior knowledge, formulate

predictions about the book content. If desired, in the DR-TA the child can dictate or write the predictions.

2. Tell the children that they should listen to (read) the trade book to determine whether the material confirms or disconfirms the predictions that they made. Then have the children listen to (read) the book a section at a time.

3. After the book or story has been completed, have the children discuss their predictions, indicating which ones were confirmed and which ones were not. Help the children determine the criteria that should be used in deciding whether or not the predictions were confirmed. This portion of the DR-TA also can be dictated or written if desired.

4. If the book was not entirely read at one time, alternate periods of silent reading and discussion until the entire book has been read.

In each case, emphasize the validity of the child's reasoning rather than the accuracy of the original predictions.

Story Impressions

Story impressions are a helpful strategy for improving comprehension of narrative material such as narrative trade books or stories. Story impressions can be used successfully in second and third grades with children of average and above average ability. Children with special needs also can use this interesting strategy with teacher or tutor help.

Here are the steps that comprise story impressions:

1. Select an interesting narrative trade book at the appropriate grade level with a clearly delineated plot and clearly defined characters.

2. As you read this trade book, choose about six to eight key words from the book that will serve as the story impression clues. These clues should be about the story characters or important story events.

3. Write these clues in a list on the chalkboard or a transparency.

4. Have the children formulate a prediction about the reading material from each story clue. Number each of their predictions. Encourage the children to make logical, and also creative, predictions.

5. Have each child read the book, focusing on deciding whether or not the predictions were correct. This strategy encourages purposeful, motivated reading, which should lead to improved comprehension.

6. After the children have finished reading the entire trade book, they should re-examine their predictions. Each prediction that proved to be correct should remain as it is. Each prediction that proved to be incorrect should be corrected by having the children dictate the correct story summary opposite the inaccurate prediction.

Here are the advantages of story impressions:

- It gives children specific purposes for reading, and thus their comprehension usually improves greatly.
- It helps children learn to make valid and logical predictions.
- It encourages children to read relevant, interesting trade books and stories.

To provide an example, I have selected *The Giving Tree* by Shel Silverstein. This book is about a tree that loves a boy and wants to give parts of itself to the boy when he comes to visit it. The tree continues giving to the boy throughout his life until he is an old man. This book illustrates the joy of giving of oneself to make others' lives better.

Here are sample story impressions clues for this book.

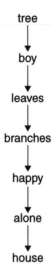

tree

boy

leaves

branches

happy

alone

house

A reading teacher or tutor can write his or her own predictions about this book in the Predictive Story Summary portion of a copy of the following reproducible activity sheet. Then find the trade book and read it. After you have read it, do not add anything to the correct predictions, but write the correct story summary opposite any incorrect predictions. Many adults may find that this activity is somewhat challenging.

1 | **2** | **3**

STORY IMPRESSIONS ACTIVITY SHEET

Predictive Story Summary　　　　**Actual Story Summary**

Wide Reading of Motivating Materials

Wide reading of interesting, motivating, relevant, easy materials is the single best way to improve reading comprehension. The main goal of such reading always should be understanding. Such reading can take place in narrative and informational trade books, predictable books, other easy-to-read books, chapter books, supplementary readers, poetry, children's magazines and newspapers, and relevant computer software. The child always should have specific purposes for reading, monitor his or her comprehension, and be prepared in some way to show that he or she has understood the material.

Question-Answer Relationships Strategies

Questioning strategies or *question-answer relationships (QARs)* can be used both as an assessment strategy and as a teaching strategy for comprehension. QAR instruction encourages children to use both prior knowledge and the reading material when answering comprehension questions. The relationship for questions with answers directly stated in the material in one sentence can be called "Right There." Children should look for appropriate words in the question and then read the sentence that contains the answer.

The relationship between questions and answers in the material that requires information by synthesizing several sentences or paragraphs is called "Think and Search." The relationship between questions for which the answers have to come from the child's own prior knowledge and result in a new creation is called "On My Own."

Reading teachers and tutors should ask all children, including those with special needs, mainly "Think and Search" and "On My Own" questions. Children should be encouraged to respond at the higher levels of comprehension. A number of reading teachers and tutors still place too much emphasis on lower-level questions at the expense of higher-level questions, because lower-level questions are much easier to construct and evaluate. If children have not been asked many "Think and Search" and "On My Own" questions, they may never become adept at answering these questions. All young children, including those with special needs, can begin to answer questions that evaluate higher-level comprehension.

Modeling the decision about the questions to ask is an important part of teaching about them. *Supervised practice* following a teacher's modeling also is very important in ensuring that children learn how to formulate and answer higher-level comprehension questions.

Poetry

Children's poetry is an important way of improving both listening and comprehension skills. Since poetry is condensed writing, every word is very important, and comprehension is thus emphasized. Poetry also encourages visual imagery because of its sensory descriptions, and it introduces delightful ideas. In addition, poetry provides opportunities for a child to learn new words, ideas, and attitudes and to experience life through the eyes of poets. Poetry has form and order and often is easy to remember.

Poetry can be used for the following purposes with young children:

- To demonstrate the pleasure of hearing interesting, motivating sounds;
- To improve the understanding of rhyming;

- To improve children's imagination and creativity;
- To provide enjoyment through the use of poetry that contains silly, creative words and humor; and
- To improve the self-esteem and self-confidence of children.

Here are some types of poetry:

- *Limerick*—Five lines of verse set in a specific rhyming pattern that usually is humorous and creative.
- *Narrative*—Poetry that tells a story or describes an event or happening.
- *Lyric*—Descriptive poetry that usually has a song or rhythmic quality.
- *Free or blank verse*—Poetry that does not rhyme.
- *Haiku*—An ancient but presently popular Japanese verse that contains three lines consisting of seventeen syllables and often dealing with nature as its subject.
- *Nonsense verse*—Poetry that usually is ridiculous.

Displaying poems in prominent places in the classroom or tutoring setting may help to create interest in poetry. Place appropriate pictures or illustrations near the poems. Pictures and flannel boards can be used to present poetry in an interesting way. A poem can be enjoyed either indoors or outdoors or at the end of a lesson to reward children for good work.

A reading teacher or tutor can create his or her own personalized poems for the class or the student(s) being tutored. The following suggestions for writing poetry may help:

- Use frequent rhyming.
- Vary the rhythm pattern.
- Use rhythms that encourage moving, singing, or chanting.
- Use themes and concepts that are familiar to the children.
- Use words that children can easily understand.
- Make each line an independent thought.
- Use as many action verbs as possible.
- Include as many visual images as possible in each line.

Some books with poetry that are likely to appeal to young children can be found in Appendix XIV.

Visual Imagery

Visual imagery, sometimes called *mental imagery*, is an interesting strategy for improving the comprehension of young children. It is effective if children are given material that lends itself well to constructing mental images of what they have read. Creating visual images enhances the use of prior knowledge, improves the ability to make predictions and inferences, and can increase retention of what is read.

One reason that visual imagery is effective is that it is an *active process*. Creating one's own mental images often is more effective than is using someone else's creations. Imaging is a fairly easy skill to teach and use.

One way of improving mental imaging ability is to have children read high-interest material and ask them to attempt to picture the main characters, the setting, or the events in the book. Some useful titles for this purpose are listed in Appendix XV.

The Herringbone Technique

The *herringbone technique* is effective in improving reading comprehension ability at the second-grade reading level and above. This strategy helps children to find important information in either narrative or content material by asking the following six basic comprehension questions: *Who? What? When? Where? How?* and *Why?*

Construct a fish outline or a plain outline and put it on poster board. Feel free to use the reproducible diagram on the next page. If you laminate the outline, it can be used again and again. Young children usually like the fish outline better. Show the outline of the strategy on the chalkboard or a transparency. Be sure to explain and demonstrate thoroughly, and provide supervised practice for the children before asking them to complete it independently or with a partner(s). Once the strategy is clear, have the child dictate (write) the main idea on the horizontal line and the appropriate details that answer the six target questions on the slanted lines of the outline. Depending on the reading material, they can complete the herringbone form either as they are reading (usually preferable) or when they have finished.

After children have completed this technique, conduct a follow-up group discussion. Help the children determine that the material does not always contain all of the information needed to complete the herringbone diagram and that sometimes the information required on the outline is not very helpful in understanding the material. If a few children think that some of the missing information may be important, encourage them to locate it using other resources.

Strategies Using Puppets

Puppets are very useful in teaching reading skills, especially for young children, including those with special needs. Sometimes a puppet may be the only tool that can motivate children to practice reading. Using a puppet often transforms the stress of the difficult task into highly motivated practice.

Koos (1986) stated this about using puppets:

Imagine a lifeless puppet lying on a table. Suddenly, a child slips his [her] hand into the puppet and it awakens to a life and personality of its own. Magic happens, and the world of make-believe begins. Children love to pretend, and puppetry allows them to create. (p. 56)

Name: _____ **Grade:** _____

HERRINGBONE DIAGRAM

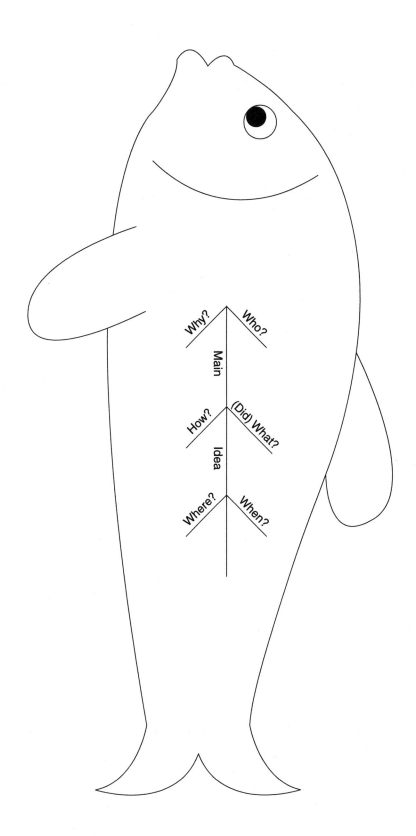

Why? Who?

Main

How? (Did) What?

Idea

Where? When?

Using puppets is an example of *applied* or *creative reading*—the highest level of the reading process. Here are several ways to use puppets:

- Have the children present simple puppet skits and plays. Some of these can follow up on trade books or stories that have been heard or read.

- Provide props and puppet theaters so children can use them in puppet skits and plays.

- Locate resources in the local community that provide puppet presentations: groups of puppeteers, high school or elementary school classes, and individuals who are adept at puppet presentations.

- Have children use puppets while reading parts aloud in a trade book or story.

- During tutoring sessions have the child be a puppeteer.

- Encourage shy children to use puppets while talking with each other or with a reading teacher or tutor.

Puppets can be placed into two general categories—those operated with the *hands and fingers* or those that *dangle on a string*. The latter are called *marionettes. Hand puppets* are very popular with young children since they are quite easy to construct and use. Moving arms and pliable faces on puppets enhance their use for characterization and action. Rubber, plastic, and papier-mâché heads are durable, and cloth faces encourage a wide variety of facial expressions.

Here are the directions for constructing several motivating puppets. You can modify the puppets as you wish.

Baby Deer Bag Puppet

Materials Needed

Brown lunch bag, brown and black construction paper scraps, white poster paint, scissors, white glue.

Directions for Constructing the Baby Deer Puppet

1. Fold back the two bottom corners of a flattened brown bag to form the nose of the deer. Glue the folded corners to hold them in place.

2. Cut eyes and a nose from the black construction paper. Glue the nose on the bottom of the bag between the two folder corners. Glue the eyes on above the nose.

3. Cut two ears for the deer from the brown construction paper. Glue them in place above the eyes.

4. Dip an index finger in the white paint and paint white spots on the baby deer.

Here is an illustration of this puppet.

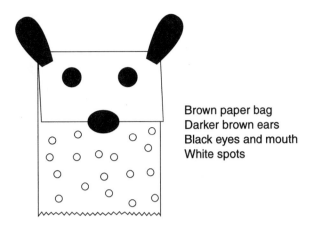

Brown paper bag
Darker brown ears
Black eyes and mouth
White spots

Coat Hanger Puppets

Materials Needed

Coat hangers, old nylon stockings, cloth tape, yarn, felt scraps, buttons, wiggle eyes, scissors, glue.

Directions for Constructing the Coat Hanger Puppets

1. Stretch each hanger into a diamond shape, and then pull the stocking over it and tie it at the bottom.

2. Bend the hook into an oval and tape it in place so it won't poke the children.

3. Decorate the puppets in whatever way you would like. Be as creative as possible.

4. Name these puppets and present a simple puppet show with them.

Tooth Puppet

Materials Needed

Paper plate, crayons or markers, glue, packing peanuts.

Directions for Constructing the Tooth Puppet

Draw a face on the top side of a folded paper plate. Glue the Styrofoam pieces along the outside edge inside the fold of the plate so that they look like teeth. Packing peanuts that are rectangular shaped work the best. To work the puppet, hold it with both hands and then open and close the puppet's tooth-filled mouth to make it "talk."

Lamb Puppet

Materials Needed

Crayons, markers or paint, white felt, black construction paper, scissors, hot glue/hot glue gun, glue sticks (optional), cotton balls (optional).

Directions for Constructing the Lamb Puppet

1. Color or paint the lamb's face.

2. Tear apart the cotton balls and glue small pieces onto the lamb's head.

3. Cut out the head.

4. Use the head/body piece, hands, and feet as patterns. Trace and cut the head/body and leg piece out of white felt. Cut two layers for each piece. Trace and cut the hands and feet out of black construction paper.

5. *This part is to be done by an adult only.* Go to an area away from the children. Use a hot glue gun to glue the two body pieces together for the lamb around all edges except the bottom. Then use a hot glue gun or regular glue stick to glue the face onto the felt hand/body pieces and glue hands and feet onto the body piece.

Here is an illustration of the lamb puppet.

Mitten Family Puppet

Materials Needed

Glove, felt scraps, craft glue, yarn, plastic eyes, lace scrap for baby's bonnet.

Directions for Constructing the Mitten Family Puppet

1. Cut out five felt circles about 1 inch to 1½ inches for the faces of the mitten family.

2. Decorate each circle with felt cutouts for faces, ear, and hair. Glue on yarn for the hair, and glue on plastic eyes. Glue on lace trim for the baby's bonnet.

3. Glue the faces to the thumb and fingertips of the glove on the palm side. Then add lace, felt, or ribbon for decoration on the fingers of the glove.

Busy Bee Puppet

Materials Needed

Paper plate, a stretchy black glove, glue, wiggle eyes, felt, 1-inch pom-pom, pipe cleaner.

Directions for Constructing the Busy Bee Puppet

1. Color the paper plate whatever flower color you want.

2. Cut around the edge of the paper plate to make petal shapes. (See the illustration below.)

3. Cut a hole in the center of the paper plate that is large enough for an index finger to fit through.

4. Put on the glove and poke an index finger through the hole in the paper plate. The finger will be the bee puppet.

5. Glue the pom-pom to the end of the finger. Glue the wiggle eyes onto the pom-pom.

6. Cut short pieces of pipe cleaner for the antennae of the bee, and glue them onto the pom-pom. Cut thin strips of yellow felt and glue them around the finger to look like the bee's stripes.

7. Use felt and make wings for the bee and glue them on.

8. Once the glue is dry, you can slip your hand into the glove and play with the puppet. You can make your bee move around.

Colorful Uncle Sam Puppet

Materials Needed

Two-inch white plastic-foam ball, two 4-inch paper cups (colored red, white, and blue if possible), 9-inch square of blue fabric with stars, 3/16-inch to 1/4-inch by 11-inch dowel, 3-inch circle of stiff paper or light cardboard, 1/2 yard of 1/4-inch wide red ribbon, scraps of white and flesh felt, white glue or hot glue gun, straight pins, white acrylic paint, black marking pen.

Directions for Constructing the Colorful Uncle Sam Puppet

1. Glue 1/2 inch at one end of dowel into the white ball. Poke hole and insert the dowel down through center bottom of one cup.

2. Cut 9-inch by 5-inch fabric. Adult: Hot-glue 1/2 inch at lower 9 inches of fabric, right side out, inside the cup about 1/4 inch below top. Gather the top of fabric around the base of the ball, making a 1-inch collar. Then glue it. Tie ribbon around the "*gathers.*" Pull the stick down to hide the ball. Push it up to show the ball and fabric.

3. Cut 1½-inch diameter flesh felt circle for face. Cut white oval beard/mustache with an opening for the mouth. Glue the beard to the face with white glue. Make dot eyes with a marker. Paint white eyebrows.

4. Cut off lower 1½ inches of second cup to use for the top of the hat. To make it narrower, cut 3/4-inch wide vertical strip from the side, and then cut a slit from the side to center bottom. Overlap the sides about 1/4 inch, slitting the edge of the bottom so they interlock, and then glue.

5. Glue the fabric circle to the top of the paper circle for the hat brim. Glue the hat top to the brim. Glue the face and hat to the ball, securing the hat with straight pins into the ball.

Frog Puppet from a Paper Bag

Materials Needed

Paper lunch bag, paper and a printer, green paint or green construction paper, scissors, glue and/or tape, crayons or markers.

Directions for Constructing the Frog Puppet

1. The paper lunch bag should be closed and flat, and the smooth side will be the back of the puppet. The tab on the lunch bag will be the puppet's head. Underneath the tab will be the puppet's mouth. Three-fourths of the lunch bag will be the body of the puppet.

2. Make sure there is a side flap of paper into which the child can slip his or her arms.

3. Paint the front of the lunch bag green or trace the body and head of the paper bag onto green construction paper. Cut it out and glue it to the bag.

4. Print the template pieces. Color the largest circles and arms green. Color the long rectangle piece red on the front and back. Color the smallest circles black. Cut out all the pieces.

5. Glue the two white circles onto the two green circles. Now you have two eyes.

6. Take the long red rectangle and wrap it around a pencil to make it curl. This will be the frog's tongue.

7. Glue the eyes onto the top of the head so they stick up over the head.

8. Draw two tiny black lines for nostrils onto the head.

9. Lift the flap and glue the tongue underneath.

10. Glue the arms into the side flap. When you do this, glue or tape them onto the top of the flap. When you are using the puppet, its arms will reach forward instead of bending backwards.

11. Cut feet in one of the shapes below out of green construction paper. Bend the tabs at the top of the feet and glue or tape the tabs onto the inside of the paper bag. This will give the feet a "floppy" feel.

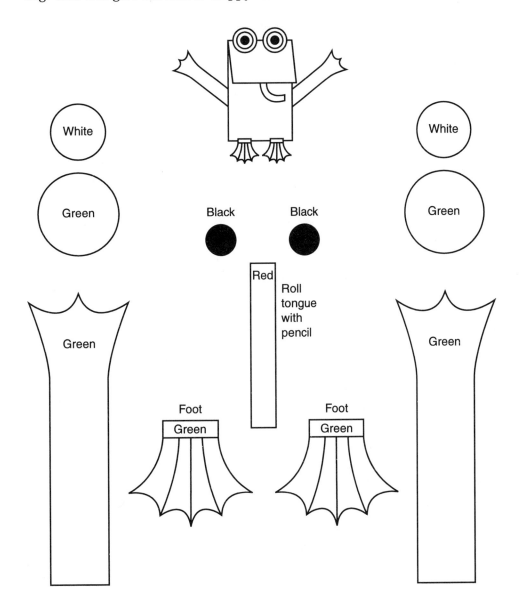

Rabbit Marionette

Materials Needed

Pieces of cardboard, cotton balls, pieces of white yarn, white thread, two 3/4-inch by 6-inch craft sticks, glue, masking tape.

Directions for Constructing the Rabbit Marionette

1. Make the rabbit body out of cardboard. Print out the pattern on the next page and transfer it to cardboard or draw your own rabbit about 3 inches by 6½ inches (make two rabbit bodies). Do the same with rabbit feet 1½ inches by 2 inches and cut out four feet.

2. Next take the cardboard body piece and place it with the plain/clean side down. Spread glue on the rabbit's body so it is completely covered, but not soaked, in glue. Set yarn pieces (one for each leg) where the rabbit's legs will go, extending about 1½ inches onto the body piece. Cover with the second rabbit body piece (good side up). Using a strong needle an adult should carefully poke a small hole for thread to go through the head between the ears about 1/4 inch or less down.

3. Make the rabbit's back feet. Take one rabbit foot piece (good side up). Cover it with glue. Place the end of leg yarn overlapping 1/2 inch to 3/4 inch on the foot where the ankle would be. Cover with the second foot piece, good side up. Repeat to make the second rabbit paw. Carefully poke small holes for thread to go through, right in the center of each foot.

4. Take the cotton balls and, gently finding the edge, unroll them. This will form "cotton sheets." When there are enough sheets to cover the rabbit's body front and back, spread glue on the front of the bunny body (all over but not too thick). Place sheets of cotton on the rabbit horizontally starting at one end of the rabbit and leaving the sheet hanging off the other edge. Cover the rabbit's face and body first, and then center a smaller length of cotton sheet centered over each ear. When the entire front of the rabbit is covered and glued, let it dry.

5. When the rabbit is dry, turn it over and spread glue on the back of the body and finish wrapping cotton sheets, adding more cotton if necessary, and let dry.

6. Wrap the rabbit feet in cotton and then let dry.

7. Make the rabbit features. Roll cotton into one 3/4-inch ball for the tail; two 1/2-inch balls for the cheeks; one 1/4-inch ball for the nose; two 1-inch flattened balls for the front paws. Make two stitches with white thread to form the toes. Place the eyes, nose, cheeks, feet, and tail on the rabbit. Let them dry.

8. Glue two craft sticks together as shown in the illustration and let dry.

9. Using a needle, pull thread through the holes on the rabbit's head and tie securely. Then let the thread extend 4 to 6 inches and wrap the end on the longest part of the craft stick, making sure the crosswise stick is on top for support, and tape it securely with masking tape. Then pull more thread through the hole on the rabbit's paw, sewing a few stitches directly to the cotton and knotting to secure the thread on the base of each foot. (Leave 14 to 16 inches of thread extending from the foot.) When both paws are finished, hold the bunny up by the craft sticks and attach the string so that the legs hang down, but the string is not loose or tight. Fasten to the craft stick (crosswise stick) with masking tape. Let the string hang down in back of the stick (see the illustration). Repeat with the other foot.

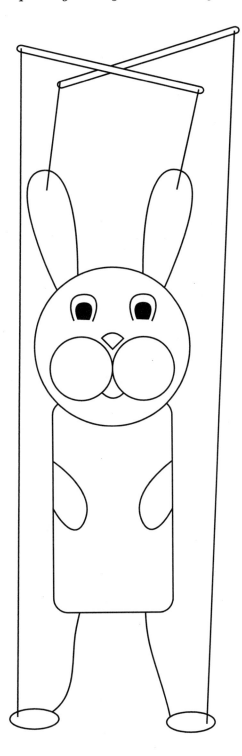

Activities to Develop Sequencing Ability

A few activities can be used with young children to help them develop the ability to place a number of items in *correct sequence*. Since sequencing is a complex reading skill, only a beginning can be made in this skill in the primary grades. Begin to teach this skill by having children place items *in correct sequence*, progressing to about four to five items in third grade. A number of third-grade children will find this task difficult. Sequencing usually starts with actual objects and then progresses to activity sheets.

Here are several suggestions for providing instruction and/or practice in placing items in correct sequence.

- Locate a simple comic strip with five or fewer frames. Cut the comic strip apart by frames and then laminate the frames. To make this activity self-checking, place the correct sequence number on the back of each comic strip frame before laminating it. Have children try to reassemble the comic strip by placing it in correct sequence. If you want, each broken-out comic strip can be placed into a large envelope.

- Omit a frame from a broken-out comic strip and have children infer what is missing and then write a description about it.

- Omit the last frame and have children infer and write an ending for the strip.

- Remove some dialogue from the balloons and have children infer and write in the appropriate dialogue.

- You also can construct your own activity sheets or purchase commercial activity sheets that emphasize sequencing. This type of activity sheet may look like the following:

Place the items on this activity sheet in the correct order.

_____ She bought a black puppy that she named "Honey."
_____ Allie wants to buy a new black puppy.
_____ She found a puppy to buy in a newspaper ad.

Activities for Improving Ability to Follow Directions

Many elementary school children have not been taught to read and follow directions. Many adults also have difficulty in reading and following directions effectively. Therefore, a beginning should be made in this important reading skill in the primary grades.

Here are several simple strategies:

- Write directions on the chalkboard for recess activities or getting into a line in the classroom. Try to encourage children into the habit of following these directions without an oral explanation from the teacher or tutor.

- Write directions on the chalkboard for paper folding or other simple activities that children can do at their seats. Have the children read and follow these directions in a step-by-step manner.

- Ask the children to write the directions for playing a very simple game. Have them read their directions and discuss whether or not they could learn to play the game from a child's written directions.

- Encourage the children to read and follow simple directions such as those found in workbooks and target arithmetic word problems without help.

Discriminating Between Real and Make-Believe and Between Fact and Opinion

Discriminating between *real* and *make-believe* and between *fact* and *opinion* are both elements of "Think and Search" comprehension, or critical reading. Since critical reading is an essential skill in a democratic society, it is important that young children make a beginning in it.

Only a few children in first grade, and a number of children in second grade, may be able to discriminate between real and make-believe. Ask children if they believe that a trade book or story that they have heard or read for themselves is real or make-believe and share reasons why they gave the answer they did. As an example, children can understand that books and stories in which animals talk or behave as humans in some way must be make-believe since animals cannot behave that way in real life.

By third grade children can be given a series of statements and asked to determine whether they are *fact* or *opinion*. Since this is a difficult skill for many young children to master, it should be presented in detail, with opportunities to practice. Here are several examples that could be contained on an activity sheet for this purpose:

Fact or Opinion

A snake is a dangerous pet for a child.	(O)
An adult cocker spaniel weighs about twenty-eight pounds.	(F)
A dog is a better pet for a child than a cat.	(O)
My mother is the best cook in our city.	(O)
A deer is an animal that eats various kinds of plants.	(F)
Most old people are quite grumpy.	(O)
A lion is an animal that lives in Africa.	(F)
Reading is the easiest subject to learn in school.	(O)
It is safer to fly in an airplane than to ride in an automobile.	(F)
It is more fun to live in an apartment building than in a house.	(O)

Some key phrases can help children determine that what they are reading is make-believe, such as *once upon a time, in a make-believe land called . . ., the cat said, the pig wore a pink dress*, and others.

Other Strategies for Improving Comprehension

Many additional strategies can be used to improve various elements of comprehension. Only a few are listed here; however, you can consult the professional books in the Bibliography for many more suggestions. All of them have been used successfully in teaching and tutoring young children:

- Careful observation of punctuation marks such as periods, commas, question marks, and exclamation points;

- Putting a number of items—and later words—into the correct category (categorization or classification activities);

- Calling the attention of the children to such connecting words as *and, but, or,* and *however;*

- Allowing children to have time to answer comprehension questions without being rushed, which is especially important with higher-level questions;

- Encouraging children to use *text look-backs,* looking back in the reading material to locate the answer to a specific question;

- Writing a text for a wordless (textless) book;

- Participating in creative dramatics;

- Participating in such creative writing activities as writing an ending to an incomplete story, writing an alternative ending to an incomplete story, composing a simple poem, or personal writing as a follow-up to reading;

- Reading a book that encourages reading (A list of such books was compiled by Graves, Juel, and Graves [2003].); and

- Listening to music that encourages writing. (Music can often be very easily related to reading. Jacobi-Karna [1996] provides an extensive list of children's books that encourage musical activities.)

Reproducibles for Improving Ability in Comprehension

Following are four reproducible activity sheets for improving ability in reading comprehension. Duplicate them and use them in their present form or modify them in any way to suit the needs, abilities, and interests of specific pupils. The activity sheets are

> *Riddles*
> *Anticipation/Reaction Guide*
> *Determining Fact or Opinion*
> *Reading a Passage and Drawing a Picture About It*

RIDDLES

Read each of these riddles to yourself. Then *write the answer* to it on the line below it. You can work with a partner(s) if you want.

What Am I?

1. I live in Africa on the grassy plains.

    I have light brown fur.

    I am called the "king of all the animals."

    What am I? _____

2. I live in the big woods.

    I usually have gray fur.

    I am a wild animal that is very much like a dog.

    What am I? _____

3. I am a very large gray animal.

    I can live in a zoo or a circus.

    A person can ride high on my back.

    What am I? _____

4. I am an animal that lives in Africa.

    I have beautiful spotted fur.

    I can run faster than any other animal.

    What am I? _____

5. I am a farm animal.

    I am a clean animal, although some people don't think so.

    Another name for me is "hog."

    What am I? _____

6. I am a fairly large animal.

    A person can ride on me.

    I am often photographed in movies and on TV.

    What am I? _____

7. I am a tame animal.

   I am descended from wolves.

   I am called man's (woman's) "best friend."

   What am I?_____

8. I live in the woods.

   I am black and white.

   Other animals usually try to stay away from me.

   What am I?_____

9. I live in the woods.

   I often walk slowly.

   Since I have sharp quills other animals usually stay away from me.

   What am I?_____

10. I live in the country of Australia.

    I carry my baby in a pouch.

    I can hop for a long distance.

    What am I?_____

11. I am a small rodent.

    I often live outside unless I can find a way into a house.

    Sometimes I get caught in a trap.

    What am I?_____

12. I live on the grassy plains of Africa.

    I look somewhat like a small horse.

    I have black and white stripes.

    What am I?_____

13. I am a tame animal.

    I often am somewhat independent.

    I use a litter box when I live in someone's home.

    What am I?_____

RIDDLES *(continued)*

14. I am a farm animal.

    I usually live in a herd.

    I can be used for either milk or beef.

    What am I?_____

15. I am a small animal.

    I can have either brown, gray, black, or white fur.

    I live in trees.

    What am I?_____

16. I live on the grassy plains of Africa.

    I eat the leaves from tall trees.

    I have a very long neck.

    What am I?_____

17. I live in Africa.

    I have beautiful fur with spots.

    Since I am an endangered animal, I should never be killed for my fur.

    What am I?_____

18. I am a medium-sized animal with gray fur.

    I can hang from a tree with my rat-like tail.

    I am in danger whenever I cross city streets and highways.

    What am I?_____

19. I live in the big woods.

    I am a beautiful brown graceful animal.

    I may make a snorting type of noise.

    What am I?_____

20. I am a large animal that lives in the woods.

    I often have black fur.

    I hibernate (sleep) during the winter.

    What am I?_____

ANTICIPATION/REACTION GUIDE

This passage will tell you why people today use "*hello*" as a form of greeting. Before you read it, write T (*True*) or F (*False*) on the line under the word *Before* to show what you think is true now. After you have read the passage, write T or F on the line under the word *After* to show what you learned by reading.

Before   *After*

_____ _____   1. Thomas Edison invented the use of the word "*hello*" when he was the first person to say it over the telephone.

_____ _____   2. In ancient times people greeted each other with "*hallow*," which probably came from the old French word "*hola.*"

_____ _____   3. By the time the telephone was invented, people were saying "*hullo*," which later became "*hello.*"

_____ _____   4. Alexander Graham Bell, who invented the telephone, liked using the word "*hello*" as a greeting when talking on it.

_____ _____   5. The greeting "*hello*" was included in the dictionary shortly after the telephone was invented.

_____ _____   6. Today dictionaries promote "*hello*" as a standard greeting in our language.

The Invention of "*Hello*"

You may say "hello" softly or loudly, but the person at the other end of a telephone knows that you are greeting him or her.

Although Thomas Edison was the first person to say "hello" as a greeting over the telephone, he did not invent the use of the word "hello." This greeting had been used for centuries before the invention of the telephone in 1885.

In ancient times, people greeted each other with "hallow," which may have come from the old French word "hola," meaning "stop" or "whoa." By the time the telephone was invented, Americans were saying "hullo" to each other every day. Then it was just a small jump to using the word "hello." However, it wasn't until the telephone was invented that "hello" began to be used as a common form of greeting and as a way of establishing contact with other people.

Edison made "hello" a popular greeting and an important part of our lives. However, Alexander Graham Bell, who invented the telephone, never liked "hello" and wanted to use "ahoy" as the telephone greeting. As more people had telephones, the greeting of "hello" became more popular. Dictionaries have included the word "hello" for more than 100 years.

Alexander Graham Bell probably would not be happy that his form of greeting, "ahoy," was never used, and "hello" took its place.

DETERMINING FACT OR OPINION

Read each of these sentences to yourself. Some sentences are *true statements*, while the others are *statements of opinion*. In the blank in front of each sentence write the letter *F* if the statement is true, or write the letter *O* if the statement is an opinion.

_____ 1. A small dog is a better pet for an older person than a large dog.

_____ 2. Dingoes, or wild dogs, are quite commonly found in Australia.

_____ 3. It never snows on the island of Barbados, which is located in the southern Caribbean.

_____ 4. It is more interesting to read a book than to play a computer game.

_____ 5. A rattlesnake is a poisonous snake that can be found in the southwestern state of Arizona.

_____ 6. All children enjoy reading a Harry Potter book by J. K. Rowling.

_____ 7. My mother is the best mother that any child could have.

_____ 8. Midway Airport is located on the south side of the city of Chicago.

_____ 9. Fall is the most beautiful season of the year in the Northeast.

_____ 10. Boys are better in sports than are girls.

_____ 11. Salt Lake City is the capital of the state of Utah.

_____ 12. Many children today are not getting enough exercise.

_____ 13. Alaska is the most interesting state in the United States to visit.

_____ 14. A hamster is a better pet for a young child than a ferret.

_____ 15. Both English and French are spoken in the eastern part of Canada.

_____ 16. A maple tree is a deciduous tree that loses its leaves in the fall.

_____ 17. A golden retriever is a larger dog than a cocker spaniel.

_____ 18. A tornado is an example of a natural disaster.

_____ 19. Every child in the United States likes to eat pizza.

_____ 20. Joey's father is a plumber for the Jackson Company.

_____ 21. Everyone should attend college after high school.

_____ 22. The state of Florida usually is quite warm in the winter.

_____ 23. Thanksgiving always occurs in the month of November.

_____ 24. Since dragonflies eat many mosquitoes during the summer, they are considered helpful insects.

_____ 25. "Holly" is a good name for a dog.

READING A PASSAGE AND DRAWING A PICTURE ABOUT IT

Read this passage about *ostriches* (a kind of bird). Then *choose something from the passage* that especially interested you and *draw a picture* about it underneath the passage.

Ostriches

Ostriches are large flightless birds that are native to Africa. They are the largest living birds on the earth, weighing up to about 250 pounds and standing up to about eight feet tall.

The male ostrich has soft black feathers on its back with white primary feathers on its wings and tail, while the female and all young ostriches have brownish feathers to help camouflage them. Both males and females have bare necks and thighs. The skin is blue or pink in ostrich males and pinkish gray in females. Both males and females have long mobile necks, small heads, large eyes, long powerful legs, and two toes on each foot. Their voice is either a loud hiss or a booming roar.

Ostriches eat plant shoots, leaves, flowers, and seeds. While they are eating, they often raise their heads to look for *predators*. Ostrich chicks have many predators including vultures, hyenas, and jackals. Only *15* percent of ostrich chicks live until their first birthday. Ostriches are not very social birds and usually live alone, not in packs.

Ostriches nest during the dry season. The male ostrich makes several shallow scrapes in his territory. The female then lays up to twelve eggs over the next three weeks. The *incubation period* is six weeks. Despite the constant watch of the parents, fewer than *10* percent of the ostrich eggs will hatch. The young are light brown with dark brown spots. Ostriches can live to be forty years old or more.

Ostriches have excellent vision and can run about 31 miles per hour because of their strong legs. Ostriches do not bury their head in the sand, in spite of what many people have heard.

My Picture of Something from This Passage

Appendix I

Big Book Resources

Big Book Publishers
Hummingbird Educational Resources
www.hummingbirded.com/catalog.html
E-mail: pdrake@hummingbirded.com

Just for Kids Books, Inc.
www.justforkidsbooks.com/EDUBIG.HTM
1822 E. Hopi Lane
Mount Prospect, IL 60056
847-803-8783
E-mail: webmaster@justforkids.com

Scholastic, Inc.
www.scholastic.com
800-724-6527

Rigby, Inc.
www.rigby.com
1000 Hart Road, Third Floor
Barrington, IL 60010
888-677-7537
Fax: 800-699-9459 or 407-345-4060
E-mail: ecare@harcourt.com

Some Recommended Titles: Interactive Books with Musical Participation
All About Me: About body parts and their senses, sung to the tune *"The Wheels on the Bus"*
Big Blue Ocean: About ocean creatures, sung to the tune *"Deep in the Heart of Texas"*
Feed Me 5 cookies: Introduces and reviews shapes, sung to the tune *"I'm a Little Teapot"*
5 Coconuts: About a monkey who shakes a coconut tree and catches each coconut as it
    falls, sung to the tune *"La Cucaracha"*

5 Orange Pumpkins: Children help Mrs. Farmer pick a pumpkin and move it to her table for a pumpkin surprise, sung to the tune *"This Old Man"*

Itsy, Bitsy, Medium-Sized, and Big Fat Spider: Children sort out the smallest spider, rain, and sun, sung with the traditional tune

Pretty Butterflies: Children place butterflies in various positions, sung to the tune *"Three Blind Mice"*

10 Red Apples: Children pick apples off a tree and balance them on a child's head, sung to the tune *"Are You Sleeping?"*

Other Recommended Titles

Big Hungry Bear (Big Edition). Wood, Audrey. Ages 4–8.

Bread and Jam for Frances (Giant Edition). Hoban, Russell. Ages 4–8.

Can't You Sleep, Little Bear? Waddell, Martin. Ages 4–8.

Caps for Sale (Big Edition). Slobodkina, Esphyr. Ages 4–8.

Corduroy (Giant Edition). Freeman, Don. Ages 4–8.

Curious George (Giant Edition). Rey, H. A. Ages 4–8.

Doorbell Rang (Big Edition). Hutchins, Pat. Ages 4–8.

Farmer in the Dell. Adams, Pat. Ages 4–8.

Flower Garden (Big Edition). Bunting, Eve. Ages 4–8.

Growing Vegetable Soup (Big Edition). Ehlert, Lois. Ages 4–8.

Guess How Much I Love You Big Book. McBratney, S. Ages 4–8.

Here We Go Round the Mulberry Bush. Adams, Pam. Ages 3–8.

I Love Animals (Big Edition). McDonnell, Flora. Ages 4–8.

In the Tall, Tall Grass (Big Edition). Fleming, Denise. Ages 4–8.

King Bidgoods in the Bathtub (Giant Edition). Wood, Audrey. Ages 4–8.

Appendix II

Predictable Books

Chain or Circular Story
Alligator Baby. Robert Munsch.
Farmer Joe's Hot Day. Nancy Wilcox Richards.
If You Give a Moose a Muffin. Laura Numeroff.
If You Give a Mouse a Cookie. Laura Numeroff.
Seven Little Rabbits. John Becker.
The Mitten. Jan Brett.
Why Mosquitoes Buzz in People's Ears. Verna Aardema.

Cumulative
Benny's Pennies. Pat Brisson.
Chicken Licken. Gavin Bishop.
Drummer Hoff. Barbara Emberley.
"I Don't Care!" Said the Bear. Colin West.
It's My Birthday. Helen Oxenbury.
Jack's Garden. Henry Cole.
Little Pink Pig. Pat Hutchins.
Mike's Kite. Elizabeth McDonald.
My Cat Likes to Hide in Boxes. Eve Sutton.
Seven Sillies. Joyce Dunbar.
The Cat Sat on the Mat. Brian Wildsmith.
The Gingerbread Man. Jean Richards.
The Old Woman and Her Pig. Paul Galdone.
This Is the Bear. Sarah Hayes.
Today Is Monday. Eric Carle.

Familiar Sequence (Days of the Week, Months of the Year, Etc.)
Cookie's Week. Cindy Ward.
Sunday Potatoes, Monday Potatoes. Vicky Schiefman.
The Very Busy Spider. Eric Carle.
The Very Hungry Caterpillar. Eric Carle.
Today Is Monday. Eric Carle.

Familiar Sequence (Numbers)

1, 2, 3, Animal Numbers. Bert Kitchen.

1, 2, 3 to the Zoo. Eric Carle.

10 Bears in My Bed. Stan Mack.

Anno's Counting Book. Mitsumasa Anno.

Brian Wildsmith's 1, 2, 3. Brian Wildsmith.

One Crow: A Counting Rhyme. Jim Aylesworth.

Ten Black Dots. Donald Crews.

Ten, Nine, Eight. Molly Bang.

Up to Ten and Down Again. Lisa Campbell Ernest.

Who's Counting? Nancy Tafuri.

Pattern Story

Are You There Bear? Ron Maris.

Four Fierce Kittens. Joyce Dunbar.

Henny Penny. H. Werner.

Hippity Hop, Frog on Top. Natasha Wing.

Little Pink Pig. Pat Hutchins.

Love You Forever. Robert Munsch.

Millions of Cats. Wanda Gag.

Something from Nothing. Phoebe Gilman.

Spider, Spider. Kate Banks.

The Carrot Seed. Ruth Krauss.

The Gingerbread Boy. Paul Galdone.

The Little Red Hen. Paul Galdone.

The Runaway Bunny. Margaret Wise Brown.

The Three Bears. Paul Galdone.

The Three Billy Goats Gruff. Paul Galdone.

The Three Little Pigs. Paul Galdone.

Town Mouse and Country Mouse. Jan Brett.

Question and Answer

Are You My Mother? P. D. Eastman.

Bright Star, Bright Star, What Do You See? Cassandre Maxwell.

Brown Bear, Brown Bear. Bill Martin Jr.

Have You Seen My Cat? Eric Carle.

Where's the Fish? Taro Gomi.

Where's Spot? Eric Hill.

Whose Mouse Are You? Robert Kraus

Repetition of Phrase and Rhyme

A Beautiful Feast for a Big King Cat. John Archambault and Bill Martin Jr.

A Big Fish Story. Joanne and David Wylie.

A House Is a House for Me. Mary Ann Hoberman.

A Mouse in My House. Nancy Van Laan.

Ask Mr. Bear. Marjorie Flack.

Black Crow, Black Crow. Ginger Fogelsong Guy.

"Buzz, Buzz, Buzz," Went the Bumblebee. Colin West.

Chicken Soup with Rice. Maurice Sendak.

Come Out and Play, Little Mouse. Robert Kraus.

Do You Know What I'll Do? Charlotte Zolotow.
Four Fierce Kittens. Joyce Dunbar.
Good Morning Chick. Mirra Ginsburg.
Good Night, Gorilla. Peggy Rathmann.
Go Tell Aunt Rhody. Aliki.
Happy Birthday Moon. Frank Asch.
Have You Seen My Duckling? Nancy Tafuri.
Hippity Hop, Frog on Top. Natasha Wing.
I Bought My Love a Tabby Cat. Colin West.
"I Don't Care!" Said the Bear. Colin West.
Is Your Mama a Llama? Deborah Guarino.
Jake Baked the Cake. B. G. Hennesy.
Knock, Knock, Who's There? Sally Grindley.
Little Pink Pig. Pat Hutchins.
Mama, Do You Love Me? Barbara Joosse.
Moo, Moo, Brown Cow. Jakki Woo.
"Not Me," Said the Monkey. Colin West.
One, Two, Three. Alain.
Seven Little Rabbits. John Becker.
Teeny Tiny. Jill Bennett.
The Chick and the Duckling. Jose Aruego.
The Gingerbread Boy. Paul Galdone.
The Little Red House. Norma Jean Sawicki.
The Mixed-Up Chameleon. Eric Carle.
There's a COW in the Road! Reeve Lindbergh.
The Teeny Tiny Woman. Paul Galdone.
The Very Busy Spider. Eric Carle.
Two Badd Babies. Jeffrie Ross Gordon.
Where Are You Going, Little Mouse? Robert Kraus.
Where Is My Daddy? Shigeo Watanabe.
Where's the Fish? Taro Gomi.
Who Said Red? Mary Serfozo.
Whose Mouse Are You? Robert Kraus.
You Can't Catch Me. Joan Kahn.

Appendix III

Recommended LEA Resources

Avery, C., & Graves, D. (2002). *And with a light touch: Learning about reading, writing, and teaching with first graders.* Portsmouth, NH: Heinemann.

Blair-Larsen, S., & Williams, K. (1999). *The balanced reading program: Helping all students achieve success.* Newark, DE: International Reading Association.

Coombs, M. (1996). *Developing competent readers and writers in the primary grades.* Upper Saddle River, NJ: Prentice Hall.

Cramer, R. (2003). *Principles and practices of language experience.* [http://www.literacyconnections.com/Cramer.html]

Dixon, C. (1990). *Language experience approach to reading (and writing): LEA for ESL.* Upper Saddle River, NJ: Prentice Hall.

In their own words: The language experience approach: A method to reach reluctant readers. [http://www.literacyconnections.com/In Their Own Words.html]

Neuman, S., Copple, C., & Bredekamp, S. (2000). *Developmentally appropriate practices for young children.* Newark, DE: International Reading Association.

Rasinski, T., & Padak, N. (2001). *From phonics to fluency* (pp. 119–133). New York: Longman.

Rigg, P. (1989). Language experience approach: Reading naturally. In P. Rigg and R. Van Allen (Eds.), *When they all don't speak English: Integrating the ESL student into the regular classroom* (pp. 75–76). Urbana, IL: National Council of Teachers of English.

Routman, R. (2002). *Reading essentials: The specifics you need to teach reading well.* Portsmouth, NH: Heinemann.

Sampson, M., Sampson, M. B., & Allen, R. (1995). *Pathways to literacy.* Orlando, FL: Harcourt Brace College.

Appendix IV

For Additional Reading

Beck, I., & McKeown, M. (2001). Text talk: Capturing the benefits of read-aloud experiences for young children. *The Reading Teacher, 55,* 10–20.

Crafton, L. (1991). *Whole language: Getting started . . . Moving forward.* Katonah, NY: Richard C. Owen Publishers.

Fields, M., & Stanley, W. (2003). *Let's begin reading right.* Upper Saddle River, NJ: Prentice Hall.

Glazer, S., & Burke, E. (1998). *An integrated approach to early literacy.* Boston: Allyn & Bacon.

Gurian, M., & Henley, P. (2001). *Boys and girls learn differently* (pp. 73–123). San Francisco: Jossey-Bass.

Machado, J. (2002). *Early childhood experiences in language arts: Emergent literacy.* New York: Delmar Publishers.

McGee, L., & Richgels, D. (2003). *Literacy's beginnings: Supporting young readers and writers.* Boston: Allyn & Bacon.

Morrow, L. (1999). *Family literacy connections in schools and communities.* Newark, DE: International Reading Association.

Neuman, S., & Celano, D. (2001). Books aloud: A campaign to "put books in children's hands." *The Reading Teacher, 54,* 550–557.

Neuman, S., & Roskos, K. (1993). *Language and literacy learning in the early years* (pp. 62–97). Fort Worth, TX: Harcourt Brace Jovanovich.

Reutzel, R., & Cooter, R. (2000). *Teaching children to read* (pp. 400–469). Upper Saddle River, NJ: Merrill.

Salinger, T. (1996). *Literacy for young children* (pp. 67–86). Upper Saddle River, NJ: Merrill.

Spielman, J. (2001). The family photography project: "We will just read what the pictures tell us." *The Reading Teacher, 54,* pp. 762–770.

Wood, M., & Salvetti, E. (2001). Project story boost: Read alouds for students at risk. *The Reading Teacher, 55,* pp. 76–83.

Appendix V

Chants, Finger Plays, Action Verses, and Recommended Books

See the leaves falling down,
To make a carpet on the ground,
Swish, swish, wind blows by
Swish, swish, away they fly.

Windshield wiper, windshield wiper,
What do you do today?
Slip-slap, slip-slap,
I wipe the rain away.

•

Hear the engine puff, choo-choo-choo,
Hear the whistle blow, toot-toot-too.
Hear the big bell ring, ding-dong-ding.
Hear the brakeman shout "All Aboard."

•

Jack-in-the box
Sits so still.
Won't you come out?
Yes, I will.

•

I'll touch my chin,
My cheek,
My chair.

I'll touch my head,
My heels,
My hair.

I'll touch my knees,
My neck,
My nose.
Then I'll dip down and touch my toes.

•

Big clocks make a sound like TICK-TOCK;
Small clocks make a sound like TICK-TOCK, tick-tock, tick-tock, tock-tock;
And the little tiny clocks make a sound like Tick-tock, tick-tock.

•

Here's a doughnut so big and fat,
Here's the hole, but you can't eat that!

•

I put my hands in my lap,
My feet together so.
I sit as straight as straight can be,
For that is right, you know.

•

I like to be a jumping jack
And jump out from a box.
I like to be a rocking horse
and rock and rock and rock.

I like to be a spinning top
And spin around and round.
I like to be a rubber ball
and bounce way up and down.

I like to be a big, fast train
Whose wheels fly round and round.
I like to be a pony small
And trot along the ground.

I like to be so many things—
A growly-scowly bear—
But really I'm a little child
who sits upon a chair.

•

Clap your hands, clap your hands,
Clap your hands together;
Clap your hands, clap your hands,
Lightly as a feather.

Lift your right knee, lift your left knee,
Lightly as a feather.
Lift them high, lift them low.
All lift knees together.

Tap your right toe, tap your left toe,
Lightly as a feather.
Tap the right, tap the left.
All tap toes together.

•

Left foot up, right foot in,
That's the way the dance begins;
Left hand up, right hand down,
Now we all turn round and round.

•

This is how my goldfish swims,
And birdies fly like this.
Spiders crawl right up the wall,
And elephants walk like this.

•

I like to go on tippy-toe,
Like a fairy I can go.
I can stamp so that you'd say
"An elephant's at school today."

•

I can run, I can hop,
I can spin 'round like a top,
I can stretch my arms out wide,
I can swing from side to side.

I can stand up straight and tall,
I can make myself so small,
I can kneel without a sound,
And sit cross-legged on the ground.

•

Roll your hands so slowly,
as slowly as can be;
Roll your hands so slowly,
And fold your arms like me.

•

Five little birds without any home,
　[Raise five fingers of right hand]
Five little trees in a row.
　[Raise right hand high over head]

Come and build your nests in our branches tall,
  [Cup left hand for nest—right fingers in]
We'll rock you to and fro.
  [Then rock both hands]

•

Here's a bunny
  [Raise two fingers]
With ears so funny
And here's a hole in the ground.
  [Make hole with fingers of other hand]
At the first sound she hears
She pricks up her ears
  [Straighten fingers]
And pops right into the ground.
  [Put into hole]

•

Little Robin Redbreast
Sat upon a rail.
  [Crouch like bird with two hands behind like bird's tail]
Niddle noddle went his head
  [Nod head]
And wag went his tail.
  [Use hands to make tail wagging]
Niddle noddle went his head
And wag went his tail.

•

The little mice are creeping, creeping, creeping.
The little mice are creeping through the house.
The little mice are sleeping, sleeping, sleeping.
The little mice are sleeping through the house.
The old gray cat comes creeping, creeping, creeping.
The old gray cat comes creeping through the house.
And the little mice ran away.
  [One hand represents the mice; the other hand the cat. One hand creeps, while the other comes slowly down from the air. Hands meet and one scampers behind the child's back.]

•

  [Use one hand as a boat and the other arm as the bridge]
This is the way,
All the long day,
The boats go sailing by.
To and fro,
In a row,
Under the bridge so high.

Two little blackbirds,
  [Hands close with thumbs straight up for birds]
Sitting on a hill,
One named Jack,
  [Wriggle one thumb]
The other named Jill.
  [Wriggle other thumb]
Fly away Jack.
Come back Jill.
  [Bring hands back one at a time]
Come back Jill.

●

Five rabbits were hiding
  [Clenched fist]
In the woods one day.
1–2–3–4–5 jumped out
  [Fingers come out as they count]
And then they ran away.
  [Imitate running with fingers]

●

One is a giant and stamps her feet,
Two is a fairy light and neat.
  [Skip around]
Three is a mouse and curls up small.
Four is a great big bouncing ball.

●

As high as a house
  [Reach high]
As small as a mouse
  [Crouch]
As wide as a bark
  [Feet apart, arms sideways]
As thin as a pin
  [Stand erect]

●

I have ten fingers and they all belong to me.
I can make them do things—would you like to see?
I can shut them up tight, I can open them up wide,
I can put them together, I can make them all hide.
I can make them jump high,
I can make them jump low.
I can fold them up quietly and hold them just so.
  [Finger motions as described]

The stork is such a funny bird,
She stands on one leg all night.
   [Children stand on one foot]
Her head is tucked beneath her wing
Completely out of sight.
   [Tuck head under arm]
In the morning when she wakes
Up pops her head so high
Down drops her foot
Out spread her wings
And she flies to meet the sky.
   [Spread arms and flap them]

Books for Finger Plays

Here is a short list of books that contain finger plays for young children.

Beall, P. (2002). *Wee sing children's songs and fingerplays.* BK/CD/CAS.

Brown, M. (1993). *Hand rhymes.* New York: Viking Penguin.

Poulsson, E. (1972). *Fingerplays for nursery and kindergarten.* Mineola, NY: Dover Publishing.

Weimer, T. (1986). *Fingerplays and action chants: Volume I, Animals.* Greenville, SC: PEP Publishing.

Weimer, T. (1986). *Fingerplays and action chants: Volume II, Family and Friends.* Greenville, SC: PEP Publishing.

Books with Listening Themes

These trade books stress listening carefully, critically, or with appreciation. They may motivate young children to improve the various elements of their listening skills. They also can be the starting point for discussions about improving listening skills.

Brown, M. (1959). *Nibble nibble: Poems for children.* Boston: Addison-Wesley.

Foster, J. (2002). *You little monkey! And other poems for young children.* Cambridge, England: Oxford University Press.

Frost, R. (2001). *Stopping by woods on a snowy evening.* New York: Penguin Putnam.

Fujikawa, G. (2002). *Child's book of poems.* New York: Michael Friedman Publishing.

Goldish, M. (1999). *101 science poems and songs for young learners* (Grades 1–3). New York: Scholastic.

Griego, M. (1990). *Tortillas para mara and other nursery rhymes: Spanish and English.* New York: Henry Holt.

Hale, G. (1997). *Read-aloud poems for young people: An introduction to the magic and excitement of poetry.* New York: Black Dog and Leventhal Publishers.

Lithgow, J. (2003). *I'm a manatee.* New York: Simon & Schuster.

Milne, A. A. (2001). *Complete tales and poems of Winnie the Pooh: An introduction to the magic and excitement of poetry.* New York: Penguin Putnam.

Seuss, Dr. (2003). *The toothbook.* New York: Random House.

Swift, J. (2002). *First rhymes.* New York: Barnes & Noble Books.

Trelease, J., & Prelutsky, J. (1986). *Read-aloud rhymes for the very young.* New York: Alfred A. Knopf.

Untermeyer, L. (1971). *The golden book of poems for the very young.* New York: Golden Books.

Wilkin, E. (2001). *Poems to read to very young children.* New York: Random House.

Wilkinson, B. (2002). *Secrets of the vine for young hearts.* Nashville, TN: Tommy Nelson.

Zelinsky, P. (2002). *Knick-knack, paddy whack!: A moving parts book.* New York: Penguin Putnam.

Books with Listening Games

Here are several books and CDs that contain motivating listening games for young children.

Adams, M., Foorman, B., Lundberg, I., & Beeler, T. (1998). *Phonemic awareness in young children: A classroom curriculum.* Baltimore: Paul H. Brookes Publishing Company.

Clark, V. (1997). *Music box: Exploring music with young children.* New York: BBC Worldwide America.

Curious George, Preschool Learning Games—CD. (2002). New York: Simon & Schuster.

Storms, G., Griffiths, A., Storms, J., & Hurd, C. (1995). *101 music games for children: Fun and learning with rhythm and song.* Alameda, CA: Hunter House.

Appendix VI

Wordless Books

Anno, M. (1986). *Anno's counting book*. New York: HarperCollins.

Baker, J. (1991). *Window*. New York: HarperCollins.

Bang, M. (1996). *Grey lady and the strawberry snatcher*. New York: Simon & Schuster.

Banyai, I. (1998). *Re-zoom*. Harmondsworth, England: Puffin.

Briggs, R. (2000). *Snowman*. New York: Random House.

Carle, E. (1995). *Do you want to be my friend?* New York: HarperCollins.

Cousins, L. (1992). *Kite in the park*. Cambridge, MA: Candlewick Press.

Crews, D. (1997). *Truck*. New York: HarperCollins.

Felix, M. (1995). *Plane*. New York: Harcourt.

Goffin, J. (1991). *Oh!* New York: Henry N. Abrams.

Graham, A. (2003). *Full moon soup: A wordless book that's brimful of stories!* London, England: Chrysalis Children's Books.

Hogan, M. (2000). *Dinosaur flip board*. Anaheim, CA: Disney Corporation, Mouse Works.

Liu, J. (2002). *Yellow umbrella*. La Jolla, CA: Kane/Miller.

Mayer, M., & Mayer, M. (2003). *Frog on his own*. New York: Dial.

Meader, J. (1996). *The wordless travel book*. Berkeley, CA: Ten Speed Press.

Spier, P. (1997). *Peter Spier's rain*. New York: Bantam Doubleday Dell.

Trondheim, L. (2002). *Li'l Santa*. New York: Nantier Beall Minoustchine.

Twinn, M., & Blanco, J. (2000). *Book buddy—bunny*. Bridgemead Swindon Wiltshire, England: Child's Play International.

Twinn, M., & Blanco, J. (2000). *Book buddy—koala*. Bridgemead Swindon Wiltshire, England: Child's Play International.

Vincent, G. (2000). *A day, a dog*. Asheville, NC: Front Street.

Ward, L. (1992). *The silver pony: A story in pictures*. Boston: Houghton Mifflin.

Woodring, J. (2003). *The Frank book*. Seattle: Fantagraphics Book.

Appendix VII

The Dolch Basic Sight Words

The *Dolch Basic Sight Word List*, compiled by the late Edward Dolch of the University of Illinois in 1941, is the most well-known and one of the most useful sight word lists. Although the list may appear outdated, its words are comparable to the words in newer sight word lists. These *220* words are said to make up about *70 percent* of the words found in most first readers and about *65 percent* of the words in most second and third readers.

Counting the number of words that a child recognizes on a sight word list is one way of assessing his or her approximate instructional reading level (the level at which a child can read successfully with teacher or tutor help). This table helps estimate a child's approximate instructional reading level as indicated by his or her performance on this list (McBroom, Sparrow, & Eckstein, 1944). It has proven to be a very helpful estimation of a child's instructional reading level as also evaluated by an Individual Reading Inventory (see Chapter Two).

Words Recognized	Reading Level
0–75	Preprimer
76–120	Primer
121–170	First Reader
171–210	Second Reader
Above 210	Third Reader or above

Here is a reproducible copy of the *Dolch Basic Sight Word List* for use in classrooms, tutoring situations, or homes.

Name: _____ **Grade:** _____

DOLCH BASIC SIGHT WORD LIST[*]

List 1		List 2		List 3		List 4	
1.	_____ the	1.	_____ at	1.	_____ do	1.	_____ big
2.	_____ to	2.	_____ him	2.	_____ can	2.	_____ went
3.	_____ and	3.	_____ with	3.	_____ could	3.	_____ are
4.	_____ he	4.	_____ up	4.	_____ when	4.	_____ come
5.	_____ a	5.	_____ all	5.	_____ did	5.	_____ if
6.	_____ I	6.	_____ look	6.	_____ what	6.	_____ now
7.	_____ you	7.	_____ is	7.	_____ so	7.	_____ long
8.	_____ it	8.	_____ her	8.	_____ see	8.	_____ no
9.	_____ of	9.	_____ there	9.	_____ not	9.	_____ came
10.	_____ in	10.	_____ some	10.	_____ were	10.	_____ ask
11.	_____ was	11.	_____ out	11.	_____ get	11.	_____ very
12.	_____ said	12.	_____ as	12.	_____ them	12.	_____ an
13.	_____ his	13.	_____ be	13.	_____ like	13.	_____ over
14.	_____ that	14.	_____ have	14.	_____ one	14.	_____ your
15.	_____ she	15.	_____ go	15.	_____ this	15.	_____ its
16.	_____ for	16.	_____ we	16.	_____ my	16.	_____ ride
17.	_____ on	17.	_____ am	17.	_____ would	17.	_____ into
18.	_____ they	18.	_____ then	18.	_____ me	18.	_____ just
19.	_____ but	19.	_____ little	19.	_____ will	19.	_____ blue
20.	_____ had	20.	_____ down	20.	_____ yes	20.	_____ red
	/20		/20		/20		/20

Copyright © 2005 by John Wiley & Sons, Inc.

---

[*]Shanker, J., & Ekwall, E. (1998). *Locating and correcting reading difficulties.* Columbus, OH: Merrill, pp. 261 & 263. Reprinted with permission of Merrill.

DOLCH BASIC SIGHT WORD LIST* (continued)

List 5		List 6		List 7		List 8	
1.	from	1.	away	1.	walk	1.	tell
2.	good	2.	old	2.	to	2.	much
3.	any	3.	by	3.	or	3.	keep
4.	about	4.	their	4.	before	4.	give
5.	around	5.	here	5.	eat	5.	work
6.	want	6.	saw	6.	again	6.	first
7.	don't	7.	call	7.	play	7.	try
8.	how	8.	after	8.	who	8.	new
9.	know	9.	well	9.	been	9.	must
10.	right	10.	think	10.	may	10.	start
11.	put	11.	ran	11.	stop	11.	black
12.	too	12.	let	12.	off	12.	white
13.	got	13.	help	13.	never	13.	ten
14.	take	14.	make	14.	seven	14.	does
15.	where	15.	going	15.	eight	15.	bring
16.	every	16.	sleep	16.	cold	16.	goes
17.	pretty	17.	brown	17.	today	17.	write
18.	jump	18.	yellow	18.	fly	18.	always
19.	green	19.	five	19.	myself	19.	drink
20.	four	20.	six	20.	round	20.	once
/20		/20		/20		/20	

*Shanker, J., & Ekwall, E. (1998). *Locating and correcting reading difficulties.* Columbus, OH: Merrill, pp. 261 & 263. Reprinted with permission of Merrill.

DOLCH BASIC SIGHT WORD LIST* *(continued)*

List 9

1. _____ soon
2. _____ made
3. _____ run
4. _____ gave
5. _____ open
6. _____ has
7. _____ find
8. _____ only
9. _____ us
10. _____ three
11. _____ out
12. _____ better
13. _____ hold
14. _____ buy
15. _____ funny
16. _____ warm
17. _____ ate
18. _____ fall
19. _____ those
20. _____ done
       /20

List 10

1. _____ use
2. _____ fast
3. _____ say
4. _____ light
5. _____ pick
6. _____ hurt
7. _____ pull
8. _____ cut
9. _____ kind
10. _____ both
11. _____ sit
12. _____ which
13. _____ fall
14. _____ carry
15. _____ small
16. _____ under
17. _____ read
18. _____ why
19. _____ own
20. _____ found
       /20

List 11

1. _____ wash
2. _____ show
3. _____ hot
4. _____ because
5. _____ far
6. _____ live
7. _____ draw
8. _____ clean
9. _____ grow
10. _____ best
11. _____ upon
12. _____ these
13. _____ sing
14. _____ together
15. _____ please
16. _____ thank
17. _____ wish
18. _____ many
19. _____ shall
20. _____ laugh
       /20

Copyright © 2005 by John Wiley & Sons, Inc.

*Shanker, J., & Ekwall, E. (1998). *Locating and correcting reading difficulties.* Columbus, OH: Merrill, pp. 261 & 263. Reprinted with permission of Merrill.

Appendix VIII

Books for Reviewing Individual Letter Names

Many trade books are designed to emphasize a certain letter of the alphabet or the entire alphabet. These are uniquely helpful for an adult who wants to emphasize a certain alphabet letter with the entire class, a small group, or an individual child. Most of these books are beautifully illustrated and highly motivating to young children. They can be used to teach or review the *letter names in context.*

The Letter A

Demouth, P. (1996). *Johnny Appleseed.* New York: Grosset & Dunlap.

Fowler, A. (1994). *Apples of your eye: Rookie read-about-science.* Chicago: Children's Press.

Golembe, C. (1999). *Annabelle's new home.* Boston: Houghton Mifflin.

Hutchins, A., & Hutchins, R. (1994). *Picking apples and pumpkins.* New York: Scholastic.

Lerner, H., & Goldhor, S. (1996). *What's so terrible about swallowing an apple seed?* New York: HarperCollins.

Nikola, L. (1997). *America, my land* your land* our land.* New York: Lee and Low Books.

Ray, D. (1996). *Sweet dried apples: A Vietnamese wartime childhood.* Boston: Houghton Mifflin.

Slawson, M. (1994). *Apple picking time.* New York: Crown.

Turner, A. (1993). *Apple valley year.* New York: Macmillan.

The Letter B

Capucilli, P. (1998). *Biscuit finds a friend.* New York: HarperCollins.

de Brunhoff, J. (2000). *Bonjour Babar!: The six unabridged classics by the creator of Babar.* New York: Random House.

Fox, M. (1993). *Time for bed.* San Diego: Harcourt Brace.

Ho, M. (1996). *HUSH! A Thai lullaby.* New York: Orchard Books.

Lester, A. (1991). *Isabella's bed.* Boston: Houghton Mifflin.

Macdonald, M. (1996). *Tuck-me-in tales: Bedtime stories from around the world.* Little Rock, AK: August House Littlefolk.

Miller, V. (1993). *Go to bed!* Cambridge, MA: Candlwick Press.

Sabuda, R., & Reinhart, M. (2001). *Butterflies.* New York: Hyperion Books.

Spotlight, S. (2002). *Bob's big story collection.* New York: Simon & Schuster.

Waddell, M. (1988). *Can't you sleep, little bear?* New York: The Trumpet Club.

The Letter C

Cameron, A. (1994). *The cat sat on the mat.* Boston: Houghton Mifflin.

Casey, P. (1994). *My cat Jack.* Cambridge, MA: Candlewick Press.

Coxon, M. (1991). *The cat who lost his purr.* New York: Penguin Books.

Moffat, J. (1997). *Who stole the cookies?* New York: Grosset & Dunlap.

Moore, I. (1991). *Six-dinner Sid.* New York: Simon & Schuster.

Polacco, P. (1994). *Tekvah means hope.* New York: Doubleday.

Rylant, C. (1994). *Mr. Putter and Tabby bake the cake.* San Diego: Harcourt Brace.

Sun, C. (1996). *Cat and cat-face.* Boston: Houghton Mifflin.

Young, E. (1995). *Cat and rat: The legend of the Chinese Zodiac.* New York: Henry Holt.

The Letter D

Asch, F. (1989). *The last puppy.* New York: Simon & Schuster.

Cole, J., & Calmenson, S. (1996). *Give a dog a bone: Stories, poems, jokes, and riddles about dogs.* New York: Scholastic.

Ernst, L. (1992). *Waller's tail.* New York: Macmillan.

Harper, I., & Moser, B. (1996). *Our new puppy.* New York: The Blue Sky Press.

Lewis, K. (1992). *Floss.* Cambridge, MA: Candlewick Press.

McNeal, T., & McNeal, L. (1996). *The dog who lost his Bob.* Morton Grove, IL: Albert Whiteman.

Micklethwait, L. (1995). *Spot a dog: A child's book of art.* London: Dorling Kindersley Limited.

Morris, R. (1983). *Dolphin.* New York: HarperCollins.

Reit, S. (1996). *A dog's tale.* New York: Bantam.

Rylant, C. (1994). *The bookshop dog.* New York: The Blue Sky Press.

White, N. (1995). *Why do dogs do that?* New York: Scholastic.

The Letter E

Allen, J. (1993). *Elephant.* Cambridge, MA: Candlewick Press.

Backstein, K. (1992). *The blind men and the elephant.* New York: Scholastic.

Barner, B. (1995). *How to weigh an elephant.* New York: Bantam Doubleday Dell.

Berry, J. (1996). *Don't leave an elephant to go and chase a bird.* New York: Simon & Schuster.

Coxe, M. (1997). *Big egg.* New York: Random House.

Johnson, D. (1995). *Never ride your elephant to school.* New York: Henry Holt.

Lewis, K. (1995). *My friend Harry.* Cambridge, MA: Candlewick Press.

Yates, G. (1995). *An elephant alphabet book.* Chicago: Kidsbooks.

The Letter F

Brandenberg, A. (1993). *My visit to the aquarium.* New York: HarperCollins.

Brenner, B., & Chardiet, B. (1994). *Where's that fish?: Let's-read-and-find-out science.* New York: HarperCollins.

Cohen, C. (1988). *How many fish?* New York: Scholastic.

Gergely, T. (2001). *Fire engine book.* New York: Random House.

Hest, A. (1994). *Rosie's fishing trip.* Cambridge, MA: Candlewick Press.

Pfeffer, W. (1996). *What's it like to be a fish?—Let's-read-and-find-out-science.* New York: HarperCollins.

Sharp, N. (1993). *Today I'm going fishing with dad.* Honesdale, PA: Boyds Mills Press.

Watson, D. (1996). *Tommy's Mommy's fish.* New York: Viking.

The Letter G

Chardiet, B., & Chardiet, J. (1993). *The rough, gruff goat brother's cap.* New York: Scholastic.

Cronin, D. (2002). *Giggle, gaggle, quack.* New York: Simon & Schuster.

Morozumi, A. (1997). *My friend gorilla.* New York: Farrar, Strauss, Giroux.

Munsch, R. (1998). *Get out of bed!* New York: Scholastic.

Swinburne, S. (1999). *Guess whose shadow?* Honesdale, PA: Boyds Mills Press.

Wyeth, S. (1997). *Ginger Brown: The nobody girl.* New York: Random House.

Ziefert, H. (1995). *Gingerbread boy.* New York: Viking.

The Letter H

Ben-Ezer, E. (1997). *Hosni the dreamer.* New York: Farrar, Strauss, Giroux.

Brenner, M. (1994). *Abe Lincoln's hat.* New York: Random House.

Gardella, T. (1997). *Casey's new hat.* Boston: Houghton Mifflin.

Howe, J. (1999). *Horace and Morris but mostly Dolores.* New York: Atheneum.

Johnson, D. (1993). *Never babysit the hippopotamus.* New York: Henry Holt.

Lasky, K. (1995). *She's wearing a dead bird on her head.* New York: Hyperion.

Pearson, T. (1997). *The purple hat.* New York: Farrar, Strauss, Giroux.

The Letter I

Albe, S. (1997). *I can do it.* New York: Random House.

Dabcovich, L. (1997). *The polar bear son: An Inuit tale.* Boston: Houghton Mifflin.

George, J. (1997). *Arctic son.* New York: Hyperion.

Kusugak, M. (1996). *My Arctic 1, 2, 3.* New York: Annick Press.

Yue, C., & Yue, D. (1988). *The igloo.* Boston: Houghton Mifflin.

Zeifert, H. (1998). *I swapped my dog.* Boston: Houghton Mifflin.

The Letter J

Carter, D. (1992). *Jingle bugs: A merry pop-up book with lights and music!* New York: Simon & Schuster.

Gray, L. (1994). *Fenton's leap.* New York: Simon & Schuster.

Havill, J. (1999). *Jamaica and the substitute teacher.* Boston: Houghton Mifflin.

Hru, D. (1996). *The magic moonberry jump ropes.* New York: Penguin Books.

Jonas, A. (1995). *Splash!* New York: Mulberry Books.

Tyler, M. (1996). *Flags.* Greenvale, NY: MONDO Publishing.

Walsh, E. (1993). *Hop jump.* San Diego: Harcourt Brace.

The Letter K

Cowley, J. (1991). *The kangaroo from Woolloomooloo.* North Sydney, Australia: Murdock Magazines Pty. Ltd.

Hogan, P. (1991). *The life cycle of the kangaroo.* Austin, TX: Steck-Vaughn.

Leonard, M. (1990). *Counting kangaroos: A book about numbers.* Mahwah, NJ: Troll Associates.

Lepthien, E. (1995). *Kangaroos: A new true book.* Chicago: Children's Press.

Marzolo, C. (1992). *Kenny and the little kickers.* New York: Scholastic.

Ryden, H. (1994). *Joey: The story of a baby kangaroo.* New York: Tamborine.

The Letter L

Aardema, V. (1996). *The lonely lioness and the ostrich chicks.* New York: Alfred A. Knopf.

Day, L. (1995). *The lion's whiskers: An Ethopian folktale.* New York: Scholastic.

Gliori, D. (1993). *A lion at bedtime.* Hauppauge, NY: Barron's.

Krauss, R. (1998). *Little Louie the baby bloomer.* New York: HarperCollins.

Micklethwait, L. (1994). *I spy a lion: Animals in art.* New York: Greenwillow.

Nolan, D. (1997). *Androcles and the lion.* San Diego: Harcourt Brace.

Stimson, J. (1997). *Brave lion, scared lion.* New York: Scholastic.

Wolf, G. (1996). *The very hungry lion.* New York: Annick Press.

The Letter M

Bial, R. (1997). *Mist over the mountain.* Boston: Houghton Mifflin.

Bunting, E. (1997). *On call back mountain.* New York: The Blue Sky Press.

Burton, V. (2002). *Mike Mulligan and more: A Virginia Lee Burton treasury.* Boston: Houghton Mifflin.

Demi. (1995). *The stonecutter.* New York: Crown.

Johnston, A. (1994). *Amber on the mountain.* New York: Dial Books.

Numeroff, L. (1994). *If you give a mouse a cookie.* New York: HarperCollins.

Shannon, G. (1993). *Climbing Kansas mountains.* New York: Simon & Schuster.

Wells, R. (2000). *The McDuff stories.* New York: Hyperion.

The Letter N

Bash, B. (1990). *Where birds nest in the city.* Boston: Little Brown.

Erdich, L. (1996). *Grandmother's pigeon.* New York: Hyperion.

Jenkins, P. (1995). *A nest full of eggs: Let's-read-and-find-out science.* New York: HarperCollins.

London, J. (1994). *Condor's egg.* San Francisco: Chronicle Books.

Swinburne, S. (1996). *Swallows in the birdhouse.* Brookfield, CT: The Millbrook Press.

The Letter O

Frasier, D. (1998). *Out of the ocean.* San Diego: Harcourt Brace.

Lauber, P. (1990). *An octopus is amazing: Let's-read-and-find-out science.* New York: HarperCollins.

Most, B. (1991). *My very own octopus.* San Diego: Harcourt Brace.

Pringle, L. (1993). *Octopus hug.* Honesdale, PA: Boyds Mills Press.

Schwartz, A. (1999). *Old McDonald.* New York: Scholastic.

Stefoff, R. (1997). *Octopus.* London: Cavendish.

The Letter P

Gillis, J. (1992). *In a pumpkin shell: Over 20 pumpkin projects for kids.* Pownal, VT: Story Communications.

Hall, Z. (1994). *It's pumpkin time!* New York: Scholastic.

Hundley, J. (1998). *The best thing about a puppy.* Cambridge, MA: Candlewick.

Hutchings, A., & Hutchings, R. (1994). *Picking apples & pumpkins.* New York: Scholastic.

Martin, B., & Carle, E. (2003). *Panda bear, panda bear, what do you see?* New York: Henry Holt.

Marzollo, J. (1996). *I'm a seed.* New York: Scholastic.

McDonald, M. (1992). *The great pumpkin switch.* New York: Orchard Books.

Ray, M. (1992). *Pumpkins: A story for a field.* San Diego: Harcourt Brace.

Ziefert, H. (1998). *Pushkin meets the bundle.* New York: Atheneum.

Ziefert, H. (1997). *The three little pigs.* New York: Penguin Books.

The Letter Q

Arnold, M. (1996). *Quick, quack, quick.* New York: Random House.

Avery, K. (1994). *The crazy quilt.* Glenview, IL: Good Year Books/Scott Foresman and Company.

Guback, G. (1994). *Luka's quilt.* New York: Greenwillow.

Hopkinson, D. (1993). *Sweet Clara and the freedom quilt.* New York: Alfred A. Knopf.

Kinsey-Warnock, N. (1989). *The Canada geese quilt.* New York: Penguin Books.

Mills, L. (1991). *The rag coat.* Boston: Little Brown.

Turner, A. (1994). *Sewing quilts.* New York: Macmillan.

The Letter R

Birchfield, D. (1996). *Animal lore & legend—rabbit: American Indian legends.* New York: Scholastic.

Bornstein, R. (1995). *Rabbit's good news.* New York: Clarion.

Coxe, M. (1997). *R is for radish.* New York: Random House.

Hamilton, K. (1995). *Rockaby rabbit.* Boca Raton, FL: Cool Kids Press.

Hans, S. (1995). *The rabbit's escape.* New York: Henry Holt.

Ho, M., & Ros, S. (1997). *Brother rabbit: A Cambodian tale.* New York: Lothrop, Lee and Shephard Books.

Oppenheim, S. (1995). *I love you, bunny rabbit.* New York: Bantam Doubleday Dell.

Weninger, B. (1996). *What have you done, Davy?* New York: North-South Books.

The Letter S

Carlson, N. (1996). *Sit still!* New York: Viking.

Czernecki, S., & Rhodes, T. (1993). *Singing snake.* New York: Hyperion.

Daval, M. (1996). *How snake got his hiss.* New York: Scholastic.

Dewan, T. (1997). *Top secret.* New York: Scholastic.

Gray, L. (1994). *Small green snake.* New York: Orchard Books.

Havill, J. (1999). *Jamaica and the substitute teacher.* Boston: Houghton Mifflin.

McKenna, M. (1997). *Tell me a season.* Boston: Houghton Mifflin.

Robinson, F. (1996). *Great snakes!* New York: Scholastic.

The Letter T

Demi. (1998). *The greatest treasure.* New York: Scholastic.

Doro, A. (1996). *Twin pickle.* New York: Henry Holt.

Graves, B. (1997). *Mystery of the tooth gremlin.* New York: Hyperion.

MacGill-Callahan, S. (1991). *And still the turtle watched.* New York: Dial Books.

Miles, B. (1998). *Tortoise and the hare.* New York: Simon & Schuster.

Ross, G. (1995). *How the turtle's back was cracked: A traditional Cherokee tale.* New York: Dial Books.

Shannon, G. (1996). *Tomorrow's alphabet.* New York: Greenwillow.

Turner, C. (1991). *The turtle and the moon.* New York: Penguin Books.

The Letter U

Cooney, N. (1989). *The umbrella day.* New York: Putnam & Grosset.

Laser, M. (1997). *The rain.* New York: Simon & Schuster.

Medearis, A. (1995). *We play on a rainy day.* New York: Scholastic.

Yashima, T. (1986). *Umbrella.* New York: Puffin Books.

The Letter V

Cocca-Leffler, M. (1996). *Lots of hearts.* New York: Grosset & Dunlap.

Hoban, L. (1989). *Arthur's great big valentine.* New York: HarperCollins.

Marzollo, J. (1996). *Valentine cats.* New York: Scholastic.

Shannon, G. (1995). *Heart to heart.* Boston: Houghton Mifflin.

Sharmat, M. (1996). *Nate the great and the mushy valentine.* New York: Bantam Doubleday Dell.

The Letter W

Asch, F. (1995). *Water.* San Diego: Harcourt Brace.

Chase, E. (1995). *Waters.* Buffalo, NY: Firefly Books.

Jeunesse, G. (1996). *Water the source of life: Voyages of discovery.* New York: Scholastic.

Marzollo, J. (1996). *I am water.* New York: Scholastic.

Paz, O. (1997). *My life with the wave.* New York: Lothrop, Lee and Shephard.

Simon, N. (1995). *Wet world.* Cambridge, MA: Candlewick Press.

Wick, W. (1997). *A drop of water.* New York: Scholastic.

Yolen, J. (1995). *Water music: Poems for children.* Honesdale, PA: Wordsong/Boyds Mills Press.

The Letter X

Brutschy, J. (1993). *Winter fox.* New York: Alfred A. Knopf.

Carle, E. (1998). *Hello, red fox.* New York: Simon & Schuster.

Conover, C. (1989). *Mother goose and the sly fox.* New York: Farrar, Strauss, Giroux.

Gregovich, B. (1992). *The fox on the box.* Grand Haven, MI: School Zone Publishing Company.

London, J. (1993) *Gray fox.* New York: Penguin Books.

Marshall, J. (1992). *Fox be nimble.* New York: Penguin Books.

Mason, C. (1993). *Wild fox: A true story.* Camden, ME: Down East Books.

The Letter Y

Battles, E. (1978). *What does the rooster say, Yoshio?* Chicago: Albert Whitman.

Chocolate, D. (1996). *Kente colors.* New York: Walker and Company.

Lecher, D. (1992). *Angelita's magic yarn.* New York: Farrar, Strauss, Giroux.

Radley, G. (1994). *The spinner's gift.* New York: North-South Books.

Seuss, Dr. (1958). *Yertle the turtle and other stories.* New York: Random House.

Shea, P. (1995). *The whispering cloth: A refugee's story.* Honesdale, PA: Boyds Mills Press.

The Letter Z

Hoffman, M. (1985). *Zebra: Animals in the wild.* Milwaukee: Raintree Publishers.

Meaderis, A. (1992). *The zebra-riding cowboy: A folk song from the old west.* New York: Simon & Schuster.

Most, B. (1999). *Z-z-zoink.* New York: Harcourt.

Seracusa, C. (1993). *The giant zucchini.* New York: Hyperion.

Appendix IX

Cooking and Baking Activities to Review Letter Names

Cooking and baking activities can be a motivating way for young children to review letter names and sometimes review letter-sound relationships. Several good sources of cooking and baking activities for the letter names are found in the following books:

Bickert, G., & Britt, L. (1999). *Food to grow and learn on: Activities for young children.* Nashville, TN: Incentive Publishing Company.

Ehlert, L. (1996). *Eating the alphabet.* New York: Red Wagon.

Kohl, M., & Potter, J. (2001). *Snacktivities: Edible activities for parents and young children.* Beltsville, MD: Gryphon House.

Maxwell, S. (2000). *I can cook: How to cook activity projects for the very young.* Bath, England: Anness Publishing Ltd.

Vietch, B., & Harms, T. (1981). *Cook and learn.* Reading, MA: Addison-Wesley.

Here are some cooking and backing choices for each letter of the alphabet.

The Letter A

apple sauce	apple pie	apple cobbler
apricot jam	apple butter	apple salad
apple crisp	apple turnover	apricot pie

The Letter B

butter	banana bread	biscuits
blackberry jam	blueberry jam	blackberry pie
blueberry pie	bean salad	bananas and milk
boysenberry jam	bean soup	bacon and eggs
bread	burritos	cooked broccoli

The Letter C

cake	coleslaw	cupcakes
candy	corn on the cob	corned beef and cabbage
chocolate chip cookies	cooked cauliflower	cooked carrots
custard	cookies	cottage cheese

The Letter D

deviled eggs	devil's food cake	date cookies
doughnuts	dumplings	date nut bread
devil's food cupcakes		

The Letter E

hard-boiled eggs	egg salad sandwich	fried eggplant
soft-boiled eggs	fried eggs	poached eggs
sunny-side up eggs	enchiladas	

The Letter F

fruit salad	fudge	French fries
freedom fries	frosting	fritters

The Letter G

gingerbread person	grape jelly
grilled cheese sandwich	salad with grapes

The Letter H

hamburgers	ham sandwich	hush puppies
ham and cheese sandwich	hash brown potatoes	

The Letter I

ice cream	Irish soda bread

The Letter J

jam sandwich	jelly sandwich
juice	bread and jam

The Letter K

kabob (Have the child thread cut pieces of fruit on a straw to make the kabob.)

The Letter L

lasagna	lemonade
latke (potato pancake)	limeade

The Letter M

muffins	macaroni and cheese	meatballs
macaroni salad	mashed potatoes	

The Letter N

noodles   navy bean soup

The Letter O

oatmeal   oatmeal cookies   orange juice
omelet   onion rings

The Letter P

pancakes   pasta   pear salad
peanut butter   popcorn   peanut butter and
pizza   potato soup   jelly sandwich
pork chops   pudding

The Letter Q

quick bread   quince jelly   quesadilla

The Letter R

raisin pie   raisin cookies   refried beans
raspberry cobbler   raspberry pie   cooked rice
hot rice salad   chocolate-covered raisins

The Letter S

salad   soup   strawberry jam
stone soup (Make stone   string beans
   soup as described in
   book by Brown [1947].)

The Letter T

tomato soup   tomato catsup   tacos
tortillas   tuna casserole   tuna salad sandwich
toast   tapioca pudding   turkey

The Letter U

upside-down cake (use a packaged mix)

The Letter V

vanilla ice cream   vegetable soup   vegetable lasagna

The Letter W

waffles

The Letter Y

yogurt   yogurt shake   baked yams

The Letter Z

zucchini bread   zucchini muffins   zeppole
zucchini fritters   cooked zucchini

Appendix X

Contemporary Easy-to-Read Trade Books

This list of contemporary easy-to-read trade books should help children learn to identify sight words. This list is by no means comprehensive. More suggestions may be found in "Children's Choices," an annual October feature of the *Reading Teacher* journal. Each issue of *The Reading Teacher* also includes an annotated bibliography of a number of books for young children.

Ashman, L. (2002). *Can you make a piggie giggle?* New York: Dutton.

Auch, M. (2003). *The princess and the pizza.* New York: Holiday House.

Bateman, T. (2002). *The princesses have a ball.* New York: Albert Whitman.

Bennett, W. (1997). *The children's book of heroes.* New York: Simon & Schuster.

Bourgeois, P. (1999). *Franklin's class trip.* New York: Scholastic.

Boynton, S. (1998). *Dinosaur's binkit.* New York: Simon & Schuster.

Brimner, L. (2002). *The littlest wolf.* New York: HarperCollins.

Brown, M. (2002). *Arthur, it's only rock and roll.* Boston: Little, Brown.

Brown, M. (2003). *Goodnight moon board book.* New York: HarperCollins.

Capucilli, A., & Schories, P. (1998). *Biscuit finds a friend.* New York: HarperCollins.

Cherrington, J. (1999). *What's that smell? A lift and sniff flap book.* New York: Simon & Schuster.

Child, L. (1999). *Clarice Bear, that's me.* Cambridge, MA: Candlewick.

Cole, B. (1999). *Bad habits.* New York: Dial.

Cole, B. (2002). *Twelone.* New York: Dial.

Cooper, H. (2002). *Tatty ratty.* New York: Harcourt.

Dallas-Conte, J. (1996). *Cock-a-moo-moo.* Boston: Little, Brown.

Davis, K. (2002). *I hate to go to bed.* New York: Harcourt.

Dell 'Oro, S. (2000). *Sneaky salamanders.* New York: First Avenue Editions.

Dyer, J. (2002). *Little bear won't take a nap!* Boston: Little, Brown.

Fernandes, E. (2002). *Busy little mouse.* Toronto, Canada: Kids Can Press.

Grambling, L. (2002). *The witch who wanted to be a princess.* Watertown, MA: Charlesbridge.

Hartman, B. (2002). *The wolf who cried boy.* New York: Putnam.

Hubbard, P. (1999). *Trick or treat countdown.* New York: Holiday House.

Isadora, R. (2001). *ABC pop.* New York: Viking.

Joyce, S. (1998). *ABC animal riddles.* Gilsum, NH: Peel Productions.

Leuck, L. (2002). *My monster mama loves me so.* New York: HarperCollins/Lothrop.

Lillegard, D. (1999). *The big bug ball.* New York: Putnam.

Lite, L. (1996). *Boy and a bear.* North Bend, MN: Specialty Press.

Lithgow, J. (2003). *I'm a manatee.* New York: Simon & Schuster.

London, F. (2002). *Froggy goes to the doctor.* New York: Viking.

Lum, K. (2002). *What! cried granny: An almost bedtime story.* New York: Dial.

Martin, B. (2002). *A beasty story.* New York: Silver Whistle/Harcourt.

McMullen, K. (2002). *I stink!* New York: HarperCollins/Joanna Cottler Books.

McNulty, F. (2002). *If dogs ruled the world.* New York: Cartwheel Books.

Meynard, B. (1999). *Quiet, Wyatt!* New York: Putnam Penguin.

Miller, R. (2002). *The bear on the bed.* Toronto, Canada: Kids Can Press.

Mitton, T. (2002). *Down by the cool of the pool.* New York: Orchard Books.

Munsch, R. (1988). *Love you forever.* Westport, CT: Firefly Books.

Murphy, M. (1999). *Caterpillar's wish.* London: Dorling Kindersley.

Nickle, J. (1998). *The ant bully.* New York: Scholastic.

Numeroff, L. (2002). *If you take a mouse to school.* New York: HarperCollins/Laura Geringer Books.

O'Brien, P. (2002). *Gigantic! How big were the dinosaurs?* New York: Henry Holt.

Paul, A. (2001). *Everything to spend the night from A to Z.* London: DK Ink.

Pienkowski, J. (1999), *Good night: A pop-up lullaby.* Cambridge, MA: Candlewick.

Pinkwater, D. (1999). *Ice cream Larry.* Tarrytown, NY: Marshall Cavendish.

Rex, M. (2002). *The mud monster's Halloween.* New York: Cartwheel Books.

Sabuda, R. (2003). *Alice's adventures in wonderland.* New York: Simon & Schuster.

Sabuda, R., & Reinhart, M. (2001). *Butterflies.* New York: Hyperion.

Salley, C. (2002). *Epossumondas.* New York: Harcourt.

Shannon, D. (1999). *David goes to school.* New York: Blue Sky Press.

Shannon, D. (2002). *Duck on a bike.* New York: Blue Sky Press.

Shields, C. (2002). *The bugliest bug.* Cambridge, MA: Candlewick Press.

Silverstein, S. (1986). *The giving tree.* New York: HarperCollins.

Sloat, T. (2001). *Farmer Brown goes round and round.* London: DK Ink.

Tekavec, H. (2002). *Storm is coming.* New York: Dial.

Van Fleet, M. (2003). *Tails.* New York: Harcourt.

Waddell, M. (2002). *Good job, little bear.* Cambridge, MA: Candlewick.

Wallace, K. (1999). *Ducking days.* London: Dorling Kindersley.

Ward, N. (2002). *Don't eat the teacher!* New York: Cartwheel.

Weeks, S. (2002). *My somebody special.* New York: Harcourt.

Weir, A., Cherrington, J., & Kriegman, M. (1999). *Bear's big blue house.* New York: Simon & Schuster.

Weston, C. (2002). *Lucky socks.* New York: Phyllis Fogelman Books.

Wilkes, A. (1994). *The big book of dinosaurs.* London: DK Publishing.

Yee, W. (1999). *Hamburger heaven.* Boston: Houghton Mifflin.

Zeifert, H. (1999). *Clara Ann Cookie.* Boston: Walter Lorraine Books.

Zekinsky, P. (1990). *Wheels on the bus.* New York: Dutton.

Appendix XI

Further Reading on Phonics

Blevins, W., & Lynch, J. (1999). *Phonics from A to Z.* (Grades K–3). New York: Scholastic.

Cunningham, P. (1999). *Phonics they use: Words for reading and writing.* New York: HarperCollins.

Fox, B., & Hull, M. (2001). *Phonics for the teacher of reading.* Upper Saddle River, NJ: Pearson Education.

Fry, E., Kress, J., & Fountoukidis, D. (2000). *The reading teacher's book of lists* (4th ed.). San Francisco: Jossey-Bass.

Goodman, K. (1993). *Phonics phacts.* Portsmouth, NH: Heinemann.

Heilman, A. (2001). *Phonics in proper perspective.* Upper Saddle River, NJ: Prentice Hall.

Powell, D., & Hornsby, D. (1999). *Learning phonics and spelling in a whole language classroom.* (Grades K–3). New York: Scholastic.

Rinsky, L. (1997). *Teaching word recognition skills.* Upper Saddle River, NJ: Gorsuch Scarisbrick.

Savage, J. (2000). *Sound it out! Phonics in a balanced program.* New York: McGraw-Hill.

Wilson, R. Mills, Wilson, R., Hall, M., Leu, D., & Kinzer, C. (2000). *Phonics, phonemic awareness, and word analysis for teachers: An interactive tutorial.* Upper Saddle River, NJ: Pearson Education.

Appendix XII

Trade Books for Improving Phonic Skills in Context

Many contemporary interesting trade books can be used to teach or review various phonic elements in the context of actual meaningful reading. All children, including those with special needs, need practice in reading trade books that review the various phonic elements. Although the phonic elements may have to be presented in isolation to children with special needs, they should be reinforced by reading appropriate narrative and informational trade books on the child's independent or low instructional reading level.

Reviewing Initial Consonants, Consonant Blends, or Consonant Digraphs

B

D'Allance, M. (2000). *Bear's Christmas star*. New York: Simon & Schuster.

Miller, R. (2002). *The bear on the bed*. Toronto, Canada: Kids Can Press.

Roth, C. (2002). *Little bunny's sleepless night*. New York: North-South Books.

Shields, C. (2002). *The bugliest bug*. Cambridge, MA: Candlewick Press.

Spengler, K. (2002). *The bear: An American folk song*. New York: Mondo Publishing.

C

Cronin, D. (2000). *Click, clack, moo: Cows that type*. New York: Simon & Schuster.

Martin, B. (2001). *Chicken Chuck*. New York: Winston Press.

Murphy, M. (1988). *Caterpillar's wish*. London: Dorling Kindersley.

Schotter, R. (2000). *Captain Bob sets sail*. New York: Atheneum.

Sun, C. (1996). *Cat and cat-face*. Boston: Houghton Mifflin.

D

Alborough, J. (2002). *Duck in the truck*. New York: HarperCollins.

Ehrlich, H. (2000). *Dr. duck*. New York: Orchard Press.

Shannon, D. (2002). *Duck on a bike*. New York: Blue Sky Press.

Wallace, K. (1999). *Duckling days*. London: Dorling Kindersley.

Weeks, S. (2002). *Drip, drop*. New York: HarperCollins.

F

Bourgeois, P. (2002). *Franklin says I love you.* New York: Kids Can Press.

Kelley, M. (1998). *Fall is not easy.* Madison, WI: Zino Press.

Kirkwood, J. (1997). *Fire fighters.* Providence, RI: Copper Beech Press.

London, J. (2002). *Froggie goes to bed.* New York: Viking.

Marshall, J. (1992). *Fox be nimble.* New York: Penguin.

McKissack, P. (1992). *A million fish . . . more or less.* New York: Alfred A. Knopf.

G

Chardiet, B., & Chardiet, J. (1993). *The rough gruff goat brothers rap.* New York: Scholastic.

Morozumi, A. (1997). *My friend gorilla.* New York: Farrar, Strauss, Giroux.

Numeroff, L. (2000). *What grandmas do best/what grandpas do best.* New York: Simon & Schuster.

Palatine, M. (2000). *Good as goldie.* New York: Hyperion.

Roberts, B. *Gramps and the fire dragon.* New York: Clarion Books.

Taylor, B. (1998). *A day at Greenhill farm.* New York: DK Ink.

H

Bancroft, C., & Gruenberg, H. (1993). *Felix's hat.* New York: Macmillan.

Bass, J. (2001). *Herb the vegetarian dragon.* Raleigh, NC: Barefoot Press.

Gardella, T. (1997). *Casey's new hat.* Boston: Houghton Mifflin.

Hadithi, M., & Kenneway, A. (1994). *Hungry hyena.* Boston: Little, Brown.

Stille, D. (1997). *Helicopters.* Chicago: Children's Press.

J

Egielski, R. (1998). *Jazper.* New York: HarperCollins.

Hru, D. (1996). *The magic moonberry jump ropes.* New York: Penguin.

Melmed, L. (1999). *Jumbo's lullaby.* New York: HarperCollins/Lathrop.

Seymour, T. (1999). *Jake Johnson: The story of a mule.* New York: DK Ink.

K

Anholt, C., & Anholt, L. (1992). *Kids.* Cambridge, MA: Candlewick.

Helmer, D. (1997). *The koala bear: The bear that is not a bear.* New York: Rosen.

Hogan, P. (1991). *The life cycle of the kangaroo: A new true book.* Chicago: Children's Press.

Lundell, M. (1995). *A girl named Helen Keller.* New York: Scholastic.

Marzollo, Ç. (1992). *Kenny and the little kickers.* New York: Scholastic.

L

Adler, D. (1989). *A picture book of Abraham Lincoln.* New York: Holiday House.

Gliori, D. (1993). *A lion at bedtime.* Hauppauge, NY: Barron's.

Krauss, R. (1998). *Little Louie the baby bloomer.* New York: HarperCollins.

London, J., & Long, S. (1994). *Liplap's wish.* San Francisco: Chronicle Books.

Wolf, G. (1996). *The very hungry lion.* New York: Annick Press, Ltd.

M

Bartram, S. (2003). *Playhouse.* New York: Cartwheel Books.

Graham, B. (1998). *Max's bath.* Cambridge, MA: Candlewick Press.

Krauss, R. (2000). *Mouse in love.* New York: Orchard Books.

Miranda, O. (2000). *Monster math.* New York: Harcourt.

Numeroff, L. (2000). *If you take a mouse to the movies.* New York: HarperCollins.

Rex, M. (2002). *The mud monster's Halloween.* New York: Cartwheel Books.

N

Jenkins, P. (1996). *Falcon's nest on skyscrapers: Let's-read-and-find-out science.* New York: HarperCollins.

Masner, J. (1989). *Nicholas cricket.* New York: Harper & Row.

Novak, M. (1996). *Newt.* New York: HarperCollins.

Winshinsky, F. (2000). *Nothing scares us.* Minneapolis: Carolrhoda Books.

P

Bateman, T. (2002). *The princesses have a ball.* New York: Albert Whitman.

Brooks, E. (2000). *The practically perfect pajamas.* Chesterfield, Derbyshire, England: Winslow Press.

Herman, R. (2002). *Pal the pony.* New York: Grosset & Dunlap.

Johnston, P. (1999). *The pig who ran a red light.* New York: Orchard.

Munsch, R. (2003). *Playhouse.* New York: Cartwheel Press.

Seeber, D. (2002). *A pup just for me/A boy just for me.* New York: Philomel.

Q

Arnold, M. (1996). *Quick, quack, quick!* New York: Random House.

Carle, E. (1990). *The very quiet cricket.* New York: Philomel.

Guback, G. (1994). *Luka's quilt.* New York: Greenwillow Books.

Hiatt, F. (1997). *If I were queen of the world.* New York: Simon & Schuster.

Turner, A. (1994). *Sewing quilts.* New York: Macmillan.

R

Coxe, M. (1997). *R is for radish.* New York: Random House.

Darling, K. (1997). *Rain forest babies.* New York: Walker.

Han, S. (1995). *The rabbit's escape.* New York: Henry Holt.

Ho, M., & Ros, S. (1997). *Brother rabbit: A Cambodian tale.* New York: Lothrop, Lee & Shephard.

Johnston, M. (1998). *Rhinos.* New York: Rosen.

S

Dell 'Oro, S. (2000). *Sneaky salamanders.* New York: First Avenue Editions.

Joyce, W. (2000). *Snowie rolie.* New York: HarperCollins.

Otto, C. (2002). *Spiders.* New York: Scholastic.

Spinelli, E. (2000). *Six hogs on a scooter.* New York: Orchard Books.

Weeks, S. (2002). *My somebody special.* New York: Harcourt.

Weston, C. (2002). *Lucky socks.* New York: Phyllis Fogelman Books.

T

Chardiet, B., & Maccarone, B. (1990). *The best teacher in the world.* New York: Scholastic.

Cole, R. (2002). *Truelove.* New York: Dial.

Lindberg, B. (1994). *Thomas turtle, just in time.* New York: Albert Whitman.

Miles, B. (1998). *Tortoise and the hare.* New York: Simon & Schuster.

Yorinks, A. (1999). *Tomatoes from Mars.* New York: HarperCollins.

Ziefert, H. (1996). *The turnip.* New York: Penguin.

V

Carrick, C. (1995). *Valentine.* New York: Clarion Books.

Cocca-Leffler, M. (1996). *Lots of hearts.* New York: Grosset & Dunlap.

Hoban, L. (1989). *Arthur's great big valentine.* New York: Harper & Row.

Sharmat, M. (1994). *Nate the great and the mushy valentine.* New York: Bantam Doubleday Dell.

W

Brumner, L. (2002). *The littlest wolf.* New York: HarperCollins.

Egan, R. (1997). *From wheat to pasta.* Chicago: Children's Press.

Henkes, K. (2000). *Wemberly worried.* New York: Greenwillow Books.

Jonas, A. (1997). *Watch William walk.* New York: Greenwillow Books.

Lester, H. (2002). *Hooray for Wodney Wat.* Boston: Walter Lorraine Books.

Morris, A. (1998). *Work.* New York: Lothrop, Lee & Shephard.

X

Gregovich, B. (1992). *The fox on the box.* Grand Haven, MI: School Zone Publishing Company.

London, J. (1993). *Gray fox.* New York: Penguin.

Saunders, S. (1991). *Seasons of a red fox: Smithsonian wild heritage collection.* Nowalk, CT: Trudy Management Corporation.

Y

Castenada, O. (1993). *Abuela's weave.* New York: Lee & Low Books.

Chocolate, D. (1996). *Kente colors.* New York: Walker and Company.

Lecher, D. (1992). *Angelita's magic yarn.* New York: Farrar, Straus & Giroux.

Z

Asch, F. (1998). *Ziggy piggy and the three little pigs.* New York: Kids Can Press.

Siracusa, C. (1993). *The giant zucchini.* New York: Hyperion.

Tabor, N. (1994). *Cincuenta en la cebra: Contando con los animals/Fifty of the zebra: Counting with animals.* Watertown, MA: Charlesbridge Publishing.

Vowels

Long and/or Short /a/

Breckler, R. (1996). *Sweet dried apples: A Vietnamese wartime childhood.* Boston: Houghton Mifflin.

Nickle, J. (1998). *The ant bully.* New York: Scholastic.

Oppenheim, J. (1990). *Wake up, baby!* New York: Bantam.

Robart, R. (1986). *The cake that Mack ate.* Toronto, Canada: Kids Can Press.

Slawson, M. (1994). *Apple picking time.* New York: Crown.

Long and/or Short /e/

Berry, J. (1999). *Don't leave an elephant to go and chase a bird.* New York: Simon & Schuster.

Gantos, J. (1999). *Wedding bells for rotten Ralph.* New York: HarperCollins.

Karas, B. (2000). *Bebe's bad dream.* New York: Greenwillow Books.

Mayo, M. (2000). *Emergency.* Minneapolis: Carolrhoda Books.

Long and/or Short /i/

Harper, J. (2000). *I'm not going to chase the cat today!* New York: HarperCollins.

Kirk, D. (1999). *Little miss spider.* New York: Scholastic.

McMullen, K. (2002). *I stink!* New York: HarperCollins/Joanna Cotler Books.

Otto, C. (2000). *Spiders.* New York: Scholastic.

Partes, J. (2000). *Stripe.* Minneapolis: Carolrhoda Books.

Slate, J. (2000). *Miss Bindergarten stays home from kindergarten.* New York: Dutton.

Long and/or Short /o/

Bos, B. (1995). *Ollie the elephant.* New York: North-South Books.

Buchey, J. (1994). *A sled dog for Moshi.* New York: Hyperion.

Freymann, S., & Elffers, J. (2000). *Dr. Pompo's nose.* New York: Arthur A. Levine/Scholastic.

Gralley, J. (2002). *Hogula, dread pig of night.* New York: Henry Holt.

Lobato, A. (2002). *The secret of the North Pole.* Boston: McGraw-Hill.

Most, B. (1991). *My very own octopus.* San Diego: Harcourt Brace.

Pringle, L. (1993). *Octopus hug.* Honesdale, PA: Boyds Mills Press.

Schotter, R. (2000). *Captain Bob sets sail.* New York: Anne Schwartz Books/Atheneum.

Long and/or Short /u/

Melmed, L. (1999). *Jumbo's lullaby.* New York: HarperCollins/Lothrop.

Meyers, O. (1988). *The enchanted umbrella: With a short history of the umbrella.* San Diego: Harcourt Brace Jovanovich.

O'Malley, K. (2002). *Little buggy.* New York: Harcourt.

Wormell, C. (2002). *Blue rabbit and friends.* New York: Phyllis Fogelman/Dial.

Diphthongs

Conley, D. (2001). *Get fuzzy: The dog is not a toy.* Kansas City, MO: Andrews McMeel Publishing.

Jaffe, N. (1996). The *golden flower: A Taino myth from Puerto Rico.* New York: Simon & Schuster.

Kraus, R. (2000). *Mouse in love.* New York: Orchard Books.

Morris, A. (1992). *Houses and homes.* New York: William Morrow.

Oppenheim, J. (1989). *Not now! said the cow.* New York: Bantam.

Slangerup, E. (2003). *Dirt boy.* New York: Albert Whitman.

Waber, B. (2000). *The mouse that snored.* Boston: Walter Lorraine Books/Houghton Mifflin.

Appendix XIII

Books to Promote Enjoyment of Words

Pure Enjoyment

Boynton, S. (2003). *Fuzzy fuzzy fuzzy: A touch, skritch, and tickle book.* New York: Simon & Schuster.

Brett, J. (1999). *Gingerbread baby.* New York: Putnam.

Cronin, D. (2002). *Giggle, giggle quack.* New York: Simon & Schuster.

Findlay, L. (2002). *The cat in the hat big sticker book.* New York: Bantam Doubleday Dell.

Flansburgh, J. (2002). *They might be giants.* New York: Simon & Schuster.

Gerth, M. (2000). *Ten little ladybugs.* Santa Monica, CA: Intervisual Books.

Guarino, D. (1997). *Is your mama a llama?* New York: Scholastic.

Joose, B. (1996). *I love you the purplest.* San Francisco: Chronicle Books LLC.

Keller, L. (2003). *Arnie the doughnut.* New York: Henry Holt.

Keller, L. (2003). *Open wide: Tooth school for young readers.* New York: Henry Holt.

Lichtenheld, T. (2003). *What are you so grumpy about?* Boston: Little, Brown.

McCann, J. (2003). *How to draw Scooby Doo!* New York: Barnes & Noble Books.

Myers, R. (1995). *365 knock-knock jokes.* New York: Barnes & Noble Books.

Nelson, M. (2001). *Elmo's world: Animals!* New York: Random House.

Pilkey, D. (2001). *Captain Underpants and the wrath of the wicked wedgie woman.* New York: Scholastic.

Sabuda, R. (2003). *Alice's adventures in wonderland pop-up book.* New York: Simon & Schuster.

Schwartz, A. (1985). *In a dark, dark room and other scary stories.* New York: Harper Collins.

Spotlight, S. (2002). *Bob's big story collection.* New York: Simon & Schuster.

Yoon, S. (2004). *My shimmery learning book: Colors, shapes, counting, opposites, getting dressed.* Santa Monica, CA: Intervisual Books.

Zelinsky, P. (2002). *Knick-knack paddywhack!: A moving parts book.* New York: Dutton.

Riddle Books

Aboff, M. (2004). *The giant jellybean jar.* New York: Penguin Putnam.

Balderstone, R. (1999). *What am I?* Cambridge, England: Cambridge University Press.

Big Book of Jokes and Riddles. (2003). New York: Kidsbooks Incorporated.

Carter, D. (1999). *Giggle bugs: A lift-and-laugh book.* New York: Simon & Schuster.

Cole, J., & Calmenson, S. (1995). *Ready . . . set . . . read and laugh: A funny treasury for beginning readers.* New York: Bantam Doubleday Dell.

Eisenberg, L. (2003). *Puppy love* (Riddle in the Middle Series). New York: HarperCollins.

Maestro, M., & Maestro, G. (1997). *What do you hear when cows sing?: And other silly riddles.* New York: HarperCollins.

Marzollo, J. (1997). *I spy super challenger! A book of picture riddles.* New York: Scholastic.

Appendix XIV

Poetry Books for Young Children

Here is a sample of contemporary books of poetry that can be used with young children. Many others are equally useful.

Ada, A. (2003). *Pio Peep!: Traditional Spanish nursery rhymes*. New York: HarperCollins.

Carlisle, B. (1997). *Butterfly kisses: A narrative poem celebrating the love between fathers and daughters*. New York: Golden Books.

Cole, J. (1989). *Anna banana: 101 jump rope rhymes*. New York: William Morrow & Company.

Crews, N. (2003). *The neighborhood Mother Goose*. New York: HarperCollins.

Dahl, R. (1995). *Roald Dahl's revolting rhymes*. New York: Puffin Books.

Dakos, K. (1995). *If you're not here, please raise your hand: Poems about school*. New York: Simon & Schuster.

Fleishman, P. (1992). *Joyful noise: Poems for two voices*. New York: HarperCollins.

Frederick, R. (2000). *Mother Goose's nursery rhymes*. New York: Barnes & Noble Books.

Frost, R. (2001). *Stopping by woods on a snowy evening*. New York: Dutton.

Greenfield, E. (1986). *Honey, I love and other poems*. New York: HarperCollins.

Hague, M. (2001). *Teddy bear's Mother Goose*. New York: Henry Holt.

Lobel, A. (2003). *Book of Mother Goose: A treasury of more than 300 classic nursery rhymes*. New York: William Morrow & Company.

Marzollo, J. (1999). *I love you: A rebus poem*. New York: Scholastic.

Milne, A. (2001). *Complete tales and poems of Winnie the Pooh: 75th anniversary edition*. New York: Dutton.

Novick, M. (2003). *Double delights nursery rhymes*. New York: Barnes & Noble Books.

Opie, I. (1996). *My very first Mother Goose*. New York: Scholastic.

Peterson, M. (1998). *Mother Goose*. Orlando, FL: Disney Press.

Prelutsky, J., & Corey, S. (1983). *The Random House book of poetry for children*. New York: Random House.

Sabuda, R. (1999). *Movable Mother Goose: A classic collectible pop-up.* New York: Simon & Schuster.

Seuss, Dr. (1996). *There's a wocket in my pocket: Dr. Seuss books of ridiculous rhymes.* New York: Random House.

Silverstein, S. (1996). *Falling up: Poems and drawings.* New York: HarperCollins.

Silverstein, S. (2004). *Where the sidewalk ends.* New York: HarperCollins.

Stevenson, R. (1999). *A child's garden of verses.* New York: Simon & Schuster.

Wells, R. (2002). *The very best of Mother Goose.* New York: Michael Friedman.

Wright, B. (1994). *Real Mother Goose.* New York: Scholastic.

Appendix XV

Books for Visual Imagery

Here is a sampling of trade books that can easily be used to help young children create visual images. Countless other books are equally useful.

Barrie, J. (2003). *Peter Pan: The original story.* New York: HarperCollins.

Baum, F., & Sabuda, R. (2000). *The wonderful Wizard of Oz.* New York: Simon & Schuster.

Boynton, S. (1998). *Dinosaur's binkit.* New York: Simon & Schuster.

Boynton, S. (2003). *Snuggle puppy.* New York: Workman Publishing.

Burnett, F. (1995). *Little princess.* New York: Barnes & Noble Books.

Carroll, L. (2004). *Alice's adventures in Wonderland and through the looking-glass.* New York: Barnes & Noble Books.

Catling, P. (1996). *The chocolate touch.* New York: Bantam Doubleday Dell.

Dahl, R. (1996). *James and the giant peach.* New York: Puffin.

Dahl, R. (1998). *The witches' hat.* New York: Puffin.

Grahame, K. (1995). *The wind in the willows.* New York: Barnes & Noble Books.

Gustafson, S. (1996). *Nutcracker.* New York: Barnes & Noble Books.

Lewis, C. (1994). *The lion, the witch and the wardrobe.* New York: HarperCollins.

Lofting, H. (2002). *The story of Dr. Doolittle.* New York: Barnes & Noble Books.

McBrier, P. (2001). *Beatrice's goat.* New York: Simon & Schuster.

Montgomery, L. (1991). *Complete Anne of Green Gables.* New York: Bantam Doubleday Dell.

Numeroff, L. (2000). *If you take a mouse to the movies.* New York: HarperCollins.

Rothmann, P. (2003). *The day the babies crawled away.* New York: Putnam.

Sabuda, R., & Carroll, L. (2003). *Alice's adventures in Wonderland.* New York: Simon & Schuster.

Sears, W., Sears, M., & Kelly, C. (2001). *Baby on the way.* Boston: Little, Brown.

Sendak, M. (1995). *In the night kitchen.* New York: HarperCollins.

Shriver, M. (1999). *Where's heaven?* New York: Golden Books.

Wells, R. (2001). *The McDuff stories.* New York: Hyperion.

West, T. (2000). *Journey to Orange Island.* New York: Scholastic.

Wiggins, K. (2002). *Rebecca of Sunnybrook Farm.* New York: Barnes & Noble Books.

Wilder, L. (1997). *Christmas in the big woods.* New York: HarperCollins.

Williams, M. (1996). *The velveteen rabbit: Or how toys become real.* New York: Barnes & Noble Books.

Bibliography

Works Cited

Chapter One

Allen, R. V. (1976). *Language experiences in communication.* Boston: Houghton Mifflin.

Crafton, L. (1991). *Whole language: Getting started . . . moving forward.* Katonah, NY: Richard C. Owen.

Durkin, D. (1966). *Children who read early.* New York: Teachers College Press.

Guarino, D. (1989). *Is your mama a llama?* New York: Scholastic.

Morrow, L. (1997). *Literacy development in the early years.* Boston: Allyn & Bacon.

Paulsen, G., & Paulsen, R. (1998). *The tortilla factory.* San Diego: Harcourt.

Chapter Two

Clay. M. (2002). *An observational survey of early literacy achievement.* Portsmouth, NH: Heinemann.

Learning Media. (1991). *Dancing with the pen: The learner as a writer.* Wellington, New Zealand: Ministry of Education.

Chapter Three

Abrahamson, R. (1981). An update on wordless picture books with an annotated bibliography. *The Reading Teacher, 34,* 417–421.

Brown, R., Cazden, C., & Bellugi-Klima, U. (1968). The child's grammar from one to three. In J. Hall (Ed.), *Minnesota symposium on child development.* Minneapolis: University of Minnesota Press.

Chomsky, N. (1965). *Aspects of a theory of syntax.* Cambridge: MIT Press.

Halliday, M. (1975). *Exploration in the functions of language.* London: Edward Arnold.

Lennenberg, E. (1967). *Biological foundations of language.* New York: John Wiley.

McNeil, D. (1970). *The acquisition of language: The study of developmental psycholinguistics.* New York: Harper & Row.

Miller, W. (1967). *Relationship between mother's style of communication and her control system to the child's reading readiness and subsequent reading achievement in first grade.* Unpublished doctoral dissertation at the University of Arizona, Tucson.

Neuman, S., & Roskos, K. (1993). *Language and literacy for the early years.* Fort Worth, TX: Harcourt Brace Jovanovich.

Piaget, J., & Inhelder, B. (1969). *The psychology of the child.* New York: Basic Books.

Pinnell, G., & Jaggar, A. (1992). Oral language: Speaking and listening in the classroom. In J. Flood et al. (Eds.), *Handbook of research in teaching the English language arts.* New York: Macmillan.

Skinner, B. F. (1957). *Verbal behavior.* New York: Appleton-Century-Crofts.

Stauffer, R. G. (1980). *The language experience approach to the teaching of reading.* New York: Harper & Row.

Vygotsky, L. (1978). *Mind in society: The development of psychological processes.* Cambridge: Harvard University Press.

Chapter Four

Allen, P. (1982). *Who sank the boat?* New York: Coward-McCann.

Ashton-Warner, S. (1963). *Teacher.* New York: Touchstone Press.

Cunningham, P. (1980). Teaching were, with, what, and other "four-letter" words. *The Reading Teacher, 34,* 160–163.

Dickerson, D. (1982). A study of the use of games to reinforce sight vocabulary. *The Reading Teacher, 36,* 46–49.

Durrell, D. (1980). Letter-name value in reading and spelling. *Reading Research Quarterly, 16,* 46–49.

Fry, E., Kress, J., & Fountoukidis, D. (2000). *The reading teacher's book of lists* (4th ed.). San Francisco: Jossey-Bass.

McBroom, M., Sparrow, J., & Eckstein, C. (1944). *Scale for determining a child's reading level* (p. 11). Iowa City: Bureau of Publications, Extension Service, University of Iowa.

Press, H. (2001). *The little giant book of science experiments.* New York: Barnes & Noble.

Seuss, Dr. (1950). *Bartholomew and the oobleck.* New York: Random House.

Chapter Five

Adams, M. (1990). *Beginning to read: Thinking and learning about print.* Cambridge: MIT Press.

Clymer, T. (1963). The utility of phonic generalizations in the primary grades. *The Reading Teacher, 12,* 252–258.

Cunningham, P. (1987). Action phonics. *The Reading Teacher, 41,* 247–249.

Cunningham, P. (1999). *Phonics they use: Words for reading and writing.* New York: HarperCollins.

Fry, E., Kress, J., & Fountoukidis, D. (2000). *The reading teacher's book of lists* (4th ed.). San Francisco: Jossey-Bass.

May, F. (1998). *Reading as communication.* Upper Saddle River, NJ: Prentice Hall.

Stahl, S., Osborne, J., & Lehr, F. (1990). *Beginning to read: Thinking and learning about print—A summary.* Urbana-Champaign, IL: Center for the Study of Reading.

Chapter Six

Fry, E., Kress, J., & Fountoukidis, D. (2000). *The reading teacher's book of lists* (4th ed.). San Francisco: Jossey-Bass.

Gunning, T. (1996). *Creating reading instruction for all children* (pp. 132–150). Boston: Allyn & Bacon.

Rinsky, L. (1997). *Teaching word recognition skills.* Upper Saddle River, NJ: Gorsuch Scarisbrick.

Shanker, J., & Ekwall, E. (2002). *Locating and correcting reading difficulties.* Upper Saddle River, NJ: Prentice Hall.

Taylor, W. (1953). Cloze procedure: A new tool for measuring readability. *Journalism Quarterly, 39,* 234–237.

Chapter Seven

Adams, M. (1991). *Beginning to read: Thinking about learning and print.* Urbana-Champaign, IL: Center for the Study of Reading.

Anderson, R. C., Wilson, P. T., & Fielding, L. G. (1988). Growth in reading and how children spend their time outside of school. *Reading Research Quarterly, 23,* 285–303.

Chall, J. (1987). Two vocabularies for recognition and meaning. In M. G. McKeown and M. E. Curtis (Eds.), *The nature of vocabulary acquisition* (pp. 7–17). Hillsdale, NJ: Lawrence Erlbaum.

Graves, M. (1987). Roles of instruction in vocabulary development. In M. G. McKeown and M. E. Curtis (Eds.), *The nature of vocabulary acquisition* (pp. 165–184). Hillsdale, NJ: Lawrence Erlbaum.

Graves, M., Juel, C., & Graves, B. (2003). *Teaching reading in the 21st century.* Needham Heights, MA: Allyn & Bacon.

Jacobi-Karna, K. (1996). Music and children's books. *The Reading Teacher, 49,* 56–64.

Koos, K. (1986). Puppet plays. *First Teacher, 7*(5), 56–64.

Miller, W. (2001). *The reading teacher's survival kit* (pp. 11–136). San Francisco: Jossey-Bass.

Nagy, W., & Herman, P. (1987). Breadth and depth of vocabulary knowledge. In M. G. McKeown and M. E. Curtis (Eds.), *The nature of vocabulary acquisition* (pp. 19–35). Hillsdale, NJ: Lawrence Erlbaum.

Silverstein, S. (1992). *The giving tree.* New York: HarperCollins.

Stauffer, R. G. (1975). *Directing the reading-thinking process.* New York: Harper & Row.

Stauffer, R. T. (1980). *The language-experience approach to the teaching of reading.* New York: Harper & Row.

Additional Reading

Chapter Two

Barbe, W., & Allen, H. (1999). *Reading skills competency tests: Fourth level* (p. 14). San Francisco: Jossey-Bass.

Barbe, W., & Allen, H. (1999). *Reading skills competency tests: Fifth level* (p. 14). San Francisco: Jossey-Bass.

Barbe, W., Allen, H., & Sparkman, B. (1999). *Reading skills competency tests: Readiness level* (p. 14). San Francisco: Jossey-Bass.

Barbe, W., Allen, H., & Thornton, W. (1999). *Reading skills competency tests: First level* (p. 14). San Francisco: Jossey-Bass.

Barbe, W., Allen, H., & Thornton, W. (1999). *Reading skills competency tests: Second level* (p. 14). San Francisco: Jossey-Bass.

Barbe, W., Allen, H., & Thornton, W. (1999). *Reading skills competency tests: Third level* (p. 14). San Francisco: Jossey-Bass.

Clay, M. (2002). *An observational survey of early literacy achievement.* Portsmouth, NH: Heinemann.

Chaliff, C., & Ritter, M. (2001). The use of miscue analysis with deaf readers. *The Reading Teacher, 55,* 190–200.

Ekwall, E., & Shanker, J. (1998). *Locating and correcting reading difficulties* (7th ed.). Upper Saddle River, NJ: Merrill/Prentice Hall.

Hoffman, J., Assaf, L., & Paris, S. (2001). High-stakes testing in reading: Today in Texas, tomorrow? *The Reading Teacher, 54,* 482–492.

McCabe, P. (2003). Enhancing self-efficacy for high-stakes reading tests. *The Reading Teacher, 57,* 12–20.

Miller, W. (1993). *Complete reading disabilities handbook* (pp. 64–95). San Francisco: Jossey-Bass.

Miller, W. (1995). *Alternative assessment techniques for reading & writing* (pp. 122–140, 141–175, 158-215). San Francisco: Jossey-Bass.

Miller, W. (2000). *Strategies for developing emergent literacy* (pp. 217–236). New York: McGraw-Hill.

Miller, W. (2001). *The reading teacher's survival kit* (pp. 11–136). San Francisco: Jossey-Bass.

Miller, W. (2003). *Survival reading skills for secondary students* (pp. 11–48). San Francisco: Jossey-Bass.

Reutzel, R., & Cooter, R. (2000). *Teaching children to read* (pp. 346–396). Upper Saddle River, NJ: Merrill.

Valencia, R., & Villarreal, B. Improving students' reading performance via standards-based reform: A critique. *The Reading Teacher, 56,* 612–621.

Chapter Three

Belk, J., & Thompson, R. (2001). *Worm painting and 44 more hands-on language arts activities for the primary grades.* Newark, DE: International Reading Association.

Campbell, R. (2001). *Read-alouds with young children.* Newark, DE: International Reading Association.

Dickinson, D., McCabe, A., & Sprague, K. Teacher rating of oral language and literacy (TROLL): Individualizing early literacy instruction with a standards-based rating tool. *The Reading Teacher, 56,* 554–564.

Fields, M., & Spangler, K. (2003). *Let's begin reading right.* Upper Saddle River, NJ: Prentice Hall.

Hadaway, N., Vardell, S., & Young, T. (2001). Scaffolding oral language development through poetry for students learning English. *The Reading Teacher, 54,* 796–806.

Jewell, T., & Pratt, D. (1999). Literature discussions in the primary grades: Children's thoughtful discourse about books and what teachers can do to make it happen. *The Reading Teacher, 52,* 842–850.

Mayesky, M. (1995). *Creative activities for young children.* Albany, NY: Delmar Publishers.

McGee, L. (2003). *Designing early literacy programs for at-risk preschool and kindergarten children.* New York: Guilford Publications.

Morrow, L. (1997). *Literacy development in the early years: Helping children read and write.* Boston: Allyn & Bacon.

Reutzel, R., & Cooter, R. (2002). *Strategies for reading assessment and instruction: Helping every child succeed.* Upper Saddle River, NJ: Prentice Hall.

Seifeldt, C., & Galper, A. (2000). *Active experiences for active children.* Upper Saddle River, NJ: Pearson Education.

Snow, C., Tabors, P., Nicholson, P., & Kurland, B. (1995). SHELL: Oral language and early literacy skills in kindergarten and first-grade children. *Journal of Research in Childhood Education, 10,* 37–48.

Chapter Four

Allen, R. (1976). *Language experience in communication.* Boston: Houghton Mifflin.

Brown, K. (2003). What do I say when they get stuck on a word? Aligning teachers' prompts with students' development. *The Reading Teacher, 56,* 720–733.

Brown, R., & Carey, S. (1998). *Hands-on alphabet activities for young children.* Paramus, NJ: The Center for Applied Research in Education.

Lenters, K. (2003). The many lives of the cut-up sentence. *The Reading Teacher, 56,* 535–536.

May, F. (1998). *Reading as communication* (pp. 142–172). Upper Saddle River, NJ: Prentice Hall.

Meier, T. (2003). Why can't she remember that? *The Reading Teacher, 57,* 242–252.

Muncy, P. (1995). *Complete book of illustrated reading and writing activities for the primary grades* (pp. 3–14 & 119–172). San Francisco: Jossey-Bass.

Orellana, M., & Hernandez, A. (1999). Talking the walk: Children reading urban environmental print. *The Reading Teacher, 52,* 612–619.

Pinnell, G. (1996). Ensuring success for the beginning reader. In J. Baltas & S. Shafer (Eds.), *Guide to balanced reading K-2* (pp. 36–42). New York: Scholastic.

Reutzel, D., & Cooter, R. (2003). *Teaching children to read.* Upper Saddle River, NJ: Merrill.

Richgels, D. (2002). Information texts in kindergarten. *The Reading Teacher, 55,* 586–595.

Shanker, J., & Ekwall, E. (2002). *Locating and correcting reading difficulties.* Upper Saddle River, NJ: Pearson Education.

Smith, J. (2000). Singing and songwriting support early literacy instruction. *The Reading Teacher, 53,* 646–651.

Waring, C. (1999). *Developing letter-sound connections.* Paramus, NJ: The Center for Applied Research in Education.

Chapter Five

Blevins, W., & Lynch, J. (1999). *Phonics from A to Z* (Grades K–3). New York: Scholastic.

Cunningham, P. (2000). *Phonics they use: Words for reading and writing.* New York: HarperCollins.

Dahl, K., & Scharer, P. (2000). Phonics teaching and learning in whole language classrooms: New evidence from research. *The Reading Teacher, 53,* 584–594.

Eldridge, L. (2003). *Phonics for teachers: Self-instruction methods and activitie*s. Upper Saddle River, NJ: Prentice Hall.

Fox, B. (2003). *Word identification strategies: Phonics from a new perspective.* Upper Saddle River, NJ: Prentice Hall.

Fox, B., & Hull, M. (2001). *Phonics for the teacher of reading.* Upper Saddle River, NJ: Pearson Education.

Fry, E., Kress, J., & Fountoukidis, D. (2000). *The reading teacher's book of lists* (4th ed.). San Francisco: Jossey-Bass.

Goodman, K. (1993). *Phonics phacts.* Portsmouth, NH: Heinemann.

Heilman, A. (2001). *Phonics in proper perspective.* Paramus, NJ: Prentice Hall.

Johnston, F. (2001). The utility of phonics generalizations. *The Reading Teacher, 55,* 132–143.

Powell, D., & Hornsby, D. (1999). *Learning phonics and spelling in a whole language classroom* (Grades K–3). New York: Scholastic.

Rinsky, L. (1997). *Teaching word recognition skills.* Upper Saddle River, NJ: Gorsuch Scarisbrick.

Savage, J. (2000). *Sound it out! Phonics in a balanced program.* New York: McGraw-Hill.

Wilson, R., Wilson, R., Hall, M., Leu, D., & Kinzer, C. (2000). *Phonics, phonemic awareness, and word analysis for teachers: An interactive material.* Upper Saddle River, NJ: Pearson Education.

Yopp, H., & Yopp, R. (2000). Supporting phonemic awareness development in the classroom. *The Reading Teacher, 54,* 130–143.

Chapter Six

Allen, H., & Barbe, W. (1998). *Ready-to-use vocabulary, word analysis & comprehension activities: Second-grade reading level.* Paramus, NJ: Prentice Hall.

Allen, H., & Barbe, W. (1998). *Ready-to-use vocabulary, word analysis & comprehension activities: Third-grade reading level.* Paramus, NJ: Prentice Hall.

Allen, H., Barbe, W., & Lehner, R. (1998). *Ready-to-use vocabulary, word analysis & comprehension activities: First-grade reading level.* Paramus, NJ: Prentice Hall.

Brown, M. (2000). *Goodnight moon board book and nightlight.* New York: HarperCollins.

Cheek, E., Flippo, R., & Lindsey, J. (1997). *Reading for success in elementary schools* (pp. 122–129). Madison, WI: Brown & Benchmark.

Cole, B. (2002). *Truelove.* New York: Dial.

Dahl, K., et al. (2003). Connecting developmental word study with classroom writing: Children's descriptions of spelling strategies. *The Reading Teacher, 57,* 310–319.

Edwards, W. (2002). *Alphabeasts.* Toronto, Canada: Kids Can Press.

Fry, E., Kress, J., & Fountoukidis, D. (2000). *The reading teacher's book of lists* (4th ed.). San Francisco: Jossey-Bass.

Gerth, M. (2000). *Ten little ladybugs.* Santa Monica, CA: Intervisual Books.

Gunning, T. (2001). *Building words* (pp. 199–228). Boston: Allyn & Bacon.

Gustafson, S. (1996). *Nutcracker.* New York: Barnes & Noble Books.

Koutsky, J. (2002). *My grandma, my pen pal.* Honesdale, PA: Caroline House/Boyds Mills Press.

May, F. (2001). *Reading as communication.* Upper Saddle River, NJ: Prentice Hall.

Miller, W. (2002). *Reading skills problem solver* (pp. 123–200). San Francisco: Jossey-Bass.

Muncy, P. (1997). *Complete book of illustrated reading & writing activities for the primary grades* (pp. 102–115, 250–260). San Francisco: Jossey-Bass.

Pilkey, D. (2001). *Captain Underpants and the wrath of the wicked wedge woman.* New York: Scholastic.

Shanker, J., & Ekwall, E. (2002). *Locating and correcting reading difficulties.* Columbus, OH: Merrill/Prentice Hall.

Vacca, J., Vacca, R., & Gove, M. (2002). *Reading and learning to read.* New York: HarperCollins.

Weeks, S. (2002). *My somebody special.* New York: Harcourt.

Wiggins, K. (2002). *Rebecca of sunnybrook farm.* New York: Barnes & Noble.

Zelinsky, P. (2002). *Knick-knack paddywhack!: A moving parts book.* New York: Dutton.

Chapter Seven

Barton, J., & Sawyer, D. (2004). Our students *are* ready for this: Comprehension instruction in the elementary school. *The Reading Teacher, 57,* 334–347.

Blachowicz, C., & Ogle, D. (2001). *Reading comprehension.* New York: Guilford.

Burns, P., Roe., B., & Smith, S. (2001). *Teaching reading in today's elementary schools.* Boston: Houghton Mifflin.

Clyde, J. (2003). Stepping inside the story world: The subtext strategy—a tool for connecting and comprehending. *The Reading Teacher, 57,* 150–160.

Gambrell, L., Morrow, L., & Pressley, M. (Eds.). (2003). *Best practices in literacy instruction.* New York: Guilford.

Gerber, C. (1995). *Reading for understanding—Grade 1.* New York: McGraw-Hill.

Harvey, S., & Goudvis, A. (2000). *Strategies that work: Teaching comprehension to enhance understanding.* Portland, ME: Stenhouse Publishers.

May, F. (2001). *Reading as communication.* Upper Saddle River, NJ: Prentice Hall.

McLaughlin, M., & Allen, M. (2001). *Guided comprehension: A teaching model for grades 3–8.* Newark, DE: International Reading Association.

Miller, W. (2001). *The reading teacher's survival kit.* San Francisco: Jossey-Bass.

Owocki, G. (2003). *Comprehension: Strategies for K–3 students.* Portsmouth, NH: Heinemann.

Pinnell, G., & Deford, D. (2003). *Teaching for comprehension in reading, Grades 1–3: Theory and practice.* New York: Scholastic.

Shanker, J., & Ekwall, E. (2002). *Locating and correcting reading difficulties.* Upper Saddle River, NJ: Pearson Education.

Zimmerman, S., & Hutchins, C. (2003). *7 keys to comprehension: How to help your kids read it and get it!* New York: Crown Publishing Group.

Answer Key

Chapter One

Pre-Assessment

1.	True	11.	True
2.	False	12.	False
3.	True	13.	True
4.	False	14.	True
5.	True	15.	True
6.	True	16.	True
7.	True	17.	False
8.	True	18.	True
9.	False	19.	True
10.	True	20.	True

Chapter Two

Pre-Assessment

1.	True	7.	True
2.	False	8.	True
3.	True	9.	True
4.	True	10.	False
5.	True	11.	True
6.	True	12.	True

13.	False	16.	True
14.	True	17.	True
15.	True	18.	True

Chapter Three

Pre-Assessment

1.	True	10.	True
2.	False	11.	True
3.	True	12.	False
4.	True	13.	True
5.	True	14.	True
6.	False	15.	True
7.	False	16.	False
8.	True	17.	True
9.	True	18.	False

Chapter Four

Pre-Assessment

1.	False	11.	True
2.	True	12.	True
3.	False	13.	False
4.	True	14.	False
5.	True	15.	True
6.	True	16.	True
7.	True	17.	True
8.	True	18.	True
9.	False	19.	True
10.	True	20.	True

Can You Find the Lost Animals?

```
r t (a n t e l o p e) x y w t m n o d o g g h i (n i o l)
y s (r a e b) c j f r y b d a b c x z o p y s t m o r r
(w (x o f) e g c r t m n y u g h t t u v x y z z o e r e
 o s s s (h o r s e) j j a b b x c d e e e e r o o y y v
 l (r e h s i f (c o w) r a c c x y o u u a b c f g g h o
 f) d r g g (p i g) o t u x r o j l k k m n o p q q q r r
 l o p g u (s k u n k) m o n y p q r s s t o r e e d o
 g g (t i g e r) s u r r p q z e o a a r r s s e e o f x
(t n a h p e l e) o x r (f e r r e t) t u a s e i m o y o
```

Winter Fun

VISITING

SKATING

HOCKEY

WALKING

TOBOGGANNING

SKIING

SNOWMAN

SLEDDING

Locate the Target Word as Quickly As You Can

carry (which) many what why sing made warm those whose

(which) white myself again know drink kind because wash

while (which) paper thought soon father below (which) earth

young state once (which) through food wish own wash (which)

best clean far both (which) wore seven once (which) know

(which) again when write wonder (which) ride would shoe

said wish (which) there cold today where every four one

much (which) off been went ever goes start does always two

play may (which) never sleep please because (which) wall own

done three pick hurt (which) pull us buy (which) head city

plant (which) might weight wonder (which) whale last most

young hear (which) being second late paper group along

while white face enough almost above chose (which) got

often watch (which) read grow show whip (which) maybe

just brown (which) again after eight around new must too

whip six myself again play way (which) ride will not long

Chapter Five

Pre-Assessment

1. True
2. True
3. False
4. True
5. True
6. False
7. True
8. False
9. True
10. True

11. True
12. False
13. True
14. True
15. True
16. True
17. True
18. True
19. True
20. False

Use the Clue to Write the Correct Consonant Blend

2. stream	12. stars
3. snake	13. sneeze
4. stick	14. spoon
5. spring	15. snail
6. steel	16. sport
7. stop	17. strike
8. sprain	18. scrub
9. snip	19. space
10. stockings	20. study
11. snowball	

Use the Clue to Write the Correct Digraph

2. lunch	14. thaw
3. show	15. the
4. church	16. sharp
5. chair	17. chimney
6. thin	18. cheek
7. sheep	19. there
8. chicken	20. third
9. shirt	21. chilly
10. short	22. thimble
11. chalk	23. shop
12. thumb	24. chief
13. child	25. shell

Print the Correct Vowel in Each Word

2. dog, cat

3. got, nap

4. bag, big

5. mop, pan

6. bat, not

7. tap, hot

8. six, rats

9. hop, cat

10. big, pig

11. Jim, jog

12. bid, pig

13. tip, top

14. pot, hot

15. cot, bed

16. let, lot

17. deck, dock

18. Pat, fan

19. Donald, ham

20. big, red

A Vowel Word Puzzle

2. lag, leg, log, lug

3. bet, but, bat, bit

4. bug, big, bag, beg

5. ball, bull, bell, bill

6. pen, pin, pan, pun

7. Dick, duck, dock, deck

8. peck, pack, puck, pick

9. truck, track, trick

10. pet, put, pit, pat

Hinks Pinks

2. maid braid

3. fake snake

4. brave Dave

5. dawn fawn

6. lean Jean

7. wed Ted (Fred, Ned)

8. queer deer

9. rent tent

10. glib fib

11. nice lice

12. big twig

13. stuck buck

14. hug bug

15. burn churn

16. cute flute

17. pork fork

18. torch porch

19. keen queen

20. fat rat

Chapter Six

Pre-Assessment

1. True	11. True
2. False	12. False
3. True	13. True
4. False	14. False
5. False	15. False
6. True	16. True
7. True	17. False
8. True	18. True
9. True	19. True
10. False	20. False

Illustrating Common Compound Words

No answer key

Locating Incorrect Verb Suffixes in Story Context

named, started, missed, learned, received, sitting, walking, called, loved

Attaching a Correct Suffix to a Base (Root) Word

brushes, childhood, golden, careful; quickly, girlhood, walking, lifeless; landed, sleepy, rapidly, goodness; watchful, rainy, wooden, slowly; motherhood, quicker (*or* quicken), fasten (*or* faster), toothless

Deducing Compound Words from Two Clues

cupcake, blackbird, carpool, chalkboard, earring, bluebird, jellyfish, sunlight, bookworm, turtleneck, wheelchair, toothpaste, dishwater, suntan, tugboat, stoplight, snapdragon, bandstand, streetcar

What Words Don't Belong?

1. couch; 2. drive; 3. snow; 4. dark; 5. teach; 6. heavy; 7. run; 8. kitchen; 9. clothes; 10. been; 11. eyes; 12. painting; 13. table; 14. church; 15. truck; 16. grass; 17. cupcake; 18. bicycle; 19. dishes; 20. pencil

What Is the Mystery Word?

Reading

Determining Actual Words from Context

1. birds; 2. cry; 3. shirt; 4. fries; 5. day; 6. pool (*or* hole); 7. milk; 8. skunk; 9. friend; 10. cat; 11. birthday; 12. rug; 13. socks; 14. old; 15. blue; 16. boy; 17. dog; 18. coffee; 19. truck; 20. hospital

Cloze Procedure

dogs	was
the	week
dog	barked
fall	will
she	school
owners	love
really	

Chapter Seven

Pre-Assessment

1. False	11. True
2. True	12. False
3. True	13. True
4. True	14. True
5. True	15. True
6. False	16. True
7. True	17. True
8. False	18. False
9. True	19. True
10. True	20. False

Think of a Synonym

Any answer that makes sense should be considered correct. These answers are just included for illustrative purposes.

2. mischievous, bad, destructive, poorly behaved

3. hurt, damaged

4. kindest, sweetest, most pleasant

5. beautiful, lovely

6. tasty, flavorful, appetizing, satisfying

7. frigid, frosty

8. scarlet, carnation

9. quickly, rapidly

10. difficult, challenging

11. interesting, joyful, pleasant, enjoyable

12. worn out, beat up, ancient

13. talented, competent, knowledgeable, pleasant

14. huge, gigantic, enormous

15. happy, joyful, excited, grateful, thankful

16. wealthy, affluent

17. fascinating, entertaining, remarkable

18. soiled, not clean

19. loveliest, most beautiful, prettiest, most appealing

20. brightest, most gifted

Vocabulary Word Puzzles About Animals

1. cheetah
2. tiger
3. lamb
4. fox
5. porcupine
6. rattlesnake
7. gorilla
8. wombat
9. hippopotamus
10. kangaroo
11. fisher
12. rhinoceros
13. wildebeest
14. antelope
15. squirrel
16. timber wolf
17. ferret
18. gazelle
19. zebra
20. coyote

Anticipation/Reaction Guide

1. False	4. False
2. True	5. True
3. True	6. True

Riddles

1. lion; 2. wolf (timberwolf); 3. elephant; 4. cheetah; 5. pig; 6. horse; 7. dog; 8. skunk; 9. porcupine; 10. kangaroo; 11. mouse; 12. zebra; 13. cat; 14. cow; 15. squirrel; 16. giraffe; 17. leopard; 18. opossum; 19. deer; 20. bear

Determining Fact or Opinion

1. O; 2. F; 3. T; 4. O; 5. F; 6. O; 7. O; 8. F; 9. O; 10. O; 11. F; 12. F; 13. O; 14. O; 15. F; 16. F; 17. F; 18. F; 19. O; 20. F; 21. O; 22. F; 23. F; 24. F; 25. O

Reading a Passage and Drawing a Picture About It

Drawings will vary.